Knowledge Puzzles

KNOWLEDGE PUZZLES

An Introduction to Epistemology

Stephen Cade Hetherington

The University of New South Wales

Westview
PRESS
A Member of the Perseus Books Group

Copyright © 1996 by Westview Press, A Member of the Perseus Books Group

Published in 1996 in the United States of America by Westview Press, 5500 Central Avenue, Boulder, Colorado, 80301-2877, and in the United Kingdom by Westview Press, 12 Hid's Copse Road, Cumnor Hill, Oxford OX2 9JJ

Library of Congress Cataloging-in-Publication Data
Hetherington, Stephen Cade.
    Knowledge puzzles : an introduction to epistemology / Stephen Cade Hetherington.
        p.   cm.
    Includes bibliographical references and index.
    ISBN 0-8133-2486-6 (hardcover) —ISBN 0-8133-2487-4 (paperback)
    1. Knowledge, Theory of.   I. Title.
BD161. H45   1996
121—dc20   95-40996
                                                                                CIP

The paper used in this publication meets the requirements of the American National Standard for Permanence of Paper for Printed Library Materials Z39.48-1984.

10   9   8

For Parveen,
who has taught me so much
worth knowing

Contents

Preface

0.1 The Book's Aim

Epistemology is an intriguing area of an intriguing subject—philosophy. But epistemology is also one of the more difficult areas of one of the more difficult subjects—philosophy. Students should therefore welcome whatever assistance they can get in understanding the concepts and methods of inquiry important to the discipline. My motivation for writing this book is to provide that assistance.

The book is not intended to replace or to compete with the central primary writings in epistemology. Rather, it presents many of epistemology's main ideas in a way that will help you understand those primary writings. In each chapter I introduce one main theme by way of a few puzzles (examples, questions, and issues). I have aimed to stimulate and suggest, not to exhaust (either readers or a topic). Capturing the spirit—the flavor—of a given idea is the point of each chapter.

I have tried not to favor any one epistemological theory, but instead to find questions and puzzles about each. My goal is to present as many views as I can—certainly most of the major ones—as fairly as possible, regardless of whether I agree with them. By discussing each theory or idea nondogmatically and questioningly, I seek not only to convey epistemology's questioning nature but also to remind you time after time of that nature—and of your chance to take advantage of it. Approach each idea or theory with the aim of deciding what *you* think about it.

0.2 The Book's Structure

Those who read straight through the book should find its organization clear as they proceed, one chapter leading thematically into the next. But that is not the only way to use the book, as I shall explain. Before that, though, it might be helpful if I say something about which chapters "belong" together.

Chapter 1 introduces the basic epistemological project—the attempt to understand the nature of knowledge. Chapters 2 through 4 assemble three concepts (truth, belief, and justification) fundamental to that project. So begins our attempt to understand knowledge; should we end there, too? By understanding these concepts, do we fully understand what knowledge is? Chapter 5 doubts that we do. It asks whether there is more to knowledge than is revealed in Chapters 2 through 4.

Well, is there? Chapters 6 through 15 grapple with that question: What is knowledge? These chapters contain a series of attempts to answer that question—and a collection of puzzles about those attempts. Does this plethora of possibilities suggest that it is not so easy to understand knowledge? Can we ever fully understand it? That is what Chapter 16 asks. Maybe we will never know all that could be known. I am human; you are human. Is it human to not know all? Is it also human to not fully understand the phenomenon of knowing?

Don't despair—yet. Chapter 17 considers an optimistic view of the attempt to understand knowledge, one that interprets all of us as having lots of knowledge. But like all substantive philosophical suggestions, this one is no less puzzling than those that preceded it. Maybe it is not so conceptually simple after all to accord lots of people lots of knowledge.

Should we therefore *deny* them knowledge? With that question, the door opens onto epistemology's famous *skeptical* questions. Skeptics deny us knowledge we thought we had (yes, they really do). We meet a series of them in Chapters 18 through 22.

For most people, though, it is hard to listen to skeptics without wanting to correct them, explaining to them why there is knowledge. Right now, do you, could you, believe—genuinely—that you know nothing? Chapters 23 through 25 present some classic attempts to defuse skepticism.

But skeptics never give up easily. They never have; they never will. Chapter 26 takes us back to modern skepticism's roots. It considers a particularly ancient and basic form of skepticism—one which doubts that people can even have beliefs, let alone knowledge. ("What? Can that be a serious suggestion?" Yes—and no. Wait—and see.)

It is appropriate, then, that the book begins and ends with questioning. It begins by asking what knowledge is and by calling on epistemology to answer that question. It ends (in Chapter 27) by asking whether we could ever adequately answer the question. What can epistemology hope to establish? Can we ever really understand knowledge? Surely we can *try* to understand it. But is that also the most that we can do?

0.3 Using This Book

There are several ways in which a teacher might use this book, since there are different courses for which it is suitable. A general epistemology course (touching on nonskeptical and on skeptical epistemology) could draw upon many, or even all, of the chapters, the choice reflecting a given teacher's preferences. A more specialized course concentrating on skeptical epistemology might use

Chapters 1, 2, 4, and some or all of 16 through 27. Similarly, a course focusing on nonskeptical epistemology could call on some or all of Chapters 1 through 16 and 27.

Note that many chapters contain more than one important subtopic or issue. Note, too, that each chapter begins and ends with a pertinent puzzle. These puzzles could be used in tutorial discussions or for essay questions. Note, finally, that the readings listed at the end of each chapter are not intended to be exhaustive. They are meant only to guide students toward further reading (which will guide them further still—to more reading, which will guide them even further, ever onward). Still, I hope to have listed enough readings from which to choose at least most of the material needed for some engaging epistemology courses.

Some of the chapters will also be useful for many epistemology segments in general introductory philosophy courses. Such courses often include discussion of such topics as truth (Chapter 2), belief (Chapter 3), justification (Chapter 4), Gettier cases (Chapter 5), Descartes's dreaming argument (Chapter 19), his evil demon argument (Chapter 18), and Hume's inductive skepticism (Chapter 20).

0.4 Acknowledgments

I have greatly appreciated the help given to me by Spencer Carr at Westview Press. He has been an accessible, enthusiastic, and sensitive editor. The support staff at Westview has been excellent, too. I have also valued the work of three anonymous reviewers. They made many helpful suggestions and criticisms pertaining to different stages of the manuscript. My wife, Parveen Seehra, did so as well. Her sharp questioning made my task harder, and I am grateful to her for it. This book, like my life, is richer and more enjoyable for Parveen's existence.

Stephen Cade Hetherington
Sydney, Australia

1

Introducing Epistemology

If you were to think of buying a car, and you had not already learned much about cars, wouldn't it be rash not to learn something about cars before making your choice? And if you do seek knowledge about cars, but you have not already learned much about knowledge, isn't it rash not to learn something about knowledge? If so, you've come to the right place. Read on! Isn't knowledge at least as important to the world as cars are? (Although cars can transport knowledge, they cannot even exist unless there is knowledge!)

1.1 What Is Epistemology?

Epistemology is the theory of knowledge; "theory of knowledge" is what "epistemology" means. But in practice it is many theories of knowledge, there being little agreement among epistemologists as to which theories to believe. Still, there is agreement as to which theories to discuss. I will present, for your consideration, many of those theories—their claims, concepts, arguments. But I will try not to favor any one theory in particular. That would misrepresent the general state of epistemological debate. Epistemology *is* still a debate, not yet a set of dogmas—and your contributions are welcome. As you read, try to decide which, if any, of epistemology's theories you accept (and why).

Naturally, the first concept for epistemologists to consider is *knowledge*. Here are two basic questions about it:

A   *What is knowledge?*
B   *Is there any knowledge? (Does someone—anyone—have some?)*

A zoologist might wonder "What is a cobra?" and "Are there any cobras? Where are they?" Epistemologists approach knowledge with similar care. And here are some ways in which you might respond to those basic questions.

Maybe you answer B first, and you say that there is indeed some knowledge. It would then be natural for you to provide examples of knowledge. You say that

1

there is knowledge. Then where is it? You might say that you know you are alive, or that you know what your cat's name is, or that you know that the moon is closer to Earth than Uranus is, or any number of other things. Then again, if you answer B with no, you might say why such examples are not really knowledge and why people are misled into thinking of them as knowledge. (This answer would make you a *skeptic*; we meet skeptical arguments later, starting in Chapter 18.)

If you do answer B with yes plus some examples, your next thought might be, "What do those examples have in common? Why are they knowledge?" (A zoologist dumps some writhing snakes at your feet: "Cobras," she says. "Oh yeah," you say composedly, ever the inquirer: "What makes them cobras?") You thus confront A. Having answered B by saying that there is such a thing as knowledge, you now seek to understand what type of thing it is. How is knowledge different from . . . well, anything else—such as a wish or a frog? What makes knowledge knowledge? (What makes a cobra a cobra?)

And with this question, you have begun doing epistemology (zoology of knowledge?). For at the heart of epistemology is question A. If you ignore A, trying to answer only B, you merely *list* examples of putative knowledge. That activity is not clearly epistemological. How can it provide a theory of knowledge? A list is not a theory. A list of cases of supposed knowledge is not an explanation, an understanding, of knowledge. And epistemology's aim is to explain and understand knowledge, to theorize about it (to good effect). By providing data to study, a list of cases of supposed knowledge can be part of an epistemological effort, a first step toward doing epistemology. But epistemology is a journey, not a step. The step of listing possible cases of knowledge is not epistemological unless it is followed by further steps, including attempts to answer A. To do epistemology is to theorize. And only question A clearly calls on you to theorize; B does not. Can you know that you are alive (and include this on your list, in response to B), without ever theorizing about what it is to have such knowledge (hence, without ever doing epistemology, in response to A)?

The choice of which question, A or B, to first try to answer presents you with what epistemologists call the *problem of the criterion*. If you think you can start by answering B, you are a *particularist*. Your first epistemological move would be to list particular cases of knowledge—and then, presumably, to try to understand them. But if you think you can start by answering A, you are a *generalist*, or *methodist*. Your first epistemological move would be to describe general ways, or methods, of knowing—and then, presumably, to try to apply them.

Why is the problem of the criterion a problem? There is no reason why it should be immediately apparent that it is a problem; not until section 27.1 do I attempt to explain why it is. In the meantime, I suggest that we begin our inquiries by adopting this particularist hypothesis:

UNO   You have some knowledge.

With UNO (the book's first hypothesis), we assume for argument's sake that the answer to B is yes. Then we will try to answer A by devising an account or description of whatever knowledge we assume is covered by UNO. Finally, we should be able to return to B, with a newly acquired description of knowledge, so as to think about whether UNO should be retained after all. We might decide, "Oh, since that's what knowledge is, I don't have any after all," or, alternatively, "So that's what knowledge is like? Then many of us have lots of it! UNO is true of each of us."

To think about what knowledge is does not entail concluding that anyone definitely has it. We are asking what knowledge is like *if* there is any. We begin this book by hypothesizing, for argument's sake and to provide us with possible examples to study, that there is knowledge (specifically, that you have some). That is, we shall assume—via UNO—that there is some, and then we shall spend our time testing UNO. Will it survive? Will it fall?

1.2 Why Do Epistemology?

But wait. Why does anyone ever do epistemology in the first place? Why theorize about knowledge at all?

Well, you assume that you have knowledge: UNO (in your mouth, INO: "I have some knowledge"?) is your probable answer to B. Might that answer be wrong, though? And if it is, might you have been misled by a false theory of knowledge? Perhaps you mistakenly think that you have knowledge, because you are mistaken as to what knowledge is. Now, that sounds like a rather serious mistake to make, since UNO seems like one of the more important claims that could ever be made about you. If it might be false, and if you can ascertain this only by reflecting on exactly what knowledge is, then epistemology beckons. For epistemology is where such reflections will lead you. To reflect on the nature of knowledge is to do epistemology.

To this reasoning, though, you might respond as follows:

Why would I treat as a mere hypothesis the proposition that I have knowledge? That would connote hesitation on my part about accepting that proposition. But what could be more obvious than that I have knowledge?

Thus, the most basic of all epistemological puzzles asks why we should do epistemology in the first place (and hence why we should investigate what seems not to need investigation).

Of course, one problem with your confidence about having knowledge is that, although it seems obvious to you that you have some, it might not seem so clear to the rest of us. We might have less confidence in your abilities than you do. For example, you might think that you know a lot about baseball. We might think that you do not. Isn't this something on which we need not take your word? ("You say you know that the world is flat? Okay, your word's good enough for me! If you say that you know, I must believe you.") Epistemology could have a point for us, if only because its application to you—you and your knowledge—can have a point. We can legitimately ask whether you know.

What would you do in the meantime, while we were thinking about whether you really do have knowledge? Could you simply ignore us and our epistemological reflections on you, blithely assuming that you have knowledge? If so, you would be answering B with a cheery "Of course," and then ignoring A. Yet mightn't this attitude be an intellectual equivalent of an ostrich's sticking his head in the sand? By answering B with yes, you say that you have knowledge. But, by ignoring A, you imply that you have no need to justify that confidence by explaining why you are a knower. How can you be so cavalier? Do you know that you know? Might it only *seem* obvious to you that you do not need to do epistemology in order to understand your claims to know? Mightn't you be wrong to assume that you have knowledge? Mightn't UNO be false?

I grant that it is "obvious" to you that you know—obvious in that you already, and naturally, accord yourself knowledge. But does the fact that it *seems* obvious to you make it true? Surely not all of your beliefs are true. How do you know that this one is? Are you ever wrong? I am willing to bet that you are. In fact, I am willing to bet that on each day of your life you have at least one false belief. See if you can prove me wrong! (And in your effort to prove me wrong, mightn't you find yourself doing epistemology as you reflect on your beliefs and on how to avoid having false ones?) Why, then, must you be right in thinking that you have knowledge in this particular case? If you are wrong sometimes, how can it be obvious that this is not one of those times? To try to answer this question, and hence to explain why you are right to claim knowledge, is to begin doing epistemology. For you would be attempting to say what knowledge is, and thus why you have some. You would be trying to answer A, hence to expand on your answer of yes to B. And you would no longer be acting like an ostrich about UNO's epistemological implications.

Furthermore, once you admit that you sometimes make mistakes in your thinking, at times ending up with false beliefs, isn't there another reason for you to pursue epistemology? You might be unable, without calling on epistemology, to *correct* your intellectual mistakes, your false beliefs. Don't you wish to decide which of your beliefs are false (so that, if possible, you can discard them)? Epistemology might help you to eliminate your intellectual mistakes by making clearer what is involved in gaining knowledge. If it can do that, it might help you to avoid ever being in the position of (1) admitting, with normal humility, that you make mistakes in your intellectual efforts, while (2) having no specific belief of which you say "That is mistaken." That is, epistemology might save you from a version of the so-called *preface paradox*.

This paradox poses the possibility of someone admitting fallibility but being unable to decide how he has been fallible, and hence being unable to correct his mistakes. Imagine an author admitting, in the preface to a nonfiction book, that (1) the book undoubtedly contains some mistakes, but (2) since she cannot tell which of the book's claims are false, she accepts each of them. She says that there are some false claims in the book; however, each claim in the book is only there because she accepts it, hence because she does not think that it is false. (If she had been able to decide that a given sentence was false, it would not have been retained in the book.) But if each claim in the book is one that she accepts, how can she say that nevertheless there is a false claim in the book? Since she aimed to include only truths in the book, she must think—of each claim in the book—that it is true. Isn't a false claim one that she should not accept? So is there an incoherence on her part? Maybe there is. Yet, step by step, mightn't she have been quite rational in her thinking? Can't it be rational for her (1) to accept that, since she is fallible in the way humans are, there will be mistakes in the book, but (2) to accept, of each given claim in the book, that it is not a mistake? (She reads the book again. Yep, each one of its sentences seems to her to be true.) Rational or not, though, doesn't (1) clash with (2)? And isn't it a kind of clash that your own body of beliefs might contain?

How is this puzzle to be resolved? Doing so seems to call for epistemological effort. For mightn't one of the puzzle's morals be that it can be hard, even impossible, for a person to rationally decide, without careful and possibly theoretical thought, which of her beliefs are false? You might, with humility, accept that somewhere among all of your beliefs there is a falsehood or two (or three or four or even more). But where is it? Where are they? It is hard to know; they all seem so good. So, reach for your epistemology text! Maybe the falsehood is the belief that you have some knowledge—hypothesis UNO! (Of course, that is one of your most fundamental beliefs. But can't fundamental beliefs be false?) Have you considered this possibility? Epistemologists consider it. And it is only by doing likewise—by doing epistemology—that you can hope to rationally decide whether UNO is false.

1.3 Avoiding Dogmatism

If you claimed knowledge but refused to attempt to explain or understand how you had it, you would be avoiding epistemology. (Would a university or college be like that ostrich if it described itself as furthering the growth of human knowledge but had no epistemologists among its faculty?) What price, though, would you be paying for your avoidance? The answer is simple. You would have to be *dogmatic*. You would have beliefs, and you would accept claims, on the basis of a confidence you could never explain (even to yourself).

"So what?" you might reply: "My having knowledge does not depend on my explaining how I have it. I know that I am alive, for example, even if I have no epistemological theory about how I have that knowledge."

The puzzling thing about that reply is that, ironically, if you want to avoid doing epistemology, the response is not available to you. It is not true when used by you. For it is an epistemological response itself! To offer it is to begin trying to explain what is involved in your having knowledge. You would be saying that not all knowledge involves epistemological theorizing, and you would be providing an example of some knowledge of yours (i.e., that you are alive) that does not require you to do any such theorizing. Yet, by talking in that way, you are doing some epistemological theorizing about what is (not) involved in having knowledge. You have begun doing epistemology while trying to bypass doing so!

Maybe you should just square your shoulders and continue what you have probably already begun (perhaps without realizing it); perhaps you have already spent part of your life being unwittingly epistemological. Which is it to be—dogmatism or epistemology (reflex or reflect)? If dogmatism satisfies you, close this book now—forever. If epistemology entices you, read on.

Is dogmatism ever an intellectual virtue? Can you think of circumstances in which it would help you to gain knowledge?

FURTHER READING

Audi 1988, pp. xiv–xvii. (On the general value of studying any philosophy, including epistemology.)

Chisholm 1982, Chapter 5. (On the problem of the criterion, in section 1.1.)

Makinson 1965. (For the original version of the preface paradox, in section 1.2.)

Plato, *Theaetetus* 200d–210c. (On the need to seek a theory of knowledge, considered in sections 1.2 and 1.3.)

2
Truth

Can you imagine a Truth Machine—a machine that makes a list of all facts (past, present, and future)? Its records contain all and only truths. However, it can never make a record of its having been destroyed ("I have been destroyed"); once destroyed, it cannot keep records at all. Do these conditions entail that, once created, the machine could not be destroyed? For its having been destroyed would be a fact—and any fact is recorded by the machine. Or do they entail that such a machine could never be created? Does the machine's indestructibility entail that truth itself is in some sense indestructible? Once we think there is truth in the world, can we never consistently give up that belief?

2.1 Knowledge Entails Truth

Almost all epistemologists think that knowing shares at least one thing with being a successful detective. A knower is apprised of facts. ("Just the facts, ma'am. I want knowledge.") If you know that some frogs are green, then it is a fact that some are green. In general, knowing entails being right. Knowing-that-p entails that p is a fact. (Sometimes I will use letters, such as "p," as place-holders for sentences or propositions—either specific ones or ones in general. Each time, the context will make clear whether I am referring to a specific proposition.)

Epistemologists usually make this point by saying that knowledge entails truth. Although a fact is not a truth, it is what makes a proposition true. A truth is a true proposition. If you know that some frogs are green, it is true that some frogs are green. Knowing-that-p entails p's being true. You cannot know something that is not true. Another way of saying this is that if you know that p, p is true. (Of course, you might know, of some p that is not true, that p is not true. In this case, you still know a truth—the truth that p is not true.)

2.2 Objective Truth

Even if it is true that knowledge entails truth, this truth *about* knowledge and truth might not be clearly true. For instance, you might wonder what truth is. And you might ask whether there is any truth. (These questions parallel A and B

in section 1.1.) If knowing-that-p entails p's being true, we do not fully understand knowledge unless we understand truth.

Perhaps the first puzzle about truth concerns *objectivity*. Is truth something
subjective or relative—so that there is your truth, my truth, your mother's truth,
and so on? When I say that it is a cold day and you say that it is hot, must at least
one of us be objectively wrong? Or is there always more than one "true" story
about the world? Should we be wary about the idea of there being a single,
shared world? Should we question there being facts? Is there objective truth "out
there" as a potential object of knowledge?

The answers to these questions might depend on how we define "objective
truth." Suppose we define it as follows (where "= df" means that the main concept on the left-hand side is being defined on the right-hand side):

OT   *A given proposition is objectively true = df. The proposition is true, and it
     is true whether or not anyone thinks that it is true.*

The idea behind OT is this. It is objectively true that there are clouds in the sky,
only if the existence of clouds in the sky is not dependent on us and our minds.
We do not create an objective truth's objectivity. It is made true by facts, not by
our thinking about it—and the facts exist independently of our thinking about
them. By this definition, it sounds as if it would be easy to determine whether a
given proposition was objectively true. But what if we created some specific
clouds? Would we thereby create the fact of those clouds' existence? Is the creation of a cloud the creation of the cloud's objective existence? How could it be?
If the cloud depended on us for its creation, it would not exist objectively. Yet
look at it! Isn't it clearly objectively real?

Or is OT not quite right? Imagine that you are walking in a forest. (You have
been told that it is an enchanted forest, but you do not believe this. What would
make you believe it?) You have seen no one else, and it is a hot and hazy day.
Bees around you are buzzing Louis Armstrong tunes. There is a dream-like quality to it all. You hear stomping; dozily, you look up. A heavily bearded man approaches, wearing a T-shirt displaying this message:

This message is thought by at least one person to be true.

He stomps on by. "Was he an epistemology professor?" you ask yourself. "Was he
testing definition OT?"

He might have been doing so. The message on his shirt cannot be true without
someone thinking that it is true. In other words, if it is true, this is because at least
one person thinks it is true. (Its own content entails this about it.) So, by OT, the
message is not objectively true. But does that conclusion sound correct? OT entails that it is. But is OT true (objectively true) itself? If the message is objectively
true, OT is false—and hence mischaracterizes what is involved in something's being objectively true. What would be a better definition of objective truth?

2.3 Semantic Paradox

Might there be limitations on the adequacy of any definition of objective truth? Perhaps we could never come up with a perfect definition of this concept. If you expect that we *will* be able to come up with the right definition one of these days, what evidence leads you to have that expectation? For a start, do *you* expect to be able to find a perfect definition of objective truth? If not, is that just a failing in you? Do you know someone who could do better? What if your definition of objectivity differed from your best friend's? Would this disagreement entail that there is no objective truth? Or would it just entail that the two of you had so far failed to agree on what objective truth is? Analogously, would your failure to agree on what, exactly, an atom is entail that there are no atoms?

You continue your walk through the forest. Having forgotten about the bearded man, you sit down for a moment. You look around you. You think that if ever something was real, it would be this forest. "Here, a person might find understanding and truth," you think.

What you find first, though, is another bearded man in another T-shirt sporting another message. Actually, this shirt has two messages. As the man approaches, you read the message on the front of his shirt: "What is written on the back of this shirt is true." As the man trudges past, you eagerly watch him. And what message is on his back? It says, "What is written on the front of this shirt is false." It takes you a moment . . . and then it hits you. (What does? The following reasoning does.)

The message on the front of the T-shirt says that the message on the back of the shirt is true. But the message on the back says that the message on the front is false:

FRONT: BACK is true.
BACK: FRONT is false.

Doesn't this T-shirt severely test your understanding of how truth and falsity work? Isn't there something paradoxical about its messages? Together, they seem to constitute what philosophers call a *semantic paradox*.

First, if FRONT is true, BACK is true. (For (1) FRONT says that BACK is true, and (2) for FRONT to be true is for what it says to be true.) But BACK says that FRONT is false. So, if BACK is true, and it says that FRONT is false, then FRONT is false. Hence, if you begin by supposing FRONT to be true, you are apparently forced to concede that it is false.

Second, suppose that FRONT is false. But if FRONT is false, BACK is false. (For (1) FRONT says that BACK is true, and (2) for FRONT to be false is for what it says to be false, and (3) if it is false that BACK is true, BACK must be false.) But BACK says that FRONT is false. So, if BACK is false, and it says that FRONT is false, then FRONT is true. So, if you begin by supposing FRONT to be false, you are apparently forced to conclude that it is true.

Now combine those two pieces of reasoning. Aren't you unable to consistently think of either FRONT or BACK either as true or as false? Whether you assign truth, or whether you assign falsity, you end up assigning the opposite truth value:

$$\begin{array}{c} \blacktriangleright \text{True} \\ \text{False} \blacktriangleleft \end{array}$$

You become like a dog chasing its tail—except that the tail is chasing the dog as well!

What moral should be drawn from this puzzle? (Should such T-shirts be banned?) Is it that some claims are neither true nor false? (What would this conclusion mean? What other statements might be like that? For instance, what do you make of the claim that virtue is purple with black spots? Although such a claim is not obviously a semantic paradox, it is not true either. Is it therefore false? If it is, does virtue have some color other than purple? Or is the claim neither true nor false?) If the bearded man's messages are neither true nor false, does that undermine the idea of objectivity? For does the example lead us to deny that every claim is either objectively true or objectively false? And if it does, how do we rationally decide which claims are either objectively true or objectively false?

2.4 Rejecting Objective Truth

Perhaps we could draw an even stronger moral. Might there be no objective truth or objective falsity? Would that explain why it is hard to understand what objective truth is (as section 2.2 suggested), and why not all claims are either objectively true or objectively false (as section 2.3 contemplated)?

This is a serious issue meriting serious thought. And that is what you are giving it as you continue through the forest. Indeed, so absorbed are you in your reflections that you almost bump into yet another densely bearded man. He is standing in the middle of the path (looking rather depressed). Sure enough, his T-shirt displays a message. This one is stark:

There is no objective truth.

What do you make of this message? Could it be true? But wouldn't its being true entail that it was not objectively true that the message was being displayed or that it even existed? How coherent an implication of the displayed message is that? And could there really be no objective truth? If something is really the case, it is something that is objectively true. So, if there really is no objective truth, the message (which says that there is no objective truth) is objectively true. But this makes the message false! For there is the objective truth that there is no objective truth! The state of affairs that obtains if the message is true is a fact that makes the message false.

So, the idea of the message's being true is puzzling—apparently paradoxical. The fact of the message's being displayed—there, in front of you—seems as real as the man himself. (But maybe the forest is enchanted, after all.) The message's existence seems to be at odds with its content. Does this discrepancy make the message, and its existence, really—truly—paradoxical? Or might it be only apparently paradoxical? (Are M. C. Escher's apparently paradoxical pictures really paradoxical?)

Must we therefore say that the message could not be true and hence that it is false? Is the message paradoxical only if we suppose that it is true? If it is false, it is not obviously paradoxical, since its being false just amounts to there being at least one objective truth, and there seems to be nothing self-defeating or contradictory in supposing there to be at least one objective truth. Could we all wear T-shirts saying "There is at least one objective truth; maybe you are looking at it right now"? In other words, is there at least some objective truth in the world?

2.5 Finding the Objective Truths

But where is such truth to be found? It is one thing to be told that truth exists, and quite another to be told how to rationally decide which claims are true. ("I assure you, Watson, I have worked out, by the unaided power of my intellect, that there really does exist a three-tailed snake that meows like a cat. It is what killed this man. All that you have to do is find it.")

One natural way to seek truth is to seek knowledge and knowers. If a knower is someone who is somehow "in touch with" truths (as section 2.1 explained), then to gain knowledge is to be "in touch with" some truth. Your thinking would be like this:

1 *For any proposition p and for any person, if the person knows that p, then p is true. [From section 2.1.]*
2 *I know that there is an eagle perched on my head.*
3 *So, it is true that there is an eagle perched on my head. [From 1 and 2.]*

Your reasoning would be logically valid; 3 does follow from 1 plus 2. And if 1 is true, all that remains is for you to decide when it is that you do satisfy premises like 2. More generally, you have to decide who knows what.

And with this we return to our fundamental epistemological questions—A and B (presented in section 1.1). What is knowledge? Is there any—and if so, where is it? Let us discuss these questions directly.

It is true that West Virginia is in the United States. So, is it true that it is true that West Virginia is in the United States? If it is, is it true that it is true that it is true that West Virginia is in the United States? If it is, is it true that it is true that it is true that it is true that West Virginia is in the United States? How long must this pattern continue? Must it continue forever? What would stop it? How many truths are there in the world? How can we count them?

FURTHER READING

Moser 1989, pp. 23–35. (On the idea, in section 2.1, that knowledge entails truth.)
Chisholm 1977, Chapter 5. (On semantic paradox, in section 2.3.)
Plato, *Theaetetus* 151e–152c, 161c–e. (On the idea, in section 2.4, that truth is relative.)

3

Belief

You: I believe that I'll get the job.
Friend: I believe you're wrong about that.
You: Do you think that I won't get the job?
Friend: No, I think you don't really believe that you will.
You: You're wrong. And how can you know better than I do what I believe?
Me: But why can't your friend know this better than you do?

3.1 Does Knowledge Entail Belief?

We are considering the hypothesis (in response to question B in section 1.1) that you have some knowledge (e.g., you know that you are alive). We are testing that hypothesis by trying to answer question A (also in section 1.1). We want to understand what knowledge is. If knowledge is like a jigsaw puzzle, we will shake its component pieces loose and then put them together again, so as to better understand the puzzle.

We have thought about one of those pieces—truth. Does knowledge entail truth (as section 2.1 suggested)? If it does, and if you know that you are on top of Mount Everest, it is true that you are up there. To know is to be right—to discover a truth.

But surely it is more than that. Here comes another possible piece of the knowledge jigsaw puzzle. Seemingly, there are truths that escape your knowledge. Some do so because they are too "far" from you. There are facts about sheep in the outback of Australia that no one expects you to know. But even when a fact is "nearby," you can lack knowledge of it. You might not have noticed that your soup contains a live butterfly, for example (swimming the butterfly stroke).

Such a consideration takes us to a standard epistemological idea—namely, that to know p, you must make p an object of your thought. Indeed, most epistemologists say, you need to have a *belief* in p. (Some put this by asking you to feel

13

sure that p or to accept that p.) Part of what it is for you to know that you are on top of Everest is for you to believe that you are on top of it.

Belief is not enough for knowledge, though. (Do you seriously say that all of your beliefs are cases of knowledge? If you do, retreat to section 1.2.) Still, belief is apparently a first step toward knowledge. Even if not all beliefs are instances of knowledge, maybe all instances of knowledge are beliefs. Maybe knowledge entails belief. Maybe knowledge is a kind of belief.

3.2 Is Saying Believing?

For now, let's say that knowledge is a kind of belief. Does this assumption help us to decide who has knowledge? It might increase our understanding of knowledge by partially answering question A in section 1.1. Is it thereby easier for us to answer question B?

Perhaps you think that it is. To answer B fully includes deciding who has knowledge. If knowledge is a kind of belief, we can attribute instances of knowledge to someone only if we can decide what his beliefs are. So, if we attribute beliefs, we are part of the way toward attributing knowledge.

How should we do that? Should we do it by attending to what the person says? Do his words reveal his beliefs? They do not if he is lying. But let's discuss what is hopefully the more usual case, where someone uses words in a way that seems sincere, even to himself.

Today your friend says that basketball is a great game. Naturally, you then assume that he believes that basketball is a great game. Tomorrow, however, he tells you that basketball is a lousy game. ("Call that a good game? No way.") Should you say, tomorrow, that he does not believe that basketball is a great game? In general, if a person says "p," when should you—and when shouldn't you—infer that he believes that p?

Suppose that your friend says, "Basketball is a great game," but his next utterance is "I'm such a joker!" Should you think that he was not serious when he said that basketball is so good? What if, two seconds later, he again exclaims "I'm such a joker!"? Does this statement negate his previous claim about being a joker? (Should you infer that he was joking about being such a joker?) Or does it reinforce the previous claim about being a joker? (If you assume that, so long as your friend keeps on talking, he is bound to say enough to enable you to resolve this kind of ambiguity, go to Chapter 21 for a possible surprise.)

Perhaps an experiment could settle matters. Imagine that, on each of the next thirty days, you speak to your friend at 2:14 P.M. On each occasion you ask him, "Do you like basketball?" Unfortunately, each day's answer reverses the previous day's. On one day he falls over himself in his praise for the game; on the next, he is beside himself with contempt for it; the day after that, basketball is sublime; the following day, it is just sub. On the thirtieth day, you end the experiment, baffled.

What are you to conclude? Should you trace your friend's sequence of answers to the fickleness of his beliefs about basketball? You could say that on every second day he believes that basketball is wonderful, while on every other day he believes that it is woeful. Or you could conclude that he has no such beliefs and that, because his stated opinions change so much, he lacks all beliefs as to the merits of basketball. You will take the latter view if you think of belief as a stable, settled, view. How stable is stable enough, though? Can a belief come and go, flickering in and out of a mind like a strobe light?

Just what, then, is the relationship between claiming p and believing p—for example, between your friend's saying "I like basketball" and his believing that he likes it? Once you think that you can answer this question, try out your answer on the following story from the American philosopher Saul Kripke.

Pierre—born, raised, and living in France—learns about a city called "Londres." He says, sincerely, "Londres est jolie." One day he wins a mystery flight (destination unspecified). It leaves him in a city whose signs identify it as "London." Pierre looks around and says, "London is ugly." He never retracts his earlier claim (which used "Londres"). He never translates "Londres" as "London," or vice versa, and hence never becomes aware of a possible inconsistency in his claims or beliefs.

What beliefs should we attribute to Pierre? Must we accord him the belief that London is pretty, on the basis of his saying "Londres est jolie" (which translates as "London is pretty")? By the same token, must we accord him the belief that London is ugly, on the basis of his saying "London is ugly"? How can we accord Pierre only one of these two beliefs? Should we accord him both beliefs? But how can we do that? Wouldn't he thereby believe that London is both pretty and ugly? Isn't that an inconsistent belief (one that logically cannot be true)? Wouldn't we be seeing Pierre as a walking, talking, impossibility? Is there a way to interpret Pierre as being a consistent believer? (Shouldn't that always be your aim when interpreting another person's utterances?)

3.3 Using Beliefs to Find Beliefs

Maybe there are problems with the idea that someone can attribute a belief to another person. Might that be what sparks the puzzling questions in section 3.2? For example, perhaps no one else knows what your beliefs are. (Can only you know what it is that you know?) Is belief "private," so that only you can know what your beliefs are and only I can know what my beliefs are? Do you believe(!) that only you can know what it is that you believe?

If so, and if knowledge is a kind of belief, you can never know that another person has knowledge. For you can never know what it is that he believes. You know, at most, what it is that *you* know.

Even that knowledge might be beyond you, though. It is one thing to say that only you can know what your beliefs are; it is another to say that you *can* know what they are. After all, won't your efforts just give you beliefs as to what it is that you believe? Suppose, for example, that you said to yourself, "Do I believe that I am tall? Yes, I do." Would the latter affirmation only be a belief, too—a belief that you believed that you were tall? If so, then in order to decide whether you have a simple belief that you are tall, you are now calling on a more complex belief—the belief that you believe that you are tall.

But how would you know that you had the new belief? "That's simple," you say. "I would mentally tell myself that I believed that I was tall." But if you talked to someone else about this belief, they would find it just as difficult to infer your beliefs on the basis of what you said as you would find it to infer what your fickle friend believed about basketball (in section 3.2). Why would it be any less difficult for *you* to infer your own beliefs from what you said (even if you said it to yourself)? What makes the new, more complex belief any easier for you to locate within yourself than the first one was?

For instance, if you sought to know whether you were tall, and hence you asked whether you believed that you were tall, of how much use would you find the following advice: "Look into yourself, and see whether you have that belief"? Can you literally see a belief within yourself? If not, won't you derive, at best, a belief that you have the belief that you are tall? Surely the more complex belief is no easier for you to find within your mind than the first one was. So, won't you now need another belief (the belief that you believe that you believe that you are tall) in order to decide for yourself that you believe that you believe that you are tall? Isn't this getting a touch out of control?

Can you end this search, then? Or must you endlessly rely on one belief after another, each "locating" the previous one? (Such endlessness is called an *infinite regress*, something we consider in more detail in Chapter 22.) The worry is that if you have to engage in that endless search, you can never answer the underlying question. Using one belief to decide whether you have another does not resolve the basic epistemological problem, which is whether you can ever know that you have even one given belief. For how do you know of the presence of the belief that does the locating? (This puzzle applies to any belief, including one about whether someone *else* has a belief. So, it also applies to your attempts in section 3.2 to decide what beliefs are possessed by Pierre and your friend the possible basketball fan.)

3.4 Again, Does Knowledge Entail Belief?

As we saw in section 1.1, epistemologists focus on knowledge. So, the puzzles presented in sections 3.2 and 3.3 affect them only if knowledge is a kind of belief (as section 3.1 posits). Might it be, however, that knowledge is not a kind of belief? If knowing that you are alive does not entail believing that you are alive, it is not vital for epistemologists to decide whether you have that belief. Instead, they can discuss knowledge without thinking about belief.

How could it be true that knowledge does not entail belief? Here are two ways in which that might be so.

First, might knowledge and belief be different kinds of things? People often make claims like this: "I don't believe that I'm tall; I *know* that I am." Do you make such claims? (But should we take them literally? Need we concede that they are true?)

Second, perhaps one can have knowledge without realizing it. Consider Anne, an unconfident but successful oral examinee. Although she gets the right answers, she has little confidence in her answers. When asked what year Descartes was born, she hesitates and says, "I don't think this is right, but ... 1596." Descartes was, indeed, born in 1596; her answer is correct. This happens repeatedly. She is asked many questions, and she answers many of them correctly—but none of them confidently. She continually disclaims belief in the answer she is about to offer; just as continually, though, her answer is correct.

Does the correctness of Anne's answers reveal her knowledge (of biographical details of famous philosophers)? Do her claims that she does not believe her answers reveal her lack of belief in those answers? If the answer to each of these questions is yes, the case falsifies the thesis posed in section 3.1—that knowledge entails belief. Anne knows that Descartes was born in 1596, but she does not believe that he was. Thus, not all knowledge is a kind of belief.

Do you accept this interpretation of Anne's situation? Is it a case in which someone knows p but does not believe p? To answer this question, you need to answer the following two questions.

1. Is Anne's lack of confidence in her answers a decisive indication of her lack of belief? (If you think that it is, make your way back to section 3.2 and again reflect on how close a link there is between what a person says and what she believes.)

2. Is the correctness of Anne's answers a decisive indication of her having knowledge? If you think that it is, here are two possible explanations of your reaction. On the one hand, you might say that *each* time Anne gets an answer right, she has knowledge. If so, are you saying that truth (Anne's getting a true answer) is all that she needs in order to have knowledge? (If you are, proceed to Chapter 4, where we ask whether more than truth is needed for knowledge.) On the other hand, you might think that it is Anne's reliability in gaining true answers—the fact that so many of her answers are true—that constitutes her having knowledge each time. (If so, wait until Chapter 6, where we consider whether such reliability is enough for a person's having knowledge.)

Imagine a newsreader who says, at the end of each broadcast, "I'm Mary Mary. That's tonight's news. And, as ever, the views expressed throughout the bulletin are not necessarily mine. In fact, they're not mine at all. I do not believe anything I have said in this bulletin." Could Mary be telling the truth? Can you nevertheless gain knowledge from the bulletin? (What if on one day—as ever, being quite contrary—Mary adds "This is because I have no beliefs at all." Can she say this and mean it? Would you believe her? What could she have in place of beliefs?)

FURTHER READING

Moser 1989, pp. 13–23. (On the idea, in section 3.1, that knowledge entails belief; and on the link, in section 3.2, between belief and assent.)

Kripke 1979. (For the Pierre puzzle, in section 3.2.)

Plato, *Republic* 476d–478d. (For the idea, in section 3.4, that knowledge and belief are different kinds of things.)

Ring 1977. (On whether knowledge and belief are different kinds of things, in section 3.4.)

Radford 1966. (For the unconfident examinee, in section 3.4.)

4

Justification

A broken watch is correct twice a day. Suppose that Tyrone's watch is broken and always reads 9:07. He has no idea that it is broken. But, as chance would have it, he only ever consults his watch at 9:07. So, whenever he thinks or says that it is now 9:07, he is right. At those times, does Tyrone know that it is 9:07?

4.1 Does Knowledge Entail Justification?

If knowledge entails truth (section 2.1) and belief (section 3.1), is that all there is to knowledge? Is TB true?

TB   You know that p = df. You have a true belief that p.

Does your knowing that you are reading this sentence equal (1) your believing that you are reading it, plus (2) its being true that you are reading it?

Most epistemologists reject TB, saying that having a true belief is only part of what it takes to have knowledge. Although anything that is knowledge is a true belief, not all true beliefs are knowledge. Being a true belief is not enough for being knowledge. Even if truth and belief are aspects of knowledge, they are not all there is to knowledge. They are necessary to, but not sufficient for, knowledge. (Here, as elsewhere, I am talking about *propositional* knowledge—knowledge *that* such-and-such—which epistemologists tend to see as the core, or at least the most easily understood, kind of knowledge. Other types of knowledge include such things as knowledge of how to do something or knowledge of who someone is. Propositional knowledge is supposedly what scientists and other theorists seek. It is what we have if we understand ourselves and our world.) Thus, most epistemologists accept TB+ over TB:

TB+   You know that p = df. You have a true belief that p, plus something extra.

More graphically:

knowledge = ? + truth + belief

What could that something extra be? Perhaps the simplest and most usual answer is that unless a true belief is supported by an appropriate kind and amount of evidence, it is not knowledge. Epistemologists call this a belief's being *justified*. They say that you must have *epistemic* justification for the belief. ("*Epistēmē*" is the ancient Greek word for "knowledge.") This section's hypothesis is that a true belief needs to be justified if it is to be knowledge. You know that you are alive, only if you believe that you are alive and your belief is true and justified. Here is the hypothesis in general form:

JTB   You know that p = df. You have a justified true belief that p.

More graphically:

knowledge = justification + truth + belief

The justification is for the belief's truth. For instance, you think for a moment . . . and then you say that you can be thinking only if you are alive. You say that your thinking gives you good evidence that you are alive. (Your thinking makes it overwhelmingly likely to be true that you are alive!) Given this evidence, plus the fact that you are alive and your belief that you are alive, JTB tells us that you know that you are alive.

Maybe the following story will help to clarify the connections between knowledge, justification, and truth.

You find yourself at a racecourse in time for the fifth race of the day. Since you have a lazy few dollars ready to hand, you decide to bet on the race. There is a horse called "Horse" entered, and you fancy its chances. You have no evidence one way or the other; you are just guessing. (You think that, since some horse has to win, maybe a horse called "Horse" will do it. Great thinking!) Nevertheless, having made your selection, you are loyal to it. You believe that Horse will win.

You look around for a bookmaker with whom to place your bet. And now you face another decision. This racecourse has two bookmakers. The one closest to you displays this sign:

MUG PUNTERS. If you're just guessing, you're welcome here. Put your money where your beliefs are.

The other bookmaker has this sign:

PUNTERS WITH EVIDENCE. Test your evidence here. Put your money where your evidence is. (We give you better odds.)

There used to be a bookmaker with this sign:

PUNTERS WHO KNOW. If you know which horse will win, step right up.

But he would turn away all prospective customers, saying "No, I'm sorry. I can't take your business. You don't really know. You just think that you do. It wouldn't be fair of me to take your money." He went out of business. No one knows where he went.

· Anyway, few punters think of themselves as mug punters. And the odds being offered by the Evidence Bookmaker are better. Nevertheless, you must place your bet with the Mug's Bookmaker. The Evidence Bookmaker does not take only your money. He insists on you presenting your evidence. ("Money here, evidence there. Have both ready, if you please.") And you have no pertinent evidence. You are just guessing that Horse will win. Nevertheless, you believe that he will do so, and you are prepared to back this bet with (some) money. But do you know that he will win? If you do not, is a sure sign of your lack of knowledge your inability to place your wager with the Evidence Bookmaker?

Mark what happens subsequently. Horse wins! His nose edged out another nose by a nose. Your bet came good. You believed that Horse would win, and he did: Your belief was true. Does even this result, though, entail that you knew that Horse was going to win? Is the truth of a belief enough to make it knowledge?

You hurry off to collect your winnings. But to which of the two tents do you proceed? There is the Knowledge tent ("If you knew which horse would win, enter"); the advantage of collecting your winnings there is that you collect money. At the other tent, the You Got Lucky tent ("So you think you're pretty smart, eh? No, you were just lucky"), all you receive is an IOU. Only the Knowledge tent pays you with money. You can bet with an IOU won at the You Got Lucky tent—but you will never win cash by using an IOU unless your bet with the IOU is placed with the Evidence Bookmaker. Knowledge is like cash, in that it is the most desired outcome of a bet. And you gain it only when you have used evidence to place your bet and hence to back your belief. (Naturally, the belief must also be true, if you are to win money with it.)

Well, is knowledge like that? (How similar to this racecourse is the world?) A true belief is not knowledge if it is the result of guesswork. To be knowledge, it must be justified—by, for example, appropriate evidence. Does that condition sound plausible? Do you know which horses will win races, only when your predictions are justified? When does that occur? What is required? What is appropriate evidence? How do you gain it? How strong must it be? (Beginning in Chapter

6, we will consider several ways to try to understand justification and/or whatever else is needed in addition to true belief for someone to have knowledge.)

4.2 Pragmatic Justification

Some generic features of (epistemic) justification should be noted right away. First, it is not obviously the same thing as pragmatic, or prudential, justification. The latter is whatever furthers your general well-being, let's say. Epistemic justification, in contrast, bears only on such matters as your gaining truth and avoiding falsity—that is, only on your well-being as an inquirer.

Suppose that you love gambling so much that, whenever you have a day at the races, you do your job better for a few days afterward. This is so, regardless of whether your gambling ever relies on evidence. In fact, you often place bets for which you lack supporting evidence. All that matters to you is experiencing the gambling; doing so puts you in a sunny mood. So, we might say that your wagers are pragmatically justified, but they are rarely (if ever) epistemically justified. (Is there no connection at all between the two kinds of justification? Or will acting on evidence always help your life in the long run? If it will, is acting on evidence also pragmatically justified? Do all sensible people use evidence? For example, perhaps your betting ends up costing you your job. If so, even the short-term pragmatic benefits of your gambling would disappear.)

Similarly, imagine having to choose between two roads. You have been told that one of them leads to riches, the other to witches, and you have no evidence as to which is the gold-tipped one. But you choose anyway—correctly, as it transpires. Your fortune is made. Was your choice justified after all? No. It was pragmatically justified, because it has made you happier. But because you had no evidence favoring one path over the other, your decision was just a lucky guess. It was not epistemically justified.

4.3 Justification and Truth

Unlike pragmatic justification, epistemic justification is meant to have some close connection with truth. Epistemic justification for a belief is justification for the belief's truth, not its usefulness or its social respectability, say. But this is not to say that a justified belief is always true. Even good evidence might not guarantee the truth of the proposition or belief it supports. There can be evidence for p's truth even if in fact p is not true. The evidence for p's truth might still be good evidence. It would be good but inconclusive. (Of course, conclusive justification would guarantee truth. Must justification therefore be conclusive? On this point, go to Chapter 17.)

For instance, imagine that it takes you many visits to the Evidence Bookmaker before you reach your goal—the Knowledge tent. You bet, with good evidence, time and time again, continually confident of your sources and your knowledge of the horses' form. But your evidence, though good, repeatedly lets you down. It is good but not conclusive. Your beliefs as to which horse will win are false, your evidence notwithstanding. Should we infer that the evidence was not good after all? Or can evidence for p's truth be good even when p happens to be false? Again, the answer depends on whether there can be good but fallible evidence. And can there be? What is your evidence for thinking that you are looking at a book? Is it conclusive evidence? Can you imagine its being misleading? We will return to these questions in later chapters.

4.4 Justification and Objectivity

Its connection with truth supposedly makes justification an *objective* quality. For most epistemologists, truth is objective (section 2.2). And evidence, in order to be justification, is supposed to objectively support (the truth of) one proposition or belief over (the truth of) another.

You look pleadingly at the Evidence Bookmaker and assure him, from the bottom of your heart, that your bet is justified. Need he believe you? Having justification is not obviously like being in pain. If you tell me that you are in pain, isn't there little (if anything) that I can do to sensibly doubt what you are saying? But if you say that you believe there is a wombat in the garden, and you say that this belief is justified (you have good evidence for its truth), can't I sensibly doubt your claim? You are laying claim to really being able to support your claim about the wombat, yet can't I decide that you are wrong because I think that your evidence is not good? I might think that you do not understand what it takes for a belief like that to be justified. Maybe I concede that you think that your belief about the wombat is justified but I believe that this thought of yours (i.e., that your wombat belief is justified) is simply false. I might believe that you have not been reading enough good epistemology books lately!

So, mightn't the Evidence Bookmaker be right to simply not take your word for it that the pain in your left big toe is good evidence that Hot Foot is going to win the seventh race? Although you think it is good evidence, justification is supposedly more objective than that. Whether your belief is justified is not obviously something that can be decisively settled just by the fact that you believe there is enough justification present. It might feel to you (sincerely, subjectively) as if your belief is rational and well supported. But such a feeling, no matter how strong, can be misleading. There might be no justification present at all.

This, in fact, is what most epistemologists would say. What evidence might they have for this view? Do you agree with them? Or is justification subjective? Is there no such thing as objective justification? But if there is none, how could you rationally say that there is none? If you are inclined to be skeptical about something as purportedly objective as justification, bide your time until Chapter 18.

Then again, might there be *degrees* of justification? If so, though, how much is needed for knowledge? Chapters 16 and 17 discuss that issue.

> *You are about to run in an Olympic 100-meter final. You have never beaten, or even run as fast as, any of the other finalists. All of the evidence, then, tells you that you cannot win. In spite of this evidence, however, you believe that you will cross the finish line first. Now, suppose that (though you do not realize it) believing that you will win has so galvanized you that you are about to rise to new heights. You Will Win—yes! Your forming your belief against the evidence will cause the belief to be true. Nevertheless, isn't your belief unjustified, since you ignored the evidence about your past performances?*
>
> *This seems to be a case where, in order to gain a true belief, you are right to ignore your evidence. How can that be so? Shouldn't evidence always be respected? Shouldn't you always form beliefs in accordance with it? Was your belief therefore irrational? Rationally speaking, was it a mistake to form that belief? (Yet feel that medal around your neck!)*

FURTHER READING

Plato, *Theaetetus* 201a–202d. (On the idea, in section 4.1, that knowledge entails justification.)

Ayer 1956, pp. 28–34. (For more on the idea, in section 4.1, that knowledge entails justification.)

Alston 1989, Chapter 7. (For a challenge to the idea, in section 4.1, that knowledge entails justification.)

Sartwell 1991. (For another challenge to the idea, in section 4.1, that knowledge entails justification.)

Feldman and Conee 1985. (On justification as evidence, section 4.1's conception of justification.)

Foley 1991. (On puzzles like the one that ends this chapter.)

5

The Gettier Problem

You believe that there is a bird loose in the next room. You believe this because you hear maniacal laughter coming from there, clearly the sound of a kookaburra in full voice. Now, it happens to be the case that there is a bird loose in that room. But it is a lyrebird, the great mimic from the Australian bush, imitating the sound of a kookaburra sitting on the old gum tree. (This one is a great mimic.) So, your belief is true—but is it knowledge? Do you know that there is a bird loose in the next room?

5.1 Gettier Cases

JTB in section 4.1 was a hypothesis about the nature of knowledge. It purports to tell us what knowledge is—justified true belief. According to JTB, if you know that you are reading this page, you believe that you are reading it, it is true that you are reading it, and you have justification (such as good evidence) for the proposition that you are reading it.

Is nothing else required of you if you are to have such knowledge? Is knowledge simply a justified and true belief? With JTB, do we now have a complete (and true) definition of knowledge?

Prior to 1963, many (perhaps most) epistemologists would have answered yes to this question. Such epistemologists, it seemed, thought that they knew what knowledge is! Certainly some of them pointed to JTB with pride. But in 1963 an American philosopher, Edmund Gettier, presented a new puzzle, one that apparently questioned JTB. Most epistemologists call the resulting philosophical challenge *the Gettier problem,* posed by what have come to be called *Gettier cases.* Let's meet two such cases. The first is basically one of Gettier's own cases.

Gettier Case 1. Smith believes that Jones will get the promotion in their office. (He has good evidence for this belief. Their boss told him that Jones would get the position.) Smith also believes that Jones has ten coins in his pocket. (Again Smith has good evidence. He has just counted the coins in Jones's pocket.) Smith combines these two beliefs into one—the belief that the person who will get the promotion has ten coins in his pocket. Call this belief b. Since Smith has good evidence for each of the two beliefs that combine to make b, he presumably has good evidence for b itself. What is more, b is in fact true. But it is true, not because *Jones* will get the position and because he has ten coins in his pocket, but because *Smith* will win the position and because he also has ten coins in his pocket. (Neither Jones nor Smith has any idea that any of this is about to happen. Nevertheless, it is.) So, b is a belief that is true and for which Smith has good evidence. It is a justified true belief. But is it knowledge on Smith's part? Does Smith know that the person who will get the position has ten coins in his pocket? Surely not.

Gettier Case 2. You are in the country, leaning on a fence, looking at a field. You see something that looks like a sheep. It is about ten feet distant, the day is clear, and your eyes are good. You are unaware of any reason to doubt that the animal is a sheep. As the wind shifts toward you, you smell a sheep, too. You even hear one. So, you think to yourself, there is a sheep in that field. And indeed there is. Your belief is true. Apparently, it is also justified. You have what seems to be good evidence for there being a sheep in that field. (If it is not good evidence, what is? Don't you trust your senses to give you knowledge? For now, let's assume that you do. In Chapter 19, we consider the idea that you should not trust them.) The catch is that what you see is not really a sheep. It is a dog dressed up as a sheep. The farmer, for reasons best known to himself, covered the dog with a sheep's fleece. So, it looks and smells like a sheep. The farmer even installed a small radio transmitter in the fleece that plays a tape recording of a sheep. It is what you heard. Still, there is a sheep in the field. The field is gently sloped, and just over a small hill, out of your sight, smell, and hearing, a sheep is peacefully munching grass. He makes your final belief true. (Remember that your final belief is that there is a sheep in the field.) So, you have a belief—your final belief—that is justified and true. But is it a case of knowledge? Do you know that there is a sheep in the field? Surely not.

What do such Gettier cases show? The standard epistemological interpretation is that they are counterexamples to JTB. That is, they apparently undermine, or refute, the hypothesis that knowledge equals justified-true-belief. Supposedly, they do this by refuting part of JTB, which claims the following two things: (1) Any case of knowledge is a justified true belief; and (2) any justified true belief is a case of knowledge. And Gettier cases purportedly disprove (2), for they are apparently cases where someone has a justified true belief that nevertheless fails to be knowledge. Such cases falsify JTB (since half of JTB is (2)). Gettier cases seem to entail that something's being a justified true belief is not sufficient for its being knowledge.

If not, there is more to something's being knowledge than its being a justified true belief. In general, if X is not sufficient for Y, something must be added to X if Y is to be present due to X being present. Seemingly, Gettier cases give us this result:

knowledge = ? + justification + truth + belief

That is, JTB+ is true:

> JTB+   *You know that p = df. You have a justified true belief that p, plus some-*
> *thing extra.*

But this standard reaction depends on the correctness of the usual reading of the Gettier cases. The usual reading is that the cases capture someone (in Case 1, Smith; in Case 2, you outside the field) with a justified true belief that is never-theless not knowledge. Is that reading correct? Do the cases reveal the insuffi-ciency of justified true belief for knowledge? That is the question, but how can you find the correct answer?

You might do what epistemologists generally do. You might see what your so-called intuitions say about the puzzle. For example, is it intuitively clear to you that, if you were looking at the dog-in-sheep's-clothing in that field, then your belief that there was a sheep in the field, although true and justified, would not be knowledge? If so, what has gone wrong in the Gettier cases? What is knowl-edge, if it is not simply a justified true belief?

I can tell you this much already. There is little agreement among epistemolo-gists as to how to answer that last question. They were, are, and might well for-ever be, perplexed. Answers have come and answers have gone—and then have come again. Such apparently simple cases are not as easy to solve as they might seem.

For instance, if you think that the problem described within a Gettier case—the reason why you lack knowledge within Case 2, say—is that your final belief wasn't *infallibly* justified by your evidence, wait for Chapter 18, where we see that to demand infallible justification is to open the door to other puzzles. Or if you think the problem is that, somewhere in your evidence for your final belief, there is something *false*, such as the belief that the animal in front of you is a sheep, move to Chapter 11. There, we find that there might be Gettier cases in which a person uses *no* false evidence. Or . . . all in good time. There have been many suggestions as to how to resolve Gettier cases, and we will discuss several of them. Doing so is important because trying to understand what goes wrong in Gettier cases should help us to understand what knowledge is. And this was what question A in section 1.1 asked us to do.

5.2 Does Knowledge Matter?

Maybe the most basic observation we can make about Case 2 is that, in it, you are fooled by circumstances. (Actually, this is true of all Gettier cases, not just Case 2. For the sake of simplicity, however, I will focus on that particular case. I shall leave it to you, with each move we make in response to Case 2, now or in subsequent chapters, to also apply the move to Case 1.) The deception is note-worthy for the following reason.

Case 2 describes you as lacking knowledge in a quite odd way. It is a way that epistemologists call *being Gettiered*. For now, we may describe it as generically as possible, saying that to be Gettiered is to have a justified true belief that is nevertheless not knowledge. Interestingly, the problem seems not to be one of which you can be aware at the crucial time. After all, if you had been aware, at the time, of being Gettiered, you would have reasoned differently. Although you still would have concluded that there was a sheep in the field, your reasoning would have been different. Being aware of the problem, you would have realized that the animal in front of you was not a sheep and that there was a sheep else-where in the field. So you would not have relied on your perceptions of the ani-mal in front of you, although you would still have concluded that there was a sheep in the field. Does the case therefore reveal you doing *as well as could have been expected* in the circumstances? Being unaware of how nonstandard a field you were contemplating, did you draw the only conclusion you could reason-ably have drawn?

And if you did, does this entail that it does not *matter* whether you are Gettiered? Does it tell us that, since the circumstances deprive you of knowl-edge, but you could not have reasoned any better in them, what they neverthe-less deprive you of (i.e., knowledge) does not matter? The idea behind this ques-tion is that if you could not have done any better in the circumstances, and if it is your not doing any better in them that leads to your lacking knowledge in them, then it is pointless to seek or value knowledge. Knowledge becomes something lying beyond all reasonable endeavor. You lack it in the Gettier case. Yet you have done all that we could reasonably expect of you. Hence, gaining knowledge, and thereby avoiding being Gettiered, is not something we could reasonably expect of you.

Is the moral of the case, therefore, that it is important to inquire as well as you can—but not important for you to gain knowledge? In short, does knowledge matter?

5.3 Doing More to Have Knowledge

But is it true that, when leaning on that fence and looking on at that weird field, you did all that you should have done? *Was* your inquiry as good as could be rea-sonably expected? Or should you have thought to yourself something along the following lines?

Wait a moment. What if I am being Gettiered? What if that isn't a sheep? Just suppose (no, I'm not joking) that it is a dog in sheep's clothing. If it is, then—so long as there is a sheep elsewhere in the field—I am still correct in thinking that there's a sheep in the field. Nevertheless, although I would be correct, I would be Gettiered: I would have a justified and true belief that there is a sheep in the field, but I would still not know that there is a sheep in the field. So, shouldn't I suspend judgment (as to whether there is a sheep in the field) until I have inspected the field more thoroughly? Shouldn't I ascertain whether the field is really as it seems to be? In short, shouldn't I check on whether I am being Gettiered?

Thus, before we concede that you inquired as well as possible, should we ask whether you have thought about the Gettier issue itself? Has Gettier presented a kind of puzzle that should make you more cautious and careful when inquiring? Presumably, you never think that you are being Gettiered and hence that you lack knowledge in this odd way. But should you routinely check on whether you are being, or have been, Gettiered? Should you exercise that kind of caution in forming beliefs? Should you continue to seek knowledge—while taking care to inquire into whether you are being Gettiered? What will you do from now on (whenever knowledge is your aim)? What should you do from now on?

I think that I have been Gettiered—and quite often. Here are two examples. (1) I was on a bus in Sydney in 1991, and I saw the headline on the back page of the newspaper being read by the person in front of me. The headline was "World Long Jump Record Broken." I thought "Wow, Carl Lewis has jumped farther than Bob Beamon's record." I had good evidence for this belief: I saw the headline (in a reputable newspaper), I knew that the World Track and Field Championships were being held, I knew that Lewis was participating, and I knew that he had been the best long jumper in the world for a decade. It never crossed my mind that the headline could have been referring to someone else; if the record was to be broken anytime soon, of course Carl Lewis would be the man to do it. But in fact it was someone else who did it: Mike Powell had broken the record. Nevertheless, Lewis had jumped farther than the old record, and so my justified belief was true. Lewis's jump, however, was too wind-assisted to count as an official record. Powell had simply jumped farther still, and he had done so without too much wind assistance. I had a justified true belief that Lewis had jumped farther than Beamon, but did I know that he had done so? (2) More recently, as I was about to turn onto a path, I saw what looked like a pile of manure beside it. "Some pile!" I thought. And it was—a pile of leaves, though. The light filtering through the leaves above had made the leaves below look like manure. . . . Now it's your turn. Have you ever been Gettiered?

FURTHER READING

Shope 1983, pp. 3–21. (On knowledge as a justified true belief, or JTB, in section 5.1.)

Gettier 1963. (For the original Gettier cases, one of which was Case 1, in section 5.1.)

Chisholm 1989, p. 93. (For a Gettier case like Case 2, in section 5.1.)

Conee 1988. (On the idea, at the end of section 5.1, that there is value in thinking about Gettier cases.)

Kaplan 1985. (On the idea, in section 5.2, that the Gettier challenge is irrelevant to responsible inquiry.)

6

Surface Reliability

Imagine someone who, throughout his life, has never been wrong; he has never believed anything false. As a professional gambler, he never bet on a losing horse; at school, his homework was always perfect. He never misjudged another person's character or capacities; he never misjudged his own character or capacities. He never . . . well, he just never. He has believed one truth after another. On his deathbed, though, he says to his friends, "I don't know anything. I've never known anything." His friends drop their jaws—but no words. Their mouths are agape, soundless. None of them know how to reply to him. What should they say? At the end of his otherwise charmed life, has he suddenly gained his first false belief?

6.1 Believing Reliably

Two days ago, you guessed that Horse would win, and he did (in section 4.1). Today you guess that a horse called Another Horse will win, and you are right about that. Tomorrow you will guess that a horse called Yet Another Horse will win; you will be right about that, too. The day after that, . . . One correct guess is an accident; two is a bigger accident; three is . . . Well, how long can such success continue until we should deny that you are only accidentally picking winners— that is, truths? Is that when it becomes more accurate to describe you as *knowing* which horse will win? If you pick the winner often enough, must we credit you with really knowing? And, interestingly, if it happens often enough, do even your few false predictions become justified? Should we endorse the following hypothesis, R, about justification and knowledge?

R   *(1) A given belief of yours is reliable if it happens to be part of a pattern of true beliefs—that is, if it is an example of a kind of belief that you often have and whose instances, when you have them, are often true. (2) A given belief of yours is justified if and only if it is reliable (in the sense described in (1)). (3) A given belief of yours is knowledge if and only if it is true and it is justified (in the sense described in (2)).*

R describes a way of being justified, and of knowing, that depends on your being *reliable* as a believer—reliable in believing truths (on a given topic, such as racing winners). The hypothesis is that forming true beliefs often enough makes you a reliable believer (a reliable reporter of truths)—and that being a reliable believer gives you justification and knowledge. Epistemologists who accept hypotheses in this spirit are called *reliabilists*. R can be seen as a first attempt at a *reliabilism* about justification and knowledge.

6.2 Reliability and Gettier Cases

Does R solve the Gettier problem? In the second Gettier case presented in section 5.1, was your final (Gettiered) belief true, yet not part of a pattern of true beliefs? Is that why it was not knowledge?

Well, suppose that you walk away from the remarkable field in this Gettier case, shaking your head. (There are a lot of flies around.) You come to another field; you pause, gazing at it. But it just isn't your day. The same thing happens to you with this field. You are Gettiered by it, too. You have a true, justified belief that there is a sheep in the field. There is a sheep in the field. But it is not what you are seeing. You have been tricked again. This field, like the previous one, contains a dog dressed as a sheep, and that is what makes you believe there to be a sheep in the field. Once again, you have good evidence for a belief that is true—but that, unfortunately, is not knowledge.

You continue walking. You reach a third field, where . . . the same thing occurs. You are Gettiered once more. You believe that there is a sheep in this field. And there is, but you are again misled by a (different) farmer's predilection for dressing his dogs in sheepskins. You trudge on, being Gettiered by one field after another. With each field in turn, you believe that there is a sheep in it. There always is, but it is never the animal in front of you, which you quite reasonably take to be a sheep. It is always a dog in sheep's clothing. The sun goes down on you, a lonely figure being Gettiered time after time.

Shouldn't you be happy, though, about the fact that in each of these cases you end up with a true belief? Your efforts to find out what is in these fields lead you—with each field—to believe that there is a sheep in it. And there always is. So, isn't this a topic on which you are a reliable believer? There is a definite pattern of true beliefs on your part. Should we therefore say that each of your beliefs (that there is a sheep in the field) is justified and might even be knowledge? Isn't that what R would have us believe?

Apparently, it is. Yet how could it be right? A Gettier case is one in which you have a justified true belief that is not knowledge. To be Gettiered is therefore to lack knowledge. How could your being Gettiered (and thus lacking knowledge) *many* times entail that you do have knowledge after all? How can being Gettiered twenty times, say, give you knowledge—when it deprives you of knowledge on each one of those occasions?

6.3 Reliability and Guesses

Isn't R vulnerable in another way, too? Can't you be repeatedly correct (without being Gettiered, as in section 6.2) while nevertheless lacking both knowledge and justification?

For example, a single true belief might just be a lucky guess. Recall your guess (in section 4.1) that Horse would win the next race. It was a lucky guess, a guess that turned out to be true. And because it was a guess, it was unjustified. In that respect, its being a guess overrode its being true. Its being true failed to make it justified, let alone to make it an instance of knowledge.

Yet if no single guess (even a correct one) constitutes a justified belief (let alone knowledge), how can repeated lucky guesses do so? If you reach a given belief via nothing more than a guess, you lack justification for the belief. So, isn't a sequence of, say, 100 guesses tantamount to 100 such lacks? (And doesn't 100 multiplied by 0 equal 0?) If (as section 4.1 noticed) no single true, but inadequately supported, belief is—simply in virtue of being true—justified or an instance of knowledge, why would an accumulation of true beliefs count as justified or as knowledge? Surely they would not. ("So what!" you might say, "I can always tell whether or not I am guessing." If you do say this, await Chapters 7 and 22, which challenge that kind of confidence.)

6.4 Restricting Reliabilism

But maybe a pattern of reliability makes for justification only in some cases. Might it depend on what kind of belief is involved? Might R be plausible for some kinds of belief but not for other kinds? (Recall that it talks of kinds of belief.)

Suppose that Madam Zelda, an amusement-arcade fortune-teller, is very successful in her predictions. Restricting herself to predicting people's career patterns and love lives, she is uncannily accurate. (She does not try to analyze her success. But she is confident that her predictions are not guesses.) Are her claims justified by that record of accuracy? R would have us believe that they are. And does her record of true predictions constitute her having knowledge of some aspects of the future? R would have us believe that it does (ignoring, for now, the Gettier problem as it arose in section 6.2).

You might say that R is wrong in this case because (you think) there is no underlying mechanism or principle generating Madam Z's pattern of true predictions. If you do say this, go to Chapter 7, where we ask how to understand such mechanisms as contributing to justification or knowledge. Leaving that issue aside for now, though, what else could tempt you to deny that Madam Z's predictions are justified or that they constitute knowledge?

Well, compare her with some scientist who is equally reliable in his predictions. Dr. Bio is a biologist who studies seals. His latest project has him charting the migration and breeding patterns of colonies of fur seals. So far, he has been doing well in his predictions. In fact, he has been doing so well that we can mention him in the same breath as Madam Zelda! *That* is how reliable his predictions have become. She deals with the movements and the mating cycles of humans (their career moves and their romances); he focuses on the analogous concerns of fur seals. Both of these thinkers are very successful in their predictions about their respective subject matters. Does this make their predictions equally justified? R seems to say that it does. Or is Dr. B more justified than Madam Z in virtue of being A Scientist? As far as knowledge and justification are concerned, is there something special about using a scientific method? (If you think so, hurry to Chapter 7 and then to the puzzle in Chapter 20 about inductive thinking—something on which scientists rely.)

What if Dr. B then has a particularly bad year while Madam Z has a particularly good one? It will be a year in which Dr. B is much less reliable than Madam Z as a predictor, a year in which she believes many more truths than he does. Would Madam Z's predictions therefore be more justified (hence closer to being knowledge) than Dr. B's? Can a good fortune-teller be better than a good scientist at gaining knowledge? (Let's assume that Dr. B is good at his job.) R seems to imply that this can be so.

We can make this comparison even more puzzling by imagining that Madam Z turns her hand to competing with Dr. B. Having heard him bragging that science is the paramount way to find out about the world, she tries to lower his confidence. She branches out, and begins discussing not only human relationships and roles but also fur seal relationships and roles. She looks into her crystal ball, thinks for a moment, and writes down how many fur seal pups will be born next year at a colony being studied by Dr. B. She gazes into the ball again and writes down the weight distributions of those pups. And so on; for each kind of datum studied by Dr. B, Madam Z has a prediction. Some of them match Dr. B's predictions; some do not. She sends hers to Dr. B and awaits word of the results.

The pupping season duly comes around, and what do we find? We find Dr. B sitting on the rocks, dolefully gazing at a page of results, all of which match Madam Z's predictions—and hence not all of which match his. Madam Z has done much better than he has as a predictor of the details of this year's breeding by the fur seals cavorting around him. From under his furrowed brow, he stares out over the furrowed ocean. Some error on his part was to be expected, he presumes; but how has Madam Z done so well? Should he concede that she knows more about such matters than he does? Should he adopt her method—"whatever it is," he thinks ruefully—in place of his own? And what is her method? Does it matter? Aren't the results what matter? Aren't hers better than Dr. B's?

He had been invited to a conference to present his results. What does he find there? He arrives just in time to hear Madam Z presenting her results. Joylessly, he curls up in a seat at the back of the auditorium. He blinks—and the talk is over. Madam Z has read out her figures as fast as she can—and then disappeared. Her entire talk was over in a flash. But is that a failing? Given how good Madam Z's figures are, shouldn't we say that her predictions are more justified, and are closer to being knowledge, than Dr. B's competing, but less accurate, predictions? His predictions were based on a lot of research and were supported by complicated reasoning. But although this way of arriving at the figures might make them more scientific than Madam Z's, it did not make them more accurate.

Should Dr. B's colleagues turn to him anyway when they are seeking recommendations as to what to expect of the seals next year? (Or should they consult Madam Z instead?) Were his less reliable predictions reached in a way, or by a method, that made them more justified than Madam Z's more reliable ones? (If you say that they were, Chapter 7 is for you.) Is there some crucial component of justification or knowledge that Madam Z's claims lack in spite of their superior reliability? That is, is reliability not always enough for justification? Or if (as R implies) reliability is all that counts, should everyone, including Dr. B and his colleagues, respect Madam Z's predictions about the seals more than Dr. B's? Should we say that, because reliability is all that matters, and because Madam Z is more reliable, she has more justification and more knowledge than Dr. B? Or is reliability not all that matters in this context? Is R wrong?

Note that, in talking about Madam Z's and Dr. B's reliability, R is talking about how reliable in *fact* they are. The reliabilist is not assuming that the reliability in question is, has been, or can be, discerned. His suggested account, R, does not assume that the reliability it talks about can ever be ascertained. It is enough if the reliability exists. There is no requirement that anyone know that the reliability exists, for example. Madam Z might be more reliable than Dr. B even if it is hard for anyone to find out that she is more reliable than him.

For instance, we might rely on Dr. B to test Madam Z's predictions. Unlike her, he has the equipment needed to ascertain which predictions are correct. Maybe this testing process can give him superior justification for beliefs as to how the breeding went (as against how it will go), and maybe this justification is important if we are to retrospectively assess the reliability of the predictions. But does this justification make his original predictions more justified (when first made) than Madam Z's? Surely not. After all, wouldn't it be possible for Madam Z's original predictions to have been more reliable than Dr. B's even if the predictions had never been subsequently tested?

Imagine that Dr. B becomes disillusioned with science and turns to selling cars instead. He never goes back to the fur seal colony to check on the breeding. Couldn't Madam Z's predictions have been more reliable in fact at the time, in spite of the fact that no one ever bothered to find out, later on, whether her predictions were more reliable? R (and hence the reliabilist) links the *fact* of reliability to the possession of justification and knowledge. You may find out whether Madam Z was a reliable predictor and therefore decide whether she has justification or knowledge. But if R is true, mightn't she have justification and knowledge without anyone's ever finding out that she has it? (Isn't that always possible? Mightn't you have knowledge you do not know that you have? This question arises in other chapters, too—such as Chapters 7 through 13.)

Suppose that, early each Monday morning, Madam Z predicts—correctly—that all of her other predictions for the coming week will be false. She has done this each week for the past twenty years, and hence has been very good (very reliable) at predicting her failures. Does she therefore know that she knows nothing else? Does she know that her fortune-telling is no good? (If she does, though, doesn't this entail that her fortune-telling is at least somewhat good?)

FURTHER READING

Unger 1968. (On accidentality, sustained patterns of true belief, and gypsy fortune-tellers.)

7

Underlying Reliability

A good thermometer is a reliable indicator of one aspect of its environment. Imagine one that gives voice to its readings. You look at it; you raise your eyebrows, questioningly. It responds, saying what the temperature is. Does it know what the temperature is? If you say no, because you assume that thermometers lack beliefs, will you credit humans who have beliefs, and who are otherwise like good thermometers, with having knowledge? Do you have any less evidence for a thermometer's knowing what the temperature is than you have for a friend's knowing what the temperature is?

7.1 Reliability and Belief-Forming Methods

Madam Zelda (whom we met in section 6.4) is a reliable predictor of some aspects of the future. But a lot of people will be reluctant to say that she knows more about the future or has better justified beliefs about it than does Dr. Bio (also from section 6.4). Dr. B seems to derive his beliefs by using a highly respectable *method* of belief-formation—a scientific method. Many people accord scientific beliefs more respect than beliefs based on fortune-telling. Even when Madam Z's fortune-telling is more successful, mightn't you have less confidence in her predictions than in Dr. B's? Would your reluctance to depend on her be due to the fact that you distrust the way, or the method, by which she attains her reliability?

Imagine, too, that Albert Einstein had died early. He had relatively little time, too little time to form many of the theoretical beliefs that made him relatively famous. So, he manifested no sustained pattern of true scientific beliefs. Hence, R would not classify his scientific beliefs (the ones that he *did* have time to form) as justified. Does this example show that R is mistaken? Or can someone have justified beliefs even when he has only a few such beliefs (and thus never establishes a sustained pattern of true beliefs)? Wasn't Einstein already thinking in a way that would have led to many true beliefs if it had been allowed to continue?

Maybe we can still capture these ideas in a reliabilist way by using R* to refine reliabilism's basic idea (as it was presented in section 6.2):

> R*   *(1) A given belief of yours is reliable if it was produced by a good method— one that was likely to result in a sustained pattern of true beliefs. (2) A given belief of yours is justified if and only if it is reliable (in the sense described in (1)). (3) A given belief of yours is knowledge if and only if it is true and it is justified (in the sense described in (2)).*

In Chapter 6, we saw that, according to R, your belief is justified if it is one of many true beliefs that you produce on a given topic. In other words, the belief is part of a surface reliability—on the surface, you are a reliable believer. But R* requires that there be a good underlying *generator* of any surface reliability you display. It makes knowledge a matter of reaching a true belief by way of a good process or method—one that was *likely* to produce surface reliability. (And, in the Gettier cases presented in section 5.1, was the problem the method by which you formed your final belief? We turn to this question in section 7.4.)

How clear is this suggestion? Does it improve on R? Or is a good method any method that happens to produce a good enough ratio of true beliefs? If it is, we need investigate R* no further, for R*'s conception of justification would collapse into R's. We could return to Chapter 6. But, for now, let's see whether we can *make* R* improve on R. To that end, consider the following two questions. (1) Which methods are the good ones? (2) Does anyone ever succeed in using any such methods? (Note how these two questions parallel A and B in section 1.1. I discuss (1) in section 7.2 and (2) in section 7.3.)

7.2 Reliability and Good Belief-Forming Methods

Which methods are the ones that can generate knowledge? Here are three candidates:

> 1   *Using one's senses (for beliefs about the physical world).*
> 2   *Using one's reason (for many kinds of beliefs).*
> 3   *Consulting Madam Zelda. (Go back to section 6.4. She's still there, thinking about whether to predict that you will return there!)*

Which of these are good ways to form beliefs so as to gain knowledge? I discuss 1 in section 7.3 and 2 in Chapter 13. In this section, let's consider the general issue of what makes a belief-forming method one that can generate knowledge. Why will so many people dismiss 3—Madam Z's fortune-telling—as being a method that will not produce knowledge? Why should you (if, indeed, you should) rely more on your senses and your reason?

One possible criterion for deciding whether a belief-forming method is good enough to produce knowledge is this. We might say that good methods (which can generate knowledge) are those which are *predictably* reliable. (Is this what "likely" means in R*?) Was the fact that Madam Z turned out to be so reliable something that was not predictable? And if you use your eyes to good effect (forming many true beliefs on the basis of what you see), is this good result something that was easily predicted? Was Madam Z's success less predictable than yours? Is this why R* seems plausible (if it does)?

Would the demand for predictability solve the problem, though? If a pattern of true belief is predictable, it is predictable (at least in principle) by *someone,* isn't it? Upon whose powers of prediction are we to rely in assessing the predictability of Madam Z's fortune-telling success or of your believing your eyes to good effect?

Well, Madam Z is in the prediction business; she's a professional. Need we do no more than ask her how predictable her success was? Suppose we ask her, and she says that she did predict her success. Does that prove that her success was predictable and hence that her predictions were justified according to R*? If we accept this answer of hers as justified, why were we reluctant in section 6.4 to accept her original pattern of success as making her claims justified? Shouldn't we be reluctant to accept her own self-recommendation? How clear is it that she can be unbiased on the question of her own reliability?

And yet, if we ask Madam Z and she says that her success was a complete surprise to her (but it has made her a better person, her subsequent life will be a more caring one, and so on), would that prove that her success was not predictable and therefore that her predictions were not justified according to R*? If we think so, on what criterion do we accept this claim of hers? Does our acceptance show that we trust her powers of prediction after all? We trust her this time; might we be trusting her now only because it suits us to do so? Yet if we do trust her now, doesn't that undermine our acceptance of what she is saying? Doesn't it show that we think at least some of her claims should be trusted? And how can we know which are the trustworthy ones?

Whom should we consult, then? If we cannot ask Madam Z, surely we cannot rely on Dr. Bio either. He is as much a party to the dispute (hence as potentially biased) as Madam Z is. To unhesitatingly accept his word is to beg the question against Madam Z, his opponent. It is to assume that, because he is a scientist, his verdict outweighs hers (in spite of her superior record of true beliefs). And whether it does is what we are still trying to decide. If Dr. B says he is to be believed over Madam Z, isn't he just pleading his own case? Might we be accepting his word simply because we want to do so? However, suppose that Dr. B says that

Madam Z's claims are more justified than his. Can we see this claim of his as justified and breathe a sigh of relief that we have solved the dispute about whether his claims are justified? But why would we accept this claim of his if he is in effect saying that we should not think of his claims as clearly justified?

The same kind of puzzle arises if we say that a good belief-forming method is one that makes it *probable* that true beliefs result from its use. Madam Z generated more true beliefs over a significant period of time than Dr. B did. So how was it more probable that he would do better than she would? Was it more to be expected—more predictable—that Dr. B would do better? Is that what it means to say that it was more probable that he would do better than Madam Z? If so, we return to the previous few paragraphs, having failed to advance the discussion at all.

Or is there some other sense in which Dr. B had a greater probability of gaining true beliefs than Madam Z did? What is that sense, though? Might it be that you think that science would support Dr. B over Madam Z and that science is to be trusted in such matters? But how do you justify that preference? Isn't it precisely the kind of preference that is challenged by Madam Z's success? Therefore, isn't it a preference you are not yet in a position to justify? (This preference is challenged even more in Chapter 20, by David Hume's famous puzzle.)

7.3 Reliability and the Senses

Suppose that, in spite of the doubts raised in section 7.2, we credit ourselves with some understanding of what makes a method appropriate for gaining justification and knowledge. We might say that at least some cases are clear. For instance, if you use your *senses,* and most of the beliefs you thereby form are true, surely those beliefs satisfy R*. Isn't the use of the senses a good method by which to form beliefs—that is, one that yields a high percentage of true beliefs, and therefore one that produces justified beliefs?

That notion sounds simple. But is it really so clear? What does it really mean to "use your senses"? Are you using them now? Or are you using them while also, and unavoidably, relying on some intuitions, some prejudices, some cultural biases, and so on? Consider this example.

Imagine that your eyes are less reliable on Tuesdays than on Wednesdays. (I don't know why this would be so; it just is. No one would believe that it is so, but it is.) Today is Tuesday, and you are reading this book, when suddenly you hear a "thud, thud." You look up, in time to see a kangaroo bounding past. You think "Wow, was that a kangaroo?" "I believe it was," you continue, stunned or not (as the case may be). Now, is this belief of yours justified, since you formed it by using your eyes? Is it justified because you used your eyes, because they are reliable, and because they are an appropriate source of surface reliability? The light is good, and your eyes are (as far as you are aware) in good working order. But beware. You have used them on a Tuesday! And that lowers your surface reliability as a user of your senses. Over the course of your life, your senses have given (and will continue to give) you fewer true beliefs on Tuesdays than on Wednesdays.

Presumably, we want to say that this discrepancy is irrelevant to how we should assess whether your belief about the kangaroo's presence is justified. Should we assess you not as a user-of-your-eyes-on-a-Tuesday but simply as a user-of-your-eyes? In that way, could Wednesday's better success rate make up for Tuesday's worse one? Could your belief thereby be justified?

The problem is that, although this might be what we want to say, on what grounds can we decide that the use of your eyes (as against the use of your eyes on a Tuesday) is *the* method by which you have formed your belief? And remember: R* requires that there be a single method by which you form your belief. The method's reliability determines the belief's justifiedness. You did form your belief on a Tuesday. Therefore, is the use-of-your-eyes-on-a-Tuesday the method by which your belief was formed?

If the method you used was the more generic one of using your eyes (as against using them on a Tuesday), your degree of reliability, as a user of that method, will be raised by your better performances on Wednesdays. But is that the right result? Since your belief has been formed on a Tuesday, shouldn't your lower reliability on Tuesdays be all that is pertinent to the justifiedness of the belief?

Can we look to science to decide such matters? The problem with this suggestion is that, at this point in the book, it is unclear that we can rely so justifiedly on science. Why would scientists be exempt from this discussion? Have we seen that (let alone why) they have justification or knowledge? Maybe Madam Zelda does know more than scientists do!

Does the urge to rely on science depend on a belief that scientists form their beliefs in reliable ways, using reliable methods—plus a belief that scientists study how eyes function, not how eyes-used-on-Tuesdays function? But, again, can a scientist avoid the current puzzle? When a scientist forms a belief, in what specific way does she form it? What special method does she use? If she forms her belief on a Tuesday, can she (or we) know that this factor is irrelevant to determining whether she has knowledge? Imagine that Dr. Bio, disillusioned with seals, is now studying vision. If he tells you that the method you have used in forming your belief about the kangaroo is that of Believing Your Eyes, but he tells you this on a Tuesday, and Tuesday is a day on which he forms few true beliefs, then . . . well, isn't he vulnerable, too? Wouldn't this fact undermine his scientific claims?

You could respond, "But perhaps Reason fares better than the senses in these respects." Why would that be so? Can't there be a Tuesday/Wednesday puzzle about even the most logical reasoning? (If you say, "No, because such reasoning is a special way to gain knowledge," Chapter 13 is for you.)

The general problem is that you (or anyone else) might not know what method you really used in forming your belief. If such knowledge is unavailable, of how much help is it to analyze knowledge or justification in terms of such methods, as R* does? (If you say that all that matters is whether you are in fact using a good method, and that awareness, let alone knowledge, of doing so is not needed, wait until Chapter 14.)

7.4 Reliable Methods and Gettier Cases

Suppose, for argument's sake, that the argument presented in section 7.3 can be evaded. That is, suppose that there are determinate facts as to what method you use to form a given belief and that we can determine what they are. Nevertheless, won't the Gettier problem still persist?

There you were (in section 5.1), using your eyes, nose, and ears in a standard way. They combined to give you a consistent story as to what animal was in front of you—namely, a sheep. So, at this stage in the story, you were apparently using a normal (and reliable) belief-forming method. What happened next? You called on logic. You made a simple deductive inference (from "That animal in the field is a sheep" to "There is a sheep in the field"). And that method, too, is presumably a reliable one.

Yet, when all was said and done, you were Gettiered, even though your final belief was true and justified. Let's suppose that, as R*(2) implies, it was justified because you used reliable methods. You combined what are, individually, reliable methods (observation and deductive reasoning), and you combined them in what is surely a standard and reliable way. If using your senses in seemingly normal conditions, and making simple deductive inferences from what your senses tell you, is not a reliable method by which to form beliefs about the world around you, what is? Still, you were Gettiered. Is R*(3)—which says that a given belief is knowledge if and only if it is true and justified in virtue of resulting from a good method—therefore false? What is the relationship between a belief's being knowledge and its being formed via a reliable method? Does the problem lie in *combining* methods? Yet isn't that something you do often? Perhaps it is important, then, for you to decide how to combine reliable methods, so as to still be using a method that is reliable enough to give you knowledge.

> *A knight dressed only in black, with no identifying marks, enters your town on a portentous evening. Holding aloft his spear, he bellows this message: "Follow me. Only by believing whatever I say will you have knowledge! There is no alternative." You stare at him, transfixed. Should you believe him? Should you follow him? If he is right, the consequences of not following him are dire. You would lack all knowledge. Can you afford to take such a risk? Is believing him an appropriate method by which to gain knowledge?*

FURTHER READING

Armstrong 1973, pp. 166–167. (On knowledge and thermometers, as in the puzzle that begins this chapter.)

Goldman 1979. (For the idea, in section 7.1, that justification is a matter of underlying reliability.)

Pollock 1984. (On understanding reliability in terms of the likelihood of gaining true beliefs, a possibility considered in section 7.2.)

Feldman 1985. (For the kind of worry in section 7.3.)

8

Causality

Unbeknownst to you, whenever there are rabbits near you, you form the belief that there are frogs near you. (Isn't life rich and wonderful?) Could such a belief ever be knowledge? If so, knowledge of what? Rabbits? Frogs? Both? Neither?

8.1 The Basic Idea of a Causal Account of Knowledge

In Chapter 6 we tried to understand knowledge and justification in terms of a simple concept of reliability. Chapter 7 refined that attempt by introducing the concept of a belief's being formed by the use of a reliable method.

But that is not the only possible way to explain how a belief can be formed in such a way that it is appropriate to say that the belief is knowledge. Instead of seeing knowledge as a true belief formed in a reliable way, perhaps it would be more helpful to think of knowledge as a true belief *caused* by the right fact. (This view would apparently discard justification as a component of knowledge; nevertheless, knowledge's not including justification is always a possibility we should bear in mind.) If you are to know that it is hot outside, must your belief that it is hot outside have been caused by its being hot outside? If you are to know that you are tall, must your belief that you are tall be caused by the fact that you are tall?

Well, what else (you might ask) could cause those beliefs? Surely the belief that it is hot cannot be caused by the fact that it is Sunday! Presumably, your belief that you are tall cannot be caused by the fact that Pittsburgh is in Pennsylvania!

Wrong! Those beliefs, in particular situations, could be caused in those ways. For example, because Pittsburgh is in Pennsylvania you often hear that it is; and hearing those words just happens to make you feel tall, whereupon you form the belief that you are tall. (In some weird way, couldn't almost any given fact cause almost any given belief?) Still, if a belief had been caused like that, perhaps it would have been caused in the wrong way to be *knowledge*. Can you know that you are tall if this belief is caused not by the fact that you are tall but by the fact that Pittsburgh is in Pennsylvania? (Would the belief have been formed irrationally?) Doesn't your belief that you are tall, in order to be knowledge of your being tall, need to be a *response* to the fact of your being tall? If so, perhaps the way in which a belief is formed must be appropriate if the belief is to be knowledge. Let's consider C:

> C   *A given belief of yours is knowledge if and only if (1) it is true, and (2) there is an appropriate causal connection between (i) your having the belief and (ii) the fact that is said by the belief to be a fact (and which, by (1), is a fact).*

C is a first attempt at a *causal* account of knowledge. It is inspired by the kind of case in which a belief-that-p is caused by the fact that p. You believe that you have red hair, and because this belief is (1) true, and (2) a response to the fact that you have red hair, your belief is knowledge. Or so it seems. Yet how often does knowledge come about in this apparently simple way? Equally, how often is it the case that you lack knowledge because your beliefs are not responses to corresponding facts in the world? Furthermore, note that C says nothing about justification. Could C have said that when there is an appropriate causal connection between your belief and the world, the belief is therefore justified?

8.2 Causality and Gettier Cases

It might seem that one advantage of C is that it allows us to understand Gettier cases. Does C show why you lack knowledge (if you do) in Gettier cases? Would satisfying C's clauses (1) and (2) have prevented you from being Gettiered?

Recall our second Gettier case in section 5.1. Standing outside a field, you are justified, but fooled, in believing that the animal in front of you is a sheep. (You are fooled because it is a dog. But you are justified because the dog is in sheep's clothing and hence your senses "tell" you that the animal is a sheep.) You infer that there is a sheep in the field. You are right. There is a sheep in the field, albeit out of your sight, smell, and hearing. So, this belief of yours is justified and true—but not knowledge. Why does it fail to be knowledge?

One possible answer to that question uses C. We might say that what makes your belief that there is a sheep in the field true is not just the fact that there is a sheep in the field. The general fact—that there is a sheep in the field—is present because a more basic fact is present—namely, that there is a *specific* sheep in the field. He is the animal you do not see, smell, or hear. (The animal you do see, smell, and hear is the dog in sheep's clothing.) We can even give this real sheep a name—Sheepish (befitting his role in the story, as he keeps shyly to his distant corner of the field). Your belief is true because of the fact that there is some sheep in the field; but that fact is only a fact because of another fact—the fact that Sheepish is in the field.

So, maybe you are Gettiered because you are responding to the wrong fact. Your belief that there is a sheep in the field is not knowledge, because Sheepish (the real sheep in the field) plays no causal role in making you believe that there is a sheep in the field. Since nothing about him helps to give you that belief, your belief is not a causal response to him in particular. What leads to your belief is your perceptual interaction with the dog, not with the sheep. By (1) seeing, smelling, and hearing what was in fact a dog, and (2) mistakenly thinking that it is a sheep, you come to believe that there is a sheep in the field. That interaction is the causal basis of your quirkily true belief. Hence, your final belief is, at base, made true by Sheepish's being in the field; yet his being in the field plays no causal role in your gaining that belief. Hence, there is a lack of "fit" between your belief and the world. What the belief says is a fact is not, at base, what causes the belief. Is this the failing in your epistemic situation? Is this lack of fit what makes you Gettiered?

To generalize this suggestion, we might say that it is always important, in knowing about the world, to have an appropriate causal interaction with the pertinent aspect(s) of the world. Must the right bit(s) of reality cause your beliefs about reality, if those beliefs are to be knowledge? C tries to capture the intuition that this is what must occur.

8.3 Appropriate Causal Connections

C posits that, to be knowledge, a belief must have an appropriate causal background. But how well do we understand the notion of an appropriate causal background? What bits of reality are the "right" bits to cause your belief?

There are at least two questions to disentangle here. (1) What methods are appropriate ones for forming your belief? (How should your belief be formed?) (2) In response to what facts must your belief be formed? (What "inputs" should your belief-forming method receive from the world around you?)

Question (1) seems to return us to Chapter 7. Epistemologists usually answer it by listing methods such as perception, memory, and reason. And why we should single out such methods in particular was our concern in Chapter 7. In the rest of Chapter 8, then, I shall focus on question (2). We can try to answer it by considering a simple variation on our Gettier example.

Suppose that the dog is only in the field, dressed as a sheep, *because* the real sheep, Sheepish, is in the field. The farmer, having been reduced to his last sheep, did not want Sheepish to feel lonely. So, having put Sheepish in the field, he had the idea of putting the dog in the field. He also wanted to keep his dog amused. It is a clever dog with a low boredom threshold. The farmer was confident that dressing it in a sheepskin, complete with a built-in tape recording of a sheep, would amuse it for a few days.

Now, isn't this scenario one in which there is a causal connection between the presence of a sheep in the field and your belief that there is a sheep in the field? The sheep's presence in the field helps to cause the presence of the dog in sheep's clothing, and the dog's presence in sheep's clothing helps to cause your belief that the thing in front of you is a sheep, which helps to cause your belief that there is a sheep in the field. In this roundabout way, doesn't the sheep's presence in the field help to cause your belief that there is a sheep in the field? Yet, if so, doesn't your belief satisfy the requirement described by C? Your belief is that there is a sheep in the field, and C requires that the corresponding fact (i.e., that there is a sheep in the field) bear an appropriate causal connection to your belief. And doesn't it do exactly that?

But your belief is still Gettiered, isn't it? (If it was Gettiered in the original version, in section 5.1, surely it still is.) Your belief is true and justified—but not knowledge.

Hence, don't we have a case in which your belief is not knowledge (because it is Gettiered), even though it does bear an appropriate causal connection to the fact that it takes to be a fact (i.e., the fact that there is a sheep in the field)? Don't we thus have a counterexample to C? And if so, doesn't C fail to explain why your belief is not knowledge of the sheep's presence? If your belief is not knowledge even though it satisfies C's requirement, then C—in making satisfaction of that requirement part of having knowledge—fails to explain why your belief is not knowledge.

Or has C's requirement not been satisfied? Although there is a causal connection between your belief that there is a sheep in the field and the fact of there being a sheep in the field, is it an appropriate causal connection (as required by C)? Perhaps the causal background of your belief is still too odd to count as appropriate.

But why would it be too odd? Within the case, you use perception (of the animal in front of you), and you use it carefully. You reason carefully, too (from the belief that the animal in front of you in the field is a sheep to the belief that there is a sheep in the field). Moreover, when reasoning like that, you retain in your memory a clear sense of how the animal in front of you looked, smelled, and sounded. What more can you do?

For instance, should you reflect more on your situation? Maybe you should check on the causal background of your belief, perhaps by reconstructing in your mind the route by which your belief came about. Or is that too onerous a task? How can you ever hope to check on the entire causal network of a given belief? Would you have to think about every shred of skin, every subatomic particle, that helped you form the belief? After all, is it possible that you are always being

Gettiered? If so, you would have to conduct this kind of background investigation for *each* of your beliefs, in order to decide whether a given belief's causal background was odd enough to have left you vulnerable to being Gettiered in this way. (Section 5.3 introduced the idea that you might have to respond to Gettier cases by being more careful in your thinking; Chapter 9 will continue the theme.)

8.4 Causality and A Priori Knowledge

In section 8.3, we asked how clearly C accounts for those kinds of knowledge for which it tries to account. But for how much knowledge can C hope to account?

C most clearly applies to empirical knowledge. Empirical knowledge is the kind of knowledge that you have, if you do indeed have it, because of how you use your senses. Thus, C might apply to knowledge of the physical world—the world with which, it seems, your senses interact causally. (You see physical objects, you hear them, smell them, taste and touch them.)

Even if you think that C helps us to understand empirical knowledge, you might suspect that it does not account for all kinds of knowledge. And our original aim (in section 1.1) was to understand all knowledge. Most epistemologists do not think that empirical knowledge is the only kind of knowledge. People also seem to have a priori knowledge. We discuss its nature in more detail in Chapter 13. But, at this stage of our inquiry, it is important to note that, when considering possible accounts of knowledge, one should give a thought to how well any suggested account explains the nature of a priori knowledge.

A priori knowledge is knowledge which, if you have it, you have by way of something other than experience. (For example, you have it via some kind of pure reason—pure thinking, unaided by the senses.) Do you know that $2 + 2 = 4$? Can such knowledge be understood by way of a causal condition, such as described in C? If so, we could use C in deciding whether you know that $2 + 2 = 4$.

Do you think that mathematical facts (e.g., the fact that $2 + 2 = 4$) can affect you causally? Can you literally be acted on by the fact that $2 + 2 = 4$? Can you literally affect it? Or do you and such facts inhabit different "realms" of reality, between which there is no causal traffic? Perhaps you exist in a physical world, while the mathematical fact exists in a nonphysical world that would have existed even if no physical world had ever existed.

If you cannot literally be acted upon by that mathematical fact, there are the following two possibilities.

1. Because you cannot causally interact with that mathematical fact, you cannot know that $2 + 2 = 4$. In that case, a condition like C, which explains absences of knowledge in terms of absences of appropriate causal interaction, explains why you do not know that $2 + 2 = 4$. (You lack the knowledge. You lack the causal

interaction. C implies that you lack the knowledge because you lack the causal interaction.)

2. You can know that 2 + 2 = 4. This is as clear as anything ever is in epistemology, or so we might claim. But because (a) you cannot interact causally with the fact that 2 + 2 = 4 (as we supposed, for argument's sake), yet (b) C accords you knowledge that 2 + 2 = 4 only if you interact causally with that mathematical fact, it follows that (c) C does not account for all knowledge. It fails to explain what is involved in knowing something like the fact that 2 + 2 = 4. (You have the knowledge. You lack the causal interaction. C says that such knowledge requires such causal interaction. So, C is wrong.)

Which is it to be? Must we choose between these two possibilities, or is there some more plausible possibility? You might say, "Yes. To know that 2 + 2 = 4 is to generalize from specific pairs being conjoined with other pairs to make quadruples, such as pairs of pears plus pairs of pears making quadruples of pears. And I can causally interact with those pears. I can count them and then eat them (thereby learning about subtraction)." But wouldn't knowledge obtained like this be empirical, not a priori? For wouldn't your pear-based knowledge really be applied, not pure, mathematical knowledge? These are puzzling questions; Chapter 13 considers a priori knowledge in more detail.

Gazing soulfully at the night sky, Mahalia directs her attention to one especially bright spot. She thinks to herself that she is seeing a star. She begins to sing, inspired. But science tells us that what is before her is light that has taken oh-so-long to reach her eyes. The star that sent that light has disappeared since the light in front of Mahalia was sent; it has since been replaced by a new star, but she is not yet receiving light from the new star. Is her belief that there is a star in that position in the sky knowledge that there is one there?

FURTHER READING

Goldman 1967. (For a causal account of empirical knowledge.)

Goldman 1976. (For an account of empirical knowledge that combines causal considerations, such as those discussed in this chapter, with the form of reliabilism discussed in Chapter 7.)

Carrier 1993. (For a causal account of all knowledge.)

9

Defeasibility

Marcia has good evidence for her husband Jim's infidelity. He has been acting furtively, staying away from home; a strange perfume clings to his clothes; and most of her friends tell her that he is being unfaithful, although they do not claim to know who the "other person" is. On the basis of this evidence, Marcia believes that Jim is being unfaithful. Unfortunately, her belief is true. Still, she has not yet asked her best (and most trusted) friend, Kim. But, were she to do so, Kim would tell Marcia that the stories are false. Does Marcia therefore not know that Jim is cheating on her? What if—though Marcia is unaware of it—Kim is the person with whom Jim is having the affair?

9.1 The Basic Idea of Defeasibility

On a causal account of knowledge such as the one discussed in Chapter 8, you have knowledge if you are causally related in the right way to the right bit of the world. You look up to see an emu striding past. This causes you to believe that there is an emu striding past. And you are right; there is no illusion. Do you therefore know that there is an emu striding past?

What you do not know is that you are in India at the time. You think you are in outback Australia. But you have been sedated, kidnapped, transported to Rajasthan, and deposited in a chair just like the one in which you were sitting in Australia. Rajasthan, though, is not a place where emus tend to exist. So, if you were to think that you are in Rajasthan, mightn't you be in two minds about whether it was an emu that you were seeing? ("This desert heat is playing tricks on me. Maybe that was a mirage. This is India, not Australia.") It is true that you are in Rajasthan. And if you were to add this truth to the evidence provided by your eyes, you might no longer have good evidence for the existence of that emu.

Does this state of affairs entail that your evidence is not so good after all? Your evidence does not take into account an important fact (i.e., that you are in

51

Rajasthan), and this overlooked fact undermines your present evidence in the following sense: Your evidence would not stay strong if you were to *add* to it a belief that you were in Rajasthan. Considered by itself, your evidence is good. But isn't it importantly incomplete? It is incomplete because it ignores a fact that, if added to it, would undermine it. Is it a *failing* of your evidence to have ignored that particular fact? Does your belief that you are seeing an emu fail to count as knowledge just because you have no idea that you are in Rajasthan?

Here is another example. Imagine being on a jury that convicts someone on the basis of evidence that clearly points to his guilt. Imagine, too, that there are facts of which you and the other jurors are ignorant and which, had you been aware of them, would have lessened the impact of the incriminating evidence. Is your verdict of guilty, made in ignorance of these other facts, therefore not knowledge of the person's guilt? Assume that the defendant did do what he was accused of doing. In that sense, he was guilty and hence deserved to be adjudged guilty. Your verdict was true. It was justified, too. But was it justified after an examination of all the evidence that should have been considered?

Defeasibility theorists might well deny you knowledge in these cases. The basic idea behind defeasibility accounts of knowledge is that sometimes your justified true belief is not knowledge, because the justification is importantly incomplete. Your belief has not taken into account all of the important evidence, for example. There is some fact which, if you were to take it into account, would seriously weaken your justification—and which you therefore should have taken into account. Different defeasibility theorists then differ over how to analyze this "should." In what sense is a given fact one that you should have considered, thereby allowing it to affect your evidence? This question is what is at stake in the rest of this chapter (and the next).

A generic defeasibility account might well take the following shape:

> D   *(1) A given belief of yours is knowledge if and only if it is true and undefeatedly justified. (2) A belief is undefeatedly justified = df. (i) It is justified by a body of evidence e (in a way that might be described by some other theory of justification), and (ii) there are no facts which are such that (a) if beliefs in them were to be added to e, you would have a body of evidence e+ that does not justify your belief, and (b) you should add beliefs in them to e.*

Let's call the troublesome facts referred to in D(2)(ii) *undercover* facts. (They are often called *defeaters*. They defeat what, if not for them, would be good enough justification.) First, like undercover spies, they escape your attention. You are unaware of them. Or you are aware of them, but you do not include this awareness in your evidence. Second (again like undercover spies), you should look for them, or at least not allow them to escape your attention. Third (still like undercover spies), they undo you. They defeat your evidence, denying you knowledge.

Suppose that your belief (from section 4.1) that Horse will win the next race is based on hearing a claim to that effect, made by a man in a LOUD check coat, chewing on a cigar, with this label on the back of his coat: "Owner of every horse in every race today—except for Horse, in the fifth race." You think, "There's someone whose prediction of a win by Horse will be knowledgeable but unbiased." Placing your money on Horse, you contentedly await the fifth race.

But that man, on whose word you are staking so much, is not what you think he is. He is a clown from a nearby circus. That's why his hair is so big and red! The sign was put on his back by the drummer from the circus band. The clown did not notice that the sign was on his back—although, even if he had, he would not have cared. If you were to be given this information, would you retain your prediction about Horse? Or would you spring from your seat, aiming to retrieve your money from the bookmaker? (Imagine the story you would tell him about the sign and the clown! Picture his undoubted sympathy!)

Presumably your prediction would no longer be justified. Assuming that you did have some justification for your belief, then the fact that the man was a clown, if you learned of it, would weaken your justification for thinking that Horse would win. And wouldn't it be easy enough to learn of his being a clown? If all of this is so, it seems that (by D) the fact about the clown is an undercover fact. It defeats what justification you formerly had. It prevents your belief that Horse will win the next race from being knowledge.

9.2 Defeasibility and Gettier Cases

D is not meant to be the final word on defeasibility, of course. But does it at least provide a general strategy for understanding what goes wrong in Gettier cases? A defeasibility theorist would claim that the problem in a Gettier case is that an undercover fact exists. As you gaze at that odd field described in section 5.1, at least part of what is making you Gettiered is the following fact:

UF   *The animal in front of you is a dog in sheep's clothing.*

Is UF an undercover fact? It clearly has two of the three required features. (1) Although it is a fact, you are unaware of it when standing beside the field (being tricked by it). (2) Were you to become aware of UF and add a belief in it to your evidence, you would no longer be justified in believing there to be a sheep in the field.

But does UF have the third feature necessary to being an undercover fact? That is, is it a fact of which, while standing outside the field, you *should* be aware? If you say no, you might like to revisit section 5.2. If you say yes, then you think that UF has the third of the three features attributed by D to undercover facts. Hence, you would be providing an explanation, using D, of why your belief that there is a sheep in the field does not count as knowledge. The idea would be that, by D, the justification that you are relying upon (supplied by your senses), although fine in its own way, is inadequate. It seems good to you only because UF is hidden from you. Yet UF should not have remained hidden from you. This fact, plus UF's *being* hidden from you, has deprived you of knowledge that there is a sheep in the field.

9.3 Which Facts Are Undercover Facts?

D requires that there be no undercover facts. It accords you knowledge that p, only if there are no facts that (1) you have not taken into account in justifying your belief that p, (2) you should have taken into account in justifying your belief that p, and (3) would have taken away your justification for believing p if you had taken them into account in justifying your belief that p. D does not require that your evidence include an awareness of every fact that would undermine your justification, were you to become aware of it. But D does require that there not be any such facts of which you *should* be aware but are not.

How much does this requirement ask of you? How demanding is D? The answer to this question depends on how many facts around you at any given time are pertinent to your justification. The following example illustrates how hard, in a given case, it can be to determine which facts are pertinent to a given belief's justification.

Suppose you are told by your college president that you have won a coveted scholarship. This is good evidence that you have won it; I assume that you have indeed won it. (Congratulations.) As you contentedly open the gate to your house and wander toward your front door, you believe that you have won the scholarship. The belief is true and you have good evidence for its truth. Is the evidence good enough, though? Do you know that you have won?

If you are asked this question (by a local reporter) as you approach your front door, you might cite your evidence. You refer to the college president's testimony, saying that you expect to receive official notification of the result soon. "Maybe the letter is in today's mail. I should hurry inside and check. Excuse me, please."

Hurry, hurry. There is a letter waiting for you on the table in your hall. Written on official college letterhead paper, it does say that you won the scholarship.

So far, so good. But imagine that a malcontented member of the college administration had typed up a letter telling you that you had not won the scholarship. He was interrupted while putting it into an envelope to send to you. If he had sent it, it would have been the letter waiting for you. If he had sent it, would you know (right now, when approaching your front door and the waiting false letter) that you had won the scholarship?

Suppose, however, that the misleading letter never did get sent. One of the malcontent's colleagues asked to see it first (to check on whether "congratulations" had been included). As a result, the unpleasant prank was averted. But would that matter? Only a lucky accident averted the unfortunate event. As you fumble for your key, while standing outside the door, does the fact that you almost had to contend with the prank letter defeat your justification for believing that you won the scholarship?

Imagine, instead, that the false letter was sent, but that on the next day you get a letter saying that the previous letter was a prank and should not be believed. The new letter says that you did win the scholarship. Since this new letter coheres with what the college president told you, again you believe that you won. But a friend now tells you that she won the scholarship; she shows you a letter to that effect. The letter bears the same date as your second letter (the one saying that you won). What should you think? Should you suspend belief as to whether you won? Should your friend do likewise? Should the two of you hurry to the administration building, intent on finding out the truth? What if the person whom you ask for advice is the prankster—who, although he has been fired, has not yet left the building? Suppose the explanation of the apparently contradictory letters is that the prankster sent your friend's letter, too; his deeds were discovered an hour later. Corrective letters were immediately sent. You have received yours; your friend's letter awaits her inside her front door.

There are two rooms, A and B. You stand outside A, thinking, "There's a frog in that room. I just know there is." Having it on excellent authority that this is so, you have justification for your belief. And the belief is true. But you always want as much evidence as possible; that's the kind of person you are. You begin opening the door (hesitantly, so as not to inadvertently squash any frog). As you begin doing so, the frog begins leaving the room through a small vent connecting A with B. You hesitate; so does the frog. Hearing your name called (by someone with a rather croaky voice), you abandon your quest for more evidence; you close the door, and the frog stays where he is. If you had continued with your investigation, though, the frog would have continued his exit. You would have found no frog in the room. Is this an undercover fact? Because of it, do you fail to know that there is a frog in the room?

FURTHER READING

Lehrer and Paxson 1969. (For the basic idea of defeasibility, in section 9.1; and on defeasibility and Gettier cases, in section 9.2.)

Harman 1973, Chapter 9. (On the basic idea of defeasibility, in section 9.1; and on defeasibility and Gettier cases, in section 9.2.)

Lycan 1977. (On the difficulty, in section 9.3, of understanding defeasibility more precisely.)

10
Social Defeasibility

You insist that you are six feet tall; no one else agrees with you about this. "But," you say, "here is a tape measure. According to it, I am six feet tall." Everyone else around you still rejects your claims. Does it follow that you do not know how tall you are? Perhaps you have the only correct tape measure in town, the other tape measures being faulty fakes. But even if that is so, could the very fact that everyone else disagrees with you be evidence against your knowing your own height? Isn't their disagreement with you a reason, rationally speaking, for you to withdraw your claim as to your height?

10.1 Realistic Defeasibility

Perhaps we can capture the generic notion of defeasibility that was presented in Chapter 9 by saying that, for you to know that p, there must be no realistically accessible facts that would spoil your justification for p, were you to become aware of them and were you to add this awareness to your evidence for p. Undercover facts are realistically accessible facts of which your evidence takes no account. D* is much the same as D in section 9.1; the only part that has been changed is (2)(ii)(b):

> D* *(1) A given belief of yours is knowledge if and only if it is true and undefeatedly justified. (2) A belief is undefeatedly justified = df. (i) It is justified by a body of evidence e (in a way that might be described by some other theory of justification), and (ii) there are no facts which are such that (a) if beliefs in them were to be added to e, you would have a body of evidence e+ that does not justify your belief, and (b) it would be realistic to ask you to add beliefs in them to e.*

Given D*, undefeated justification can be described as justification that no realistically accessible fact can shake.

For instance, suppose you believe that there is no Loch Ness Monster: Call this belief b. You have a lot of justification for b. You have watched the loch for hours, seeing no monster, and you have used underwater cameras to no avail. And b is true, since nothing satisfies the popular definition of "Loch Ness Monster" (i.e., a large creature, apparently prehistoric, unlike any other animal presently known, living in Scotland's Loch Ness). But do you know that there is no Loch Ness Monster? Suppose that there is a monster, living in a deep and distant cavern connected to the loch, revealing himself to no one, never setting snout in the loch itself. (He is shy.) If anyone were to see him, though, that person would surely say, "Look! It's the Loch Ness Monster," because he looks exactly as a Loch Ness Monster is supposed to look. The only problem is that he does not live in the loch itself. So, strictly, this animal's existence does not falsify b. For b says there is no Loch Ness Monster, and this animal does not satisfy the popular definition of "Loch Ness Monster." Still, if you were to become aware of the animal's existence, passing it on a little-used neighborhood road, say, and you were to add this awareness to your evidence for b, wouldn't you then have a body of evidence that does not support b? Wouldn't your evidence then suggest that there is a Loch Ness Monster, and hence that b is false? Nevertheless, at present you remain unaware of the fact (call it f) of the animal's nature and existence. So, f is a fact of which you are unaware and which would undermine your evidence for b, were it to be added to your current evidence for b. By D*, therefore, if f is realistically accessible to you, you do not know that there is no Loch Ness Monster.

But *is* f realistically accessible to you? Or is that single animal's lonely existence a fact of which you could never, realistically speaking, become aware? Is it therefore irrelevant to whether you know that there is no Loch Ness Monster? Does it leave such knowledge intact? Do you still have that knowledge?

10.2 Social Defeasibility

D* limits undercover facts to facts of which it is realistic to ask you to be aware. Which facts are like that? One possibility is that this question should be answered in *social* terms. Are the facts to which it is realistic to make your knowledge answerable those which other people around you would think of as relevant, perhaps because they are aware of those facts? (Even if those people are wrong about something's being a fact, the fact that they think it is a fact might still matter. We return to this issue in section 10.3.) Can we say, then, that knowledge is a true belief, the justification for which is *socially* undefeated? Is something like SD true?

SD   *(1) A given belief of yours is knowledge if and only if it is true and it is socially undefeatedly justified. (2) A belief is socially undefeatedly justified = df. (i) It is justified by a body of evidence e (in a way that might be de-*

> *scribed by some other theory of justification), and (ii) there are no facts which are such that (a) if beliefs in them were to be added to e, you would have a body of evidence e+ that does not justify your belief, and (b) most other people (among those around you) are aware of them, perhaps believing them to be facts.*

No one who lives near you is aware of that single, reclusive monster. On the contrary, they would say that many people have tried—and all have failed—to find any such animal. You are aware of that general failure, too. It is part of your evidence for thinking there is no Loch Ness Monster. Seemingly, then, your belief that there is no Loch Ness Monster satisfies SD. Your belief is true and justified, and there are no facts (1) that would disturb your justification if you were aware of them, and (2) of which other people around you are aware. If so, and if SD is true, you know that there is no Loch Ness Monster. Does this example give us some evidence that SD *is* true?

10.3 Social Defeasibility and Gettier Cases

How well does SD analyze Gettier cases? Let's consider two of them.

Case 1. Imagine going on a holiday to country X. (It is a place where dogs and sheep are banned! "Safe from Gettier," you think. But little do you know . . .) On your first day there, X's leader is assassinated. You hear a shot and some screams. Someone runs past, fleeing, gun in hand; he tells you that there has been an assassination. You believe him. Do you therefore have good evidence for that belief? Let's suppose so. Moreover, your belief is true. There has indeed been an assassination. (You act on your belief, too. You scuttle back to your hotel room, determined to lie low for a few days in order to avoid possible social upheaval.) It seems that you have a justified and true belief that there has been an assassination. But do you know that there has been one?

The (possible) problem with concluding that you have knowledge in this situation is that everyone around you (elsewhere in the hotel and outside on the street) has heard a government denial of the assassination. You did not. By the time the denial was broadcast, you were in your hotel room, listening to Beethoven. (And he has a loud voice.) Everyone else in the area believes that there was no assassination; you, too, would have believed this, had you heard the official denial. Consequently, your true belief (that there was an assassination) is present only because, quite by chance, you have been shut off from important evidence. Although the denial was false, it is important evidence. Does the fact of the denial, along with the fact that people around you accept it, imply that you do not know that there was an assassination? Have you been Gettiered, by having a justified true belief that fails to be knowledge?

And if you have, does SD tell us why that is so? Aren't you Gettiered for the following complex reason?

(1) There has been an official denial that the assassination occurred. (2) If you were aware that there had been such a denial, your justification (for thinking that an assassination occurred) would be severely weakened. (3) Other people around you have heard the denial, and they believe it to be true.

Point (1) describes the undercover fact. Point (2) explains how that fact—if it is realistically accessible—defeats your justification. And point (3) tells us why (on social grounds) that fact is realistically accessible. In this way, does SD give us some understanding of why your belief is Gettiered?

Of course, the case might not be so clear-cut. For example, what if only some of the people outside your hotel think there has been an assassination? How much of a group must believe the denial if it is to be relevant to whether your belief is justified? What if only 50 percent of the people believe the denial? What if 84 percent of them do so? Is there a clear answer to these questions? If you assume that there is, hasten to the puzzles presented in Chapter 16. But if there is no clear answer to them, does this imply that SD is unworkable?

Case 2. Does SD explain our central Gettier case (the one about the dog in sheep's clothing, first presented in section 5.1)? Looking at that field, being tricked by the dog under the sheepskin, you used your senses and your reason normally. ("It looks, sounds, and smells exactly like a sheep. So there is a sheep in that field.") Now, a crucial part of your being Gettiered is UF (described in section 9.2)—the fact that the dog is concealed under that fleece. But would UF be classified as an undercover fact by SD—that is, would that fact be a realistically accessible defeater of your justification for thinking that there is a sheep in the field?

It seems that we must answer no to this question. For a start, there is no one else with you when you are looking at the field. Hence, no one around you is aware of UF. And if we imagine there being people around you, won't they be like you in this way—standing outside the field, being tricked by UF? So, SD seems not to treat UF as being realistically accessible to you. And yet UF does seem to defeat your justification. Is SD therefore unable to adequately explain your being Gettiered by that field's contents, since it cannot explain why UF defeats your justification?

10.4 Restricted Social Defeasibility

If the dog-in-sheep's-clothing case is a problem for SD (as section 10.3 suggested), is this because SD does not recognize that even a majority of people can be Gettiered by a given situation? There could be hundreds of people standing with you, surveying that field, none of them aware of UF. Even when everyone around you correctly believes there to be a sheep in the field, can't you all lack knowledge? Can't even a group be Gettiered? If so, agreeing (even correctly) with everyone else around you can still leave you short of knowledge.

Can this problem be avoided if we acknowledge that, when it comes to having knowledge, some people's views *matter* more than others? For example, in the dog/sheep case, although anyone else in your situation would be Gettiered, too, this does not entail that no one could do better. Your situation might be faulty. And there is someone who will realize that UF is a fact, hence to whom you could profitably listen. I am referring to the farmer (the one who dressed that dog in that sheepskin). Imagine him wandering over to join you (and anyone else) outside that field. Should we say that, because he can easily inform you of UF's presence, UF is a realistically accessible fact after all? Or is it not realistically accessible to you, because you would not *believe* the farmer? Picture him approaching you and spinning his yarn—and his story. How would you react to his tale? Would you turn tail? But if UF *is* realistically accessible, owing to the farmer's ability to tell us of it, maybe we should revise SD accordingly:

> SD* *(1) A given belief of yours is knowledge if and only if it is true and socially undefeatedly justified. (2) A belief is socially undefeatedly justified = df. (i) It is justified by a body of evidence e (in a way that might be described by some other theory of justification), and (ii) there are no facts which are such that (a) if beliefs in them were to be added to e, you would have a body of evidence e+ that does not justify your belief, and (b) those people who are best placed to assess such matters are aware of such facts, perhaps believing them to be facts.*

In general, who are these special—authoritative—people? Is it always clear? The farmer seems like a promising candidate in our dog/sheep case. He knows about UF (if anyone does), and he is close at hand, able to tell you about UF. But, in the Loch Ness Monster case in section 10.1, suppose that there is a man—with the unlikely name of Joch Ness (no, I'm not joching)—who has seen that animal that everyone would think of as being a Loch Ness Monster. Does Joch's existence (along with his evidence) imply that, once again, you do not know that there is no Loch Ness Monster, since you would be unaware of a pertinent fact of which the best-placed person is aware? Part of what makes it hard to answer that question is that Joch is as shy as the animal itself. He happened upon the monster by accident, but he lives alone, talking to no one. Even if he were to meet you, he would not tell you about the creature. Is his expertise still relevant to whether you know that there is no Loch Ness Monster? Or does Joch need to be realistically accessible to you? Is knowledge a matter of having justification that takes account of the opinions of people who are (1) authoritative on the subject at hand, and (2) close at hand? How does a hermit manage to gain knowledge? In each case, who are the people whose views on your evidence are authoritative?

Is there always some one (or more) special person whose views set a mark against which everyone else's attempts at knowledge should be judged? In every situation, is there an Ideal Knower, an Expert?

When knowledge (rather than fashion, say) is at stake, are the pertinent people those who are most likely to inculcate true beliefs in you? If that is how to interpret SD*, perhaps it is simply specifying a supposedly reliable belief-forming *method*—one that is likely to lead to your having true beliefs. (On this kind of approach to knowledge, revisit Chapter 7.) Or are the pertinent people those who will not lead you astray, those who will keep your reasoning free of falsehoods? (If you think they are the right people against whom to be judged, proceed to Chapter 11.) Or are the right people those who, in turn, share beliefs with other right people? If so, SD* is starting to sound circular. How could we ever independently determine who are the right people? Are the best scientists those who agree with . . . well, the other best scientists? Is that all there is to being a leading scientist? Is pleasing The Experts what matters in knowing?

Consider a published physics paper, with tens of authors, where the experiments and measurements are so complicated and cumbersome that no small subset of the listed authors could have conducted them, thereby gaining the knowledge captured in the paper as a whole. Is it therefore the group as a whole that has that knowledge? Can knowledge be the preserve of a group rather than of an individual? If the research wins a Nobel Prize, should The Group, and not the individuals within it, make the journey to Sweden, in order to receive the prize?

FURTHER READING

Annis 1978. (On the basic idea of social defeasibility, in section 10.2.)
Harman 1973, pp. 143–145. (For a case like the assassination one, in section 10.3.)
Hardwig 1985. (On the physics puzzle that ends this chapter.)

11

False Evidence

Jerome, a prosecutor, is confident that his 101 pieces of evidence give him knowledge of the accused's guilt. The trial goes as Jerome hoped. Verdict: "Guilty." But suppose that one piece of his evidence—the piece that swayed the jury in their decision—is false. The members of the jury, like Jerome, mistakenly thought that it was true. Does it follow that none of them know that the accused did the deed? Would it worry you, if you were either Jerome or a member of the jury, if you were ever to learn of the falsity?

11.1 Avoiding All Falsity

Defeasibility (Chapters 9 and 10) focuses on whether your justification includes all of the truths it should include. Now let's consider the other side of that coin. Maybe what matters more is that you have no *false* reasons or evidence in your justification. Could the key to Gettier cases be the fact that they are cases where a person relies on some false evidence?

In some Gettier cases, at least, false evidence is used. In the second Gettier case described in section 5.1, you infer (from the belief that the animal in front of you is a sheep) that there is a sheep in the field. This final belief of yours is true. There is a sheep in the field (Sheepish by name and nature). But, it seems, that belief is not knowledge. Is this because part of your evidence is false? The animal in front of you is no sheep; it is a dog in sheep's clothing. Yet you relied on the belief that it is a sheep. You thereby used some false evidence. Is that why your final belief is not knowledge? Since (from section 2.1) knowledge is only of what is true, how can it emerge from what is false? In response to Gettier cases, then, perhaps we should endorse the following thesis:

F   *A given belief of yours is knowledge if and only if (1) it is true, and (2) it is justified (in a way that might be described by some other, more specific, theory of justification), but without your relying on any false evidence or reasons.*

Note that, in some cases, F(2) could be satisfied because your belief is justified in a way that does not require you to have any evidence or reasons at all. This would be an *externalist* way of being justified, which is discussed in Chapter 14. But most epistemologists would interpret F(2) as requiring you to have some evidence, none of it false.

11.2 Avoiding Significant Falsity

Perhaps F is too demanding, though. Must you avoid *all* falsity in order to gain knowledge? The dog/sheep Gettier case makes it look as if you must do so. But let's consider a slightly different case. Suppose that, while you are watching the animal in front of you (the dog in sheep's clothing), the field's real sheep—Sheepish—wanders into sight. Seeing him, you think about him what you think about the dog: "That is a sheep in that field." So, now you have had that thought about two animals—once about Sheepish and once about what is really the dog. Not surprisingly, therefore, you again infer the further belief that there is a sheep in the field. But is this belief still Gettiered, as it was previously (when you were reacting only to the disguised dog)? Or is your belief now *knowledge* that there is a sheep in the field?

The distinctive feature of this revised dog/sheep case is that your evidence is now an interesting mix of true and false. There is the new evidence concerning Sheepish and the original evidence stemming from the disguised dog. You have a false belief that the animal that has been in front of you all along is a sheep, plus a true belief that the animal that has just come onto the scene is a sheep. (You do not realize that the former belief is false; you take both beliefs to be true. That is why you now include both in your evidence.) Does this combination of evidence let you know that there is a sheep in the field? Or does it deny you such knowledge? Does the true evidence within it give you knowledge? Or does the false evidence within it deprive you of knowledge? In other words, when you use both pieces of evidence should we say that, because you have true evidence that would, by itself, help you to know that there is a sheep in the field, you have such knowledge? (That is, does your true evidence override your false evidence?) Or should we say that your false evidence undermines your true evidence? (That is, is the falsity of the false evidence an undercover fact that defeats your justification?) You do not think that your evidence is partly false. You think that it is all true. But does the fact that some of it is false deprive you of knowledge?

One reason why we might say that you can know there is a sheep in the field, in spite of your evidence including a false belief that the animal in front of you is a sheep, is that we might not regard that falsehood as *significant*. We might say that knowledge can be based on evidence, some of which is false, so long as no significant elements of it are false. In the original dog/sheep case, the falsehood in your evidence (your belief that the animal in front of you is a sheep) is significant because it constituted your entire evidence. But in the present revised case, you have another good (and wholly true) body of evidence on which to base your conclusion. Does this make the falsity in your evidence too insignificant to deprive you of knowledge?

To consider whether that could be so, think of your overall evidence as comprising two paths of evidence leading to the one belief (that there is a sheep in the field). Each path contains a belief that a specific animal in front of you is a sheep; only one of these two beliefs is true. (The one about the dog is false. The one about Sheepish is true.) So, you could arrive at your belief that there is a sheep in the field by relying wholly on true evidence, following just one of the two paths of evidence. You could use your perception of Sheepish instead of your perception of the dog in sheep's clothing. Does this possibility imply that the falsity in your overall set of reasons is not vital? If so, that is because, since you *could* use your true evidence instead of your false evidence, you have enough true evidence to adequately justify your belief that there is a sheep in the field. If you were to discard the false evidence, you would still have enough true evidence "left over" with which to justify your conclusion that there is a sheep in the field. Yet, because your evidence does include some that is false, you do not satisfy F's condition. If, nevertheless, you do know that there is a sheep in the field, perhaps F is too strict a condition on knowledge. Should we replace it with F*?

F*   *A given belief of yours is knowledge if and only if (1) it is true, and (2) it is justified (in a way that might be described by some other, more specific, theory of justification), but without your relying on any ineliminable, or inessential, false evidence.*

In our revised Gettier case, you have more than one reason to conclude that there is a sheep in the field. You have a belief about the animal in front of you (the dog), and you have a belief about the animal that has just wandered past (Sheepish). F* allows us to say that (1) the former belief's falsity is not crucial to whether you know that there is a sheep in the field, and hence (2) you can still have that knowledge. In theory, you could eliminate the false belief from your reasons; you would still have enough true justifying reasons.

Is that the key to knowing? Find the false reasons you do not need. Discard them. Work with what is left. Once you do that, though, aren't you back to satisfying F? So, is F* satisfied by you only insofar as you could satisfy F? On F*, you have knowledge only because you can eliminate all falsity from your reasoning—and to do that is to satisfy F. Is F therefore the key?

11.3 Why Avoid Falsity?

Is it really so bad to have falsity in your evidence? You probably think that it is. Very likely, you try to avoid falsity, and anything you include in your evidence at least seems to you to be true. (Its apparently being true is part of the reason why you have included it as evidence.) On F, you have knowledge only if you eliminate falsity from your evidence. (And on F*, you have knowledge only if you eliminate all the falsity that matters.) Thus, if you seek knowledge, and if F is right, shouldn't you try to satisfy F?

Why bother, though? Even in Gettier cases the problem might not always be that you are being led astray by false reasons. Perhaps there are Gettier cases where you lack knowledge without relying on false reasons.

For example, suppose that you are standing outside the field (yes, THE field). Again, you are looking at the dog in sheep's clothing. But this time you do not say to yourself "That animal is a sheep." Rather, you think, "I have *good evidence* for thinking that the animal in front of me is a sheep." (And aren't you right about this? Although the animal is not a sheep, your senses give you fine evidence for thinking that it is.) Your true belief *about* your evidence for there being a sheep in the field then *becomes* your evidence for thinking that there is a sheep in the field. On the basis of this new kind of evidence, you again conclude that there is a sheep in the field. And, in reasoning like that, you use no false evidence. You do not use the false belief that the animal in front of you is a sheep; you use the true belief that you have good evidence for thinking that the animal in front of you is a sheep. Apparently, therefore, you still end up with a true and justified belief that there is a sheep in the field.

Yet aren't you still Gettiered (without having used any false evidence)? You are reacting to the dog in sheep's clothing, not to Sheepish. But it remains Sheepish who makes your final belief true. (Although he is the sheep in the field, your final belief is not a response to him. It remains a response to the dog.) Doesn't that belief fail to be knowledge? Don't you still fail to know that there is a sheep in the field? You look at what seems like a straightforward sheep (though really it is anything but that); you think you have good evidence for thinking there is a sheep in the field; you conclude that there is one there; and there is—but it is Sheepish, out of sight. Aren't you Gettiered?

If so, is this in spite of having relied on no false reasons? If it is, F is false. You can have a belief that is true and justified and that does not rely on any false evidence but that nevertheless fails to be knowledge. And if that is so, why is it important to avoid falsity in one's reasoning?

11.4 Avoiding More Falsity by Thinking Less

One way in which you no doubt try to avoid falsity in your thinking is by reflecting on your evidence, sifting the true from the false. But if (as we might conclude from section 11.3) avoiding falsity is not crucial, could you simplify your life, while losing no knowledge, by thinking *less*—specifically, doing less of that careful thinking that is meant to eliminate falsity from your thoughts? Would it be acceptable for you to become less reflective about your evidence, particularly about whether it is true? That is a puzzling idea. Being less reflective about truth and falsity is not an obvious way to gain knowledge.

So, it is worth asking whether thinking harder about the truth value of one's evidence is always helpful. For instance, might such thinking confuse you about how good your evidence is? At this stage of the book, we have found no agreement on what knowledge is. Confronted by a specific case of supposed knowledge, we might struggle to decide whether it is knowledge. At first, you might be confident that your evidence is good and true. But then you pause, reflecting on the fact that evidence can be misleading. You realize that you might even be in a Gettier situation. You begin to question how good your evidence is. You become tentative in your acceptance of the evidence. You hesitate, suspending judgment. Belief departs; hence, so does knowledge. Yet, maybe your evidence was excellent. If you had not thought so much about it, and had not doubted its worth, you might have retained your evidence and your belief—and therefore kept your knowledge. So, what should you do? Think more? Think less?

Here is a more general worry, too. Why should thinking more about your evidence always help you to separate the true from the false evidence? Could it even hinder you in this regard? For, with each new thought about the evidence, more evidence is created. Your thoughts about your evidence become evidence! And if choosing the true evidence was already difficult, it remains so. You will rely on new specimens of a kind of thing (evidence) that you have already conceded is hard to assess for truth. Will your using more such specimens make your task easier? By doing more thinking, you give yourself more data through which to sift, and this process might only give you more false beliefs to eradicate! Your beliefs about your evidence might be false and misleading. You might be more and more swamped by these beliefs, unable to separate the true ones from the false ones.

Suppose that, in our revised Gettier case (section 11.2), you are about to form the belief that there is a sheep in the field, and you are using only true evidence—the evidence about Sheepish. You choose to rely on seeing him wandering past; you ignore what would be the false evidence—the evidence of the animal (the dog) in front of you. But then you engage in the following careful thinking:

> It is generally better to have more evidence rather than less. So, I should also use the evidence about the animal in front of me. But evidence can be false. Hence, maybe the animal that just wandered past, although it looked like a sheep, was something else (a wombat dressed up as a sheep?). This makes it even more important to use the evidence of the animal in front of me. Even if the animal that just wandered past is not really a sheep, the one in front of me wouldn't be a second fake! That would be too large a coincidence!

In this way, you add false evidence to your true evidence. By thinking more, trying to be more responsible in your thinking, you call on false evidence. You outwit yourself! Does that mistake ruin your overall body of evidence? (To answer this question, perhaps we would need to go back to section 11.2.) The point right now is that it might have done so. By thinking more, aiming to be more responsible in your thinking, you have possibly deprived yourself of knowledge!

That is hardly a pleasing prospect. You are probably thinking hard while reading this book. Does that lower your chances of knowing about knowledge? Would it be better (in order to know) for you to reflect less rather than more? Should you think less well if you are to have knowledge? ("Surely not. That sounds paradoxical!" Then wait until Chapter 15, where you will discover why it can also be puzzling to require *more* thinking of someone if she is to have justification and knowledge.)

> *You open a book at a drawing of what you believe to be a fifty-sided figure. You infer that you are seeing a many-sided figure—as, indeed, you are. But the figure actually has forty-seven sides. Hence, your evidence for your belief that the figure is many-sided is partly false. Does your mistake about the exact number of sides imply that you do not know that the figure is many-sided? When does false evidence matter to your knowing, and when does it not?*

FURTHER READING

Harman 1973, pp. 46–50, 120–124. (On the basic idea of the no-false-evidence account of knowledge, in section 11.1.)

Lehrer 1965. (On the question, in section 11.2, of whether the no-false-evidence account is correct.)

Feldman 1974. (For a Gettier case like the one in section 11.3.)

Elgin 1988. (On the idea, in section 11.4, that being more intelligent and imaginative can deprive one of knowledge.)

12

Induction

There was a time when no one in Great Britain thought that there were any swans other than white ones. But there were black swans in Australia (and still are). So British zoologists were wrong when they thought that all swans were white. Nevertheless, were they inductively justified in their belief? What does this tell us about induction—and about us?

12.1 Induction and Gettier Cases

Might the problem in our main Gettier case (first described in section 5.1) be that you use some *inductive* thinking in deriving your belief that there is a sheep in the field? You seem to use both deductive and inductive thinking. You reasoned like this:

> 1   *That thing in the field has the characteristic appearance of a sheep.*
> 2   *That thing in the field is a sheep. [From 1.]*
> 3   *There is a sheep in the field. [From 2.]*

Whereas the inference from 2 to 3 is deductive, the inference from 1 to 2 is inductive. This is because 1 does not logically entail 2. The fact that something appears to be a sheep does not logically ensure that it is one. And perhaps this kind of lack of a logical guarantee helps to generate the problem in Gettier cases. Might the Gettier case simply remind us that inductive thinking is untrustworthy? We ask: Is everything that appears to be a sheep really a sheep? The Gettier case answers: No! The thing in front of you appeared to be a sheep, but it was really a dog in disguise. Although 3 happens to be true, and hence your use of induction did not prevent your final belief from being true, maybe what prevented your final belief from being knowledge (that there is a sheep in the field) was, in part, the fact that you used induction.

If that were so, the problem could take either of two forms. (1) Perhaps induction never provides enough justification. Could it be that all uses of induction are to be avoided? (If you think that they are, you will appreciate Chapter 20, where we discuss skepticism about any use of induction.) (2) Alternatively, since induction is not a logically foolproof way to reason, possibly there are bad ways and good ways to use it. We would just have to be careful to use it in the good ways. Perhaps in the Gettier case, your use of induction (in inferring 2 from 1) was simply not good enough. Should we therefore try to decide what is involved in using induction well? Let's see if we can do so.

12.2 What Is Good Inductive Thinking?

Deductive thinking involves logically conclusive reasoning; inductive thinking does not. The latter usually begins with observations (e.g., of white swans) and derives a universal generalization (e.g., "All swans are white") or a prediction (e.g., "The next swan you see will be white"). Such thinking runs logical risks. No matter how many people from a given country you have met, isn't it logically risky to conclude that everyone from that country is friendly, or white, or bald, or anything else? You risk stereotyping the country's inhabitants; you thereby court mistake. (But what if you have met almost everyone from the country? You have met all but one of the 5,456,827 inhabitants. So far, everyone has been friendly. Are you justified in inferring that everyone from there is friendly?)

   Is good inductive thinking a matter of having *enough* inductive data ready to hand? Do you need to run enough tests—enough different kinds of tests? Must you interview a large and varied enough sample of a population, for instance? So, is the inference from 4 to 5 a possible example of good inductive reasoning?

   4   *In the course of a rich and varied life, I have encountered many things*
        that appeared to be sheep. And, it transpired, all of them were sheep.
   5   *Whenever something appears to be a sheep, it is a sheep.*

   Although 4 does not logically entail 5, it seems to provide 5 with good inductive support. It records that you have experienced many instances of the kind of relationship that 5 claims holds universally. According to 5, something's appearing to be a sheep is always part and parcel of its being a sheep; according to 4, in your experience this has always been so. Does 4 inductively justify 5?

   And can we generalize this example? Is a universal claim, such as 5, at least somewhat justified by a record of pertinent observations such as those recorded by 4? If you have met many people from a particular country, and they have all been friendly, aren't you at least somewhat justified in concluding that everyone from that country is friendly? That is, do these examples reveal one form that inductive justification (if there is any) can take? (In Chapter 20, we ask whether, indeed, there is any. These questions—what is inductive justification, and is there any?—are special cases of questions A and B in section 1.1.) The examples at least provide a natural way to begin formulating what it is for inductive justification to be present. Thus, consider GI:

> GI *One way for at least some beliefs to be justified is for them to be inductively justified. One way for a belief to be inductively justified is if (1) it is a universal generalization ("All Xs are Ys"), and (2) the justification for it consists of instances of it. ("This X is Y. So is this X. This X is, too. In fact, all of the Xs observed so far have been Ys.")*

12.3 The Paradox of the Ravens

Seemingly, if we are to know what constitutes good inductive thinking (inductive thinking that provides justification and hence that can lead to inductive knowledge), we must know how our experiences, as summed up in a claim like 4, can confirm a claim such as 5. The inference from 4 to 5 seems to be as good a candidate as any for one where inductive justification is transmitted (in this case, from 4 to 5). If so, what makes it inductive justification (rather than merely inductive thinking)? GI seems to answer that question. But is GI true?

It seems to be true. GI implies that 4 provides inductive justification for 5. By 4, you have experienced many cases in which things that are apparently sheep turn out to be sheep. You have thus experienced many instances of the universal generalization 5. By GI, those instances of 5 (reported in 4) provide inductive justification for 5. What could be more straightforward? (You experience many cats, all of which purr; by GI, these experiences inductively justify the belief that all cats purr. You experience many apples, all tasting different from oranges; by GI, these experiences inductively justify the belief that apples taste different from oranges. And so on.)

What do you say to the following puzzle, then? It is a version of the *paradox of the ravens*—so named because the first version of the paradox talked about ravens. I will present a version which talks about . . . yes, sheep.

By a standard rule of logic, 5 is equivalent to 6:

> 6 *Whenever something is not a sheep, it does not appear to be one.*

Generally, wouldn't we expect whatever justifies a given claim to justify anything equivalent to that claim? If so, and if 6 is equivalent to 5, anything that justifies 5 should also justify 6. (To give another example, any evidence that someone is your mother is also evidence for her being your female parent.) This reasoning supports JE:

> JE *Whatever justifies a given proposition also justifies any logically equivalent proposition.*

Suppose that we accept JE. Then there is a puzzle as to whether we can combine JE with GI. By GI, experiences of things that are not sheep, and that do not appear to be sheep, provide inductive justification for 6. Your experiences of chocolate bars help to confirm 6. ("A chocolate bar is not a sheep, and it does not appear to be a sheep.") So do your experiences of shoes and ships and sealing wax and cabbages—and kings. But do such experiences provide inductive support for 5? How can a chocolate bar (by neither looking like, nor being, a sheep) provide any justification for the claim that whatever appears to be a sheep is a sheep? Surely, experience of a chocolate bar is quite irrelevant to justifying 6.

However, GI plus JE taken together apparently implies that the chocolate bar *is* just as relevant as is something that looks like a sheep and is a sheep. By JE, whatever is inductive support for 5 is inductive support for 6—and vice versa. But, by GI, (1) apparent sheep that are really sheep provide inductive support for 5; and (2) chocolate bars that neither look like, nor are, sheep provide inductive support for 6. So, by JE, those chocolate bars also provide inductive support for 5. And what could be odder than that? How can we avoid this result? Should we reject GI? But then how can we ever determine what inductive justification is? Should we deny JE instead? Yet doesn't our experience of very tall men being able to dunk basketballs provide some inductive justification for the claim that people who cannot dunk basketballs are not very tall men?

What kind of instance, therefore, does provide inductive justification for a universal generalization?

12.4 The Problem of Grue

Presumably, instances of universal generalizations provide inductive justification for those generalizations (if they do) because they provide justification for the world having a stable and specifiable nature. Your experiences of apparently observing sheep, and the fact that they have been veridical experiences (accurate ones), supposedly justify you in thinking that all such experiences are veridical. Such a thought is a belief in the *stability* of the world, at least in some respects.

So, if we were to think of our experiences as not providing evidence for such stability and predictability, would we have to say that our experiences provided no inductive justification? If reasoning in accord with experience will lead you badly astray time and again in the future, you should not rely on your experiences in thinking about what the world is going to be like. Would it no longer be clear what is inductively justified by what? The following puzzle raises this worry (a version of Nelson Goodman's *problem of Grue*).

Select some arbitrary time—maybe this very moment (call it NOW). Is it possible that, right NOW, the world's sheep are suddenly changing into frogs? Of course not. Well, into what are they turning? Nothing. Why on earth would you expect them to change their fundamental nature at all? There is no evidence for any such hypothesis; it is an absurd idea. And yet . . . Is it possible that, unwittingly, we have been quietly gathering inductive evidence for that remarkable occurrence? Clearly, none of us think that we have been doing so. But could we be wrong?

Let's suppose that we have often apparently encountered sheep. We have seen, smelled, touched, and/or heard what seemed to be sheep. And they were sheep. So, many apparent sheep have been observed, all of which were in fact sheep. Whatever has looked, smelled, and so on, like a sheep has been a sheep. Your experiences of what have seemed to be sheep have thus provided you with inductive justification for believing that anything appearing to be a sheep is a sheep. You infer 5 from 4, thereby inductively justifying 5.

Doesn't that give you good inductive reason to believe that any future encounters with apparent sheep will be meetings with real sheep? By being inductively justified in thinking that whatever seems to be a sheep is a sheep, you are also inductively justified in thinking that whenever, in the future, something seems to be a sheep, it is one. In other words, because your past observations of what have seemed to be sheep were accurate, you have inductive justification for thinking that, in the future, whatever seem to be sheep will be sheep.

So far, this is standard inductive thinking. Now begins the puzzle. Consider a new term—"Shog." A shog is something that:

(1) is a sheep and has been observed (before NOW), or (2) is a frog and (as of NOW) is yet to be observed.

The puzzle is called the problem of Grue because Goodman's original version used the term "grue"—which stands to "green" and "blue" as "shog" stands to "sheep" and "frog." In any case, prior to NOW, anything that has appeared to be a sheep is a thing that has been observed. Insofar as it appeared to you to be a sheep, it was observed by you. Yet if all such things are sheep, they are shogs. By having been observed to be sheep, they satisfy (1) of the definition of "shog." And to satisfy "p" in "p or q"—the form taken by the definition of "shog"—is to satisfy "p or q." Standard logic tells us this, since it treats "p or q" as "At least one of p and q, maybe both." Your observations (as captured by 4) have therefore provided inductive support not only for 5 but also for 7:

5   *Whenever something appears to be a sheep, it is a sheep.*
7   *Whenever something appears to be a sheep, it is a shog.*

However, doesn't 7 entail that, after NOW, anything that appears to be a sheep (and which, as of NOW, has not yet appeared to you) will really be a frog? For, by the time it does appear to you, 7 (which you have already supported) will have led you to expect it to be a shog. But, by being a shog—and not having been observed before NOW—it is a frog. This result follows from the definition of "shog." Since the object is a shog, it satisfies that definition. But, because it has not been observed before NOW, it does not satisfy (1) of the definition. Hence, it satisfies (2) of the definition. Again, this is because the definition has the form "p or q." And to satisfy "p or q" without satisfying "p" is to satisfy "q." For, by standard logic, "p or q" is "At least one of p and q, maybe both."

If so, though, can we make sense of the concept of inductive justification? Inductive justification is justification for stability—the continuation of past patterns. If our observations of what seem to be sheep support claims that we are seeing sheep *and* claims that we are seeing frogs, what has happened to the idea that it is clear how to draw justified conclusions from our observations? Aren't we being asked to think that our observations of apparent sheep should not be interpreted as supplying evidence for the existence of sheep (as against the existence of frogs)? How plausible a thought is that?

Society does not at present use the predicate "shog." But is that just an accident of history? Could we have used it instead of "sheep" and "frog"? Maybe we have been using the wrong predicates up to NOW. Conceivably, the world is more complicated than we have realized and we *should* have been using a more complicated predicate like "shog." We seem to have just assumed that it is clear how to describe our experiences in order to justify one claim (such as 5) rather than another (such as 7). Have we been wrong about this? Do we not know what is good inductive justification for what?

> *Have your observations of what seemed to be a world around you really been observations of a woid—a woid being something that is either (1) a world and observed by you before NOW, or (2) a void and not observed by you before NOW? Yesterday you seemed to be part of a world. Were you really part of a woid? Is the world so unstable? Is it about to become a void, an emptiness? Is that what you should conclude on the basis of your experiences of it?*

FURTHER READING

Hempel 1965, Part 1. (For the original version of the paradox of the ravens, in section 12.3.)
Goodman 1955, Chapter 3. (For the original version of the problem of Grue, in section 12.4.)

13

A Priori Knowledge

(1) You (yes, you) exist. (2) Numbers exist. (3) 2 + 2 = 4. Which of these three claims is the easiest for you to know to be true? Why? Which is the hardest for you to know to be true? Why?

13.1 The Basic Idea of A Priori Knowledge

Our Gettier cases (first presented in section 5.1) featured failures to gain empirical (a posteriori) knowledge. This kind of knowledge is generally gained, if it ever is (see Chapters 19 and 20), by using one's senses. It is knowledge of the world around us. You sense the world; you experience it. If you do this well enough, you gain knowledge—a posteriori knowledge—of the world.

Is it so surprising, then, that in our Gettier cases it seems to have been your senses that led you astray? You looked, listened, and sniffed. In the dog/sheep case, your senses told you that you were in the immediate presence of a sheep. But you were not. The animal in front of you was a dog in sheep's clothing. You were led astray by those very faculties on which you must depend if you are to have knowledge of the world around you (i.e., your senses). If the animal before you had been a sheep, you would know it only by consulting your eyes, ears, nose, and so on. But in fact they have misled you. Your belief (that the animal before you is a sheep) was false.

Now, how widespread is the Gettier problem? Is there any knowledge that is present even if your experiences lead you astray? If there is, maybe it can evade the Gettier worry. Is there a "purer" kind of knowledge that you can have by using just your mind, your power of "pure reason"? Is there any such power? Is there any such knowledge?

If there is, it is what is called *a priori* knowledge:

AP   *(1) A given belief of yours is known a priori if and only if it is true and it is justified a priori. (2) A belief is justified a priori if and only if (i) it is justified (in a way that might be described by some other, more specific, ac-*

count of justification), and (ii) the justification for it does not include evidence that reports some experience(s) *of yours.*

Does a priori knowledge evade the Gettier problem? Is it a special kind of knowledge? We consider the latter question in sections 13.2 and 13.3, and the former one in section 13.4. (Note that, like F(2) in section 11.1, on a given occasion AP(2)(ii) might be satisfied by the fact that your justification does not include any evidence or reasons at all. That would be an externalist way of having a priori justification; externalism is discussed in Chapter 14.)

13.2 A Priori Knowledge and Necessary Truths

A priori knowledge might at least look special. If it is a kind of knowledge that includes justification that does not involve your having one, rather than another, specific experience of the world, then a priori knowledge apparently involves justification that comes from something other than experience. What kind of justification might that be? What, other than experiences, can justify a belief?

In order to know that there is a sheep in front of you, you need some pertinent experiences. You can experience the sheep yourself, by seeing it or hearing it, for example. Or you can rely on testimony from a trustworthy sheep-witness. Either way, you are relying on experience. To know that there is an Empire State Building in New York, you need appropriate experiences (seeing it, being told of it, and so on). You also presumably need pertinent experiences to know that horses run faster than humans. For what knowledge, if any, is experience not necessary? If experience is needed for normal, worldly knowledge, must a priori knowledge be abnormal, otherworldly knowledge?

What knowledge is like that? Must we again call on the fortune-teller whom we met in section 6.4, Madam Zelda? Does having a priori knowledge entail being more like her? Is it a matter of exercising some kind of special intuition, for instance, as she might have done? Or are there more readily explicable ways to bypass experience and still gain knowledge? Can you look at the following reasoning and Just Know, without calling on your experience of the world, that it is logically valid?

    1   Since I'm reading and thinking, it follows that I'm thinking.

And can you look at the following equation, and Just Know—again, without calling on your experience of the world—that it is true?

    2   25 + 56 = 81.

That is, are there types of knowledge—for example, logical knowledge and mathematical knowledge—that can be known a priori? Can you know 1 and 2 to be true, without referring to any of your experiences? When you try to justify the claim that 25 + 56 = 81, are you ultimately relying on your first mathematics lessons? Or can you justify the equation purely in mathematical terms, perhaps via some faculty of Mathematical Insight? Even if you cannot do so, are there others who can?

Philosophers usually call truths like 1 and 2 *necessary*. A necessary truth is a proposition that is true and could not have been false. Necessary truths contrast with *contingent* truths. A contingent truth is a proposition that is true but could have been false. It is only contingently true that there is an Empire State Building in New York; can't you imagine a slightly different New York in which no Empire State Building was ever built? It is also a contingent truth that there are no giant gorillas atop that building. Although there are none, couldn't there have been some? However, can you imagine it not being true that 25 + 56 = 81? If you cannot, is this because it logically has to be true that 25 + 56 = 81? Is it impossible for the universe to have been different in this respect? Is 2 not only true, but necessarily true?

And are necessary truths the special ones that we can know a priori? If they are propositions that had to be true, they would be true no matter what form this particular universe might have taken. Even if there had been no life in the universe, wouldn't it have been true that 25 + 56 = 81? If so, then in order to know that such propositions are true, we need not know what form this particular universe has taken. Now, how would we seek such knowledge of the universe's contingencies? Wouldn't it be by consulting our experiences—that is, our experiences of the universe? So, to say that, in order to have knowledge of necessary truths, we need not know about this universe in particular seems to be to say that knowledge of necessary truths does not require us to consult our experiences of the world. Hence, there is apparently a close connection between necessary truths and a priori knowledge. It seems that what makes a priori knowledge special is the fact that it is knowledge of a special kind of truth—necessary truths. Such thinking implies this traditional picture:

TAP   *(1) Any necessary truth can be known a priori (if it can be known at all). (2) No contingent truths (such as empirical truths about the physical world) can be known a priori. Any contingent truth is knowable (if at all) only a posteriori.*

On this picture, a priori knowledge, when present, is a special kind of knowledge directed at a special kind of truth—truths that are not about a world that is knowable only by being experienced. (But neither AP nor TAP clearly makes a priori knowledge special in the sense of meeting a particularly *high* standard of justification, such as being infallible. We discuss fallibility and infallibility in Chapters 17 and 18, respectively.)

13.3 Kripke's Puzzles

Is the difference between a priori knowledge and a posteriori knowledge that simple, though? Maybe TAP is false. Saul Kripke is the philosopher who has most famously questioned TAP. He reasons as follows. (1) Maybe there are some necessary truths (that is, truths that do not depend just on how this world is) that can be known only by way of experience (of how this world is). If there are, TAP(1) is false. For those necessary truths would not be knowable a priori. (2) Maybe some contingent truths (that is, truths that depend on the vagaries of this world) can be known without drawing on experience (of this world's vagaries). If there are, TAP(2) is false. For those contingent truths would be knowable a priori.

(1) Necessary A Posteriori Knowledge

Are there any necessary truths that are knowable only a posteriori (and hence not knowable a priori)? For short: Is there any necessary a posteriori knowledge? Is 3 like that?

> 3   *Sheep are animals.*

Sheep are indeed animals. But this fact is not something that pure thinking or sheer brainpower reveals to us. If we know that sheep are animals, don't we know it a posteriori—by experiencing sheep, experiencing animals, and noticing a close link between the properties of being a sheep and being an animal? But how close a link have we thereby discovered? Is it like the link between being friendly to other people and being liked by other people? (This is a contingent link. Even if it occurs, it might not have done so.) Is it more like the link between being tall and not being short? (That is, is it conceptually close? Is it a necessary link?)

To test the latter question, consider this scenario:

> *There is a world in which there are objects that look like sheep and sound like sheep—but which are not even animals. They are very good wind-up toys.*

In that world, do sheep fail to be animals, since the things in that world that are most like our sheep are not animals? Does such a world reveal that, although sheep are animals in our world, this truth is not writ in logical stone? If it does, 3 is merely a contingent truth—a truth that need not have been true.

Or are there simply no sheep in that world? (Those wind-up toys are the only objects in that world that even look like sheep.) If you agree that the toys would not be animals at all, but you also think that they are not sheep in the first place, are you saying that sheep do have to be animals? You would be saying that, by something's not being an animal, it is not a sheep—no matter how much like a sheep it sounds, smells, and so on. If so, you are implying that 3 is a necessary truth.

But then, if you think that (1) 3 is necessarily true, and (2) 3 can be justified only by experience, you imply that 3 is a necessary truth that can be known only via experience. That makes 3 an example of necessary a posteriori knowledge—a necessary truth knowable only through experience. And this conclusion entails the falsity of TAP(1). Do you agree with that result?

Or is 4 better than 3 at falsifying TAP(1)?

4   *Giraffes are taller than sheep.*

You can know 4, if you can, only via experience, and thus it is knowable only a posteriori. Yet wouldn't animals that looked like giraffes but that were not taller than animals that looked like sheep not really be giraffes? Alternatively, even if they would really be giraffes, would the animals that looked like sheep not really be sheep? So, isn't 4 necessarily true?

(2) Contingent A Priori Knowledge

Are there contingent truths that are knowable a priori? For short: Is there contingent a priori knowledge? Is 5 like that?

5   *Stick S is 1 meter long, where S is the standard meter in Paris, the very stick*
    that determines—throughout the world—whether a given item is 1 meter
    in length.

Can you know, just by thinking about it, that if anything is 1 meter long, the standard meter is 1 meter long? Perhaps you can, since to be 1 meter long is, by definition, to be the length determined by the standard meter. But if you do have that knowledge, then you know 5 a priori.

Yet isn't it only contingently true that S in particular is the standard meter? Mightn't some other stick have been adopted as the standard meter? If so, and if 5 can be known a priori, isn't 5 a contingent truth that you can know a priori? If so, it is a case of contingent a priori knowledge—thus falsifying TAP(2).

This example can also be explained in the following way. Suppose that you are present at the creation of the unit of measurement called the "meter." "Take a stick, any stick," you are told. Pick up stick. S will do. Its length therefore picks out—establishes—this new unit. Subsequently, a definition in terms of inches (namely, 39.37 of them) is adopted for that length that happens to be S's length. Thus, "1 meter" now means what that "inches definition" means. Stick S just happens to have been that length, hence to have satisfied the new definition, and hence to have been 1 meter long. If so, S is only contingently 1 meter long.

Nevertheless, since S did in fact set the standard that later came to be defined as 1 meter, can't we know—without checking on S's length, in order to decide whether it is 39.37 inches long—that S is 1 meter long? That is, can't we know a priori that S is 1 meter long?

13.4 A Priori Knowledge and Gettier Cases

In section 13.1 we asked whether the Gettier problem is irrelevant to a priori knowledge. Now that we might be clearer on what a priori knowledge is, we can approach that question more informedly. Thus, can you be Gettiered when you are not relying on experience for your justification? Can you be Gettiered when your target is a necessary truth, a truth that had to be true? For example, can you be Gettiered when forming a mathematical belief?

Suppose that your thinking is good, and that you derive the right answer in some mathematical equation. Still, your reasoning is lengthy (1,000 steps), and it contains two small mistakes. If you had made just one of those two mistakes, you would have come up with a wrong final answer. Luckily, you did not. You made both mistakes, and the second one canceled out the first, giving you the correct answer. And your errors did not affect the rest of your reasoning. Apart from those two mistakes, your thinking was logical and good. So, don't you have excellent justification, via your argument, for your mathematical belief? Yet, perhaps you also fail to know that the equation is true. Haven't you been Gettiered? Your final answer is true and justified, but is it knowledge? Is even Pure Reason— or the closest we can come to it—susceptible to the Gettier problem? If so, this example makes the Gettier problem even more pressing.

> *If a belief in the existence of a God is to be knowledge, would it be a priori knowledge? Would the belief be justified without reporting anyone's experiences? Could you know that there is a God without citing any of your experiences? Or would a God's existence have to be known a posteriori (via experience)? If there is a God, is this something that had to be so? That is, does a God exist necessarily, if at all? Or would a priori knowledge of a God's existence be contingent a priori knowledge?*

FURTHER READING

Moser 1987, pp. 1–9. (On the basic idea of a priori knowledge, in section 13.1; and on a priori knowledge and necessary truths, in section 13.2.)

Kripke 1980, pp. 47–63, 97–134. (On, respectively, contingent a priori knowledge and necessary a posteriori knowledge, in section 13.3.)

14

Externalism

"That was a brave act by you, rescuing that kitten from that tree."
"It was? But it was only a short tree."
"Of course it was brave. Your life was in danger as soon as you entered that field. It was a minefield."
"It was? I ... I ... I had no idea."
Was the act brave? Did the objective danger make the act brave? Or is bravery present only when fear, or at least some awareness of danger, is present?

14.1 The Basic Idea of Externalism

Meet Amy. Mathematically, she is a child prodigy. No matter how hard a calculation you ask her to perform, she provides the correct answer in a few seconds. But she can never present reasons in support of her answers. She is not conscious of having evidence in mind for her answers; and, were she to try to think hard, seeking some such evidence lurking in the recesses of her mind, she would fail. She is an idiot savant. Nevertheless, are her answers justified? Do they constitute mathematical knowledge?

How you answer that question can reveal whether you are an *externalist* about justification (and knowledge). If you say that Amy's stunning record of true answers justifies her answers, helping to make them knowledge, you would be endorsing the type of reliabilism presented in Chapter 6. You would also be exposing an externalist bent. (In a moment, I will say why.) Or you might insist that Amy has justification, but not just because of her many true beliefs: "It is because there is some underlying mechanism at work in her mind, reliably generating those true beliefs." Now you are applying the type of reliabilism encountered in Chapter 7 instead of the type which we met in Chapter 6. But still you are analyzing the situation in an externalist way.

This is because neither of those analyses requires Amy to have in mind any good evidence or reasons for her mathematical beliefs. Supposedly, she is doing something right (by being reliable), and reliabilist theories are content with this. They do not think that she consciously has to have reasons or evidence (or that she has to be *able*, by reflecting on the contents of her mind, to find reasons or evidence). (Is much the same true of the causal account of knowledge in Chapter 8?)

In contrast, recall Chapters 9 through 11 (defeasibility and the no-false-evidence accounts). These more readily capture an *internalist* way of trying to understand justification. Each makes the actual or possible possession of good evidence the key to whether a person has justification for a belief. And it is usual to interpret these accounts as attributing evidence of which the person is, or could be, easily aware (by searching her own mind). Amy would not fare so well on an internalist way of thinking about justification. We consider such thinking in Chapter 15.

Here is another example, an analogy this time. Is it possible to be in love while having no rational reasons for your feelings? "Why do you love him? Of all people, why him?" Your answer is externalist: "I don't know. I just do. I don't need reasons for feeling like this." An externalist account of justification treats having justification as like being in love in a less reasoned way. Isn't that no less love than a love that is fully reasoned? Might justification be similar? Can a belief be justified by being held in a *good but unreasoned* way (a good way, but one that does not involve your mind having, or being easily able to gain, reasons or evidence)? Externalists think that this can occur.

So, here is one way to apply the basic idea of externalism to justification. (It can as easily be applied to knowledge.)

> EX   *A given belief of yours is justified in an externalist way = df. (1) Your belief is justified (in a way that might be described by some other, more specific, account of justification). (2) Whatever it is that, by (1), makes your belief justified is not itself a piece of evidence, or a reason, in your mind. (It is not a reason of which—by reflection or introspection—you are, or can be, aware.)*

Amy's reliability, although an objective feature of her, is not something of which she is aware. Moreover, even if she were to become aware of it, and were to base her next answer partly on her new awareness of her fine record, EX would account for her justification in terms of her reliability, not her awareness of the reliability. That is, EX(1) does not entail that Amy's justification cannot involve good and reliable reasoning. But EX(2) entails that the reliability of her reasoning—that reliability being what makes the reasoning justify Amy's answer—is not itself something of which she is, or could be, aware by reflection or introspection.

Thus, externalism accounts for justification in a way that minimizes the importance of your reasons, your evidence, for a belief. EX implies that what justifies your belief is not any mentally accessible reasons or evidence that you have for the belief. EX(1) can describe something that justifies the belief. But EX(2) distinguishes between that something and your evidential perspective on the belief. Let's sum this up by saying that externalism distinguishes between justification and evidence. From a God's-eye perspective, Amy's reliability might justify her answer. Still, her mind—her perspective—contains no good evidence or support for her answer. And this state of affairs is acceptable to EX, so long as something else about Amy (such as her reliability) reflects well on her answer. (But Chapter 4 introduced the notion of justification in terms of evidence. So, keep in your mind the possibility that externalists have in their minds an unusual account of the concept of justification. Maybe they wish to bestow a new meaning on "justification.")

Part of what motivates EX is a kind of intellectual egalitarianism. An externalist might reason as follows. We should not accord justification, and hence knowledge, only to those more sophisticated individuals who seek evidence and reasons, who reflect on their evidence and reasons, and who are intellectually careful and self-reflective. Do children, and maybe even animals, have knowledge? Do children, at any rate, have justified beliefs? If so, don't they have them in an externalist way?

14.2 Externalism and Dogmatism

Let's pay another visit to Madam Zelda, our local seer from section 6.4. Imagine her predicting that you will suddenly become rich next year—you will win $900,000 in a lottery (a lotta lottery). You press her for details, asking what her reasons are for this prediction. She replies, "I don't have any reasons. I scorn them." You still seek her reasons; she provides none. No wonder; when she gazes at her crystal ball, her mind goes blank—until, with no warning, a prediction enters her mind. Then she gives voice to the prediction. Later on, she can discover or reconstruct no reasoning that she used in the course of forming her belief.

Yet none of this lessens her commitment to her prediction. And according to EX, there is no problem with saying that her prediction is justified. All that EX asks—in EX(1)—is that Madam Zelda also satisfy some other (true, and either existing or possible) account of justification. But, as EX(2) implies, this account need not give Madam Z any clearly held reasons or evidence for accepting her prediction. In fact, like Amy, she uses no reasons or evidence, seemingly with impunity. Suppose that some form of reliabilism is true and that Madam Z is a reliable predictor. If you seek truth, you cannot visit a more reliable source; if Madam Z seeks truth, she would do well to trust herself. The fact that her reliability never gives Madam Z evidence or reasons for her prediction should not deter us if we accept EX. The fact that she can never recall more than one or two of her predictions, and so can never mentally access her history of reliability, is acceptable, according to EX.

What does that reveal about EX, though? Might it reflect poorly on EX? Is externalism misguided? Madam Z has predicted sudden wealth for you, but she has no reasons in mind for doing so. Still, EX allows her prediction to be justified. If reliabilism is a correct theory of justification, EX purports to explain how a reliable belief can be justified even when the reliable believer lacks any subjective or conscious sense of how to support the belief. In this way, EX—specifically, EX(2)—supplements other theories, those acknowledged in EX(1). The reliabilist's account is filled out by the observation that despite Madam Z's reliability, she does not have any reasons or evidence as such for her reliably generated prediction. (The fact that she has been reliable does not even give her evidence for her reliability. She never thinks, "Because I am a reliable predictor, I can trust this next prediction.")

However, does externalism thereby threaten to legitimize a worrying form of dogmatism? Madam Z has no reasons for her belief, we hypothesized. But something makes her form it. And her use of this something (perhaps a reliable, yet neither understood nor consciously used, habit of foretelling the future) is what supposedly justifies the belief. Still, it gives her no accompanying evidence or reasons for her belief (including, therefore, no sense of its own contribution to her justification). So, since it supplies her with no attendant evidence or reasons for her belief's being true, isn't she like someone who insists on the truth of what he is saying without being willing or able to say anything about why it is true? Wouldn't we call this behavior dogmatic? Yet dogmatism was identified in section 1.3 as being intellectually suspect, as possibly hindering the quest for knowledge. Is there a kind of intellectual responsibility that Madam Z is avoiding—a responsibility to seek good reasons for one's claims?

The worry can be put in the following terms. When a person uses reasons, she is open to a kind of refutation from which externalism apparently tries to protect her. Yet perhaps, as an inquirer, it is a virtue to be open to at least the possibility of that kind of refutation. Could it be that if one runs from that danger, one is ceasing to inquire? If so, might this render one's associated beliefs unjustified? I will try to explain how that might occur.

Madam Z, by using no reasoning or evidence at all, uses no reasons or evidence that can be criticized. Because she is aware of none, and tells us of none, neither she nor we can discuss whether to believe her prediction. In effect, she offers us 1:

1   *You will win a lottery next year. I offer no evidence or reasons for that prediction, though.*

All that she and we can then do is await the lottery that will make the first half of 1 true or false. But, as for rational debate in advance, none is possible. Because Madam Z has no evidence or reasons for the first half of 1, there is none to be evaluated. There is only her prediction; take it or leave it.

Contrast Madam Z with Mr. Future. He claims that 2:

> 2 *You will win a lottery next year. Here is my evidence, my reason, for that prediction: . . .*

With Mr. F, there is a chance to critically assess his evidence or reasons for his prediction. That can backfire on him, of course. It makes it easier for him or us to reject his prediction on rational grounds, even before the drawing of the lottery. We can reject his reasons, refusing to believe his prediction. With Madam Z, this way of rejecting her prediction is not available, since she provides no evidence or reasons that can be rejected.

But maybe this contrast reveals a sense in which Mr. F is doing more that is *right* than Madam Z is doing. By using reasons, he is apparently open to the possibility of rational debate (within his own mind or with other people). Is that important to his not being dogmatic? And is the avoidance of dogmatism important to being justified? Can a person have justification for a belief only if he has (or could easily have) reasons that support it in a conscious and rational way? Can there be knowledge only where there is the chance of rational debate (at least within one's own mind)?

Has Madam Z therefore escaped the threat of having her reasons undermined, only because she has used none? If so, has she strayed too far from the domain of the rational? Perhaps justification is available only to those who take what is the intellectual risk of seeking reasons for their views. Perhaps knowledge, too, is like that. (And what of Amy? Is she like Madam Z in these ways? She gives correct mathematical answers with no consciously held reasons and without being able to call on any. Are her answers thereby too dogmatic, as Madam Z's seem to be? If so, are they unjustified?)

14.3 Externalism and Pointless Evidence

Suppose that, over time, Madam Z softens her attitude toward evidence. When you pay her a return visit, once more she predicts a big lottery win for you. Again you request her reasons, and this time she does not brush you aside. She says, "My crystal ball tells me what to predict. That is why I think that you are going to win the lottery." This time, at least, Madam Z is not being straightforwardly dogmatic (as she seemed to be in section 14.2).

So what, though? The avoidance of blatant dogmatism is not an end in itself. (Or is it?) What further purpose, then, is served by Madam Z's offering reasons for her prediction? (Is she merely aiming to satisfy a professional licensing requirement? Government order: "No reasons; no license.") If we were to accept an externalist account of justification, what would we say is the *point* of a person's having evidence or reasons in her mind?

After all, on EX, the evidence or reasons within a person's mind are not part of what justifies her belief. Even if Madam Z thinks of a better reason than the one about her crystal ball, she will not thereby satisfy EX. For, by EX(2), her new reasons would not be contributing to her justification. They would not be part of what is making her prediction justified. Perhaps her reliability would do so, but her reasons would not.

Does externalism therefore treat whatever evidence you have in mind as like a wheel that is unconnected to the rest of the surrounding mechanism—and hence contributes nothing to the mechanism's operation? Madam Z has evidence. She has a reason that, in her view, supports her prediction. (She does now, at any rate.) But what does it *do* for her? Should a person's evidence contribute to her being justified? If her reasons do not do that, what else do they do? Or does externalism make us see that evidence is simply not important? For example, if you know something, is evidence not needed? Do only people who lack knowledge need evidence? ("I know there's a pig in that corner. It's *some* pig. It's a terrific pig. Radiant, even—as E. B. White would have observed. I don't need evidence for its being there. I know it's there.") In general, what function does evidence fulfill in your life? Do you seek it to satisfy other people? Is it a kind of protective coloring for humans, like that which is possessed by many animals and which warns off would-be predators? Does evidence enable you to ward off would-be critics of your views? Is that its point? Would an all-knowing God require evidence?

Perhaps the most basic question posed by externalism, therefore, is whether having evidence or reasons in mind is a pointless achievement. Or is evidence (the possession of reasons) important as part of what makes a belief justified? (If you answer the latter question with yes, you lean toward internalism and away from externalism; Chapter 15 beckons. If you answer no, then what *do* you take to be the point of having evidence? Could so many of us be so wrong when we think of evidence and reasons as being important?)

> *Seeking his owner, a dog was walking along a road, nose to the ground, sniffing. Reaching a three-pronged fork in the road (spiking his nose in so doing!), he hesitated, sniffed at one of the road's continuations, then at another. At neither could he smell his owner's aroma. What did he do next? Did he sniff at the final path? Not at all; with no hesitation and no further sniffing, he set off swiftly along the final continuation of the road. Does this action reveal that he believes that his owner followed that path? If so, was the dog reasoning his way to that belief? ("She went one of these three ways. [Sniff.] She hasn't been this way. [Sniff.] Or that way. So, she went the one remaining way. See, Spot. Run.") He might have been using some specific cognitive process. Was he using evidence or reasons, though?*

FURTHER READING

Kim 1993, sections 1–2. (For an introduction to the externalism/internalism distinction.)
BonJour 1985, Chapter 3. (On the danger of dogmatism for externalism, in section 14.2.)
Wittgenstein 1953, paragraph 271. (For the metaphor, in section 14.3, of the useless wheel.)
Sextus Empiricus, *Outlines of Pyrrhonism*, I 69, in Bury 1933, p. 43. (For the core of the puz-
    zle that ends this chapter.)

15

Internalism

Socrates said that the unexamined life is not worth living. Well, how examined would a life need to be in order to be worthwhile? Is there an upper limit to how much examination a life needs? Is there a lower limit? And are all lives identical in these respects? Do some need to be more examined than others? Think about this. The quality of your life might depend on your doing so.

15.1 The Basic Idea of Internalism

If you hesitate to accept externalism (Chapter 14), perhaps you will embrace internalism instead. And the choice matters. Unless you have no justification at all (something we consider in Chapter 18), you have justification in either an externalist or an internalist way. There is no obvious middle ground.

We formulated externalism by means of EX in section 14.1. Internalism can be introduced by IN:

IN *A given belief of yours is justified in an internalist way = df. (1) Your belief is justified (in a way that might be described by some other, more specific, account of justification). (2) Whatever it is that, by (1), makes your belief justified is itself a piece of evidence, or a reason, in your mind. (It is a reason of which—by reflection or introspection—you are, or can be, aware.)*

Like EX, IN is meant to supplement other theories of justification or knowledge—those which are internalist in spirit, at any rate. Generally, they are the theories that interpret justification in terms of evidence or reasons (either consciously or accessibly within the person's mind). Defeasibility (Chapters 9 and 10) and the no-false-evidence account (Chapter 11) tend to be like that. Each sees the key to justification as the possession of appropriate evidence. Discussions of induction (Chapter 12), too, are generally internalist, since they focus on the difference between good and bad inductive evidence. A priori knowledge (Chapter 13) can be analyzed in either an externalist or an internalist manner. If Amy (introduced in section 14.1) had a priori mathematical knowledge, she had it in an externalist way. But do professional mathematicians have a priori mathematical knowledge only if they have readily available, good evidence for their mathematical beliefs?

Recall the analogy described in section 14.1 between justification and love. An externalist about love would say that you can be in love even if you have no reasons in mind to justify your feelings (and even if you could not readily think of any). An epistemic externalist interprets justification analogously, as we found in Chapter 14—that is, you can have knowledge even if you have no reasons in mind to justify that knowledge (and even if you could not readily think of any). The internalist about love, though, would deny that it can be so unreflective. "True love," he might say, "is *reasonable*. You love only if your mind can think of some reason why the other person is so wonderful." And the epistemic internalist views justification in similar terms. Unless you have easily accessible evidence in mind for a given belief, the belief is not justified. According to internalists, your justification should be internal to your mind. It is your mind that has the belief. It should also have the justification.

The alternative is to be like Madam Zelda in sections 14.2 and 14.3. At worst, you will be dogmatic, scorning the search for evidence. At best, you will have some irrelevant or pointless evidence. In neither case, say internalists, should you be credited with a justified belief. Evidence is the key to justification.

15.2 Internalism and Dogmatism

Suppose that you are still thinking about Madam Z's prediction that you will become rich next year (section 14.2). You believe her, but is your belief justified? In particular, do you have the kind of justification that would satisfy an internalist?

Unlike Madam Z, you do have evidence for the truth of her prediction. You have inquired into her professional record, deciding that it is excellent. You have talked to friends who have consulted Madam Z. You called up Madam Z's former employer (I. C. Sooth; her advertisements say "Come See Me—Because I've Already Seen You Coming to See Me"). You consulted Madam Z's professional licensing organization (the Federated Soothsayers). Everyone has told you that Madam Z is an excellent seer. ("Go see 'er," they advise.) Having found no reason to disbelieve your informants, you decided that Madam Z is indeed reliable. With this research and thinking behind you, you accept Madam Z's prediction that you will become rich next year. Is this belief justified? It is at least as justified (as supported by evidence) as many of your beliefs that are acquired by more standard means. Moreover, you seem to have supported it in a way that an internalist would applaud. You have gathered what seems to be a lot of relevant evidence.

But might that not be enough? Is there a risk, even once you have evidence that would be sanctioned by an internalist, of being too dogmatic in your acceptance of what Madam Z says? Here is how that might occur.

Whereas formerly (before believing Madam Z's prediction) you might have been receptive to all evidence bearing one way or the other on Madam Z's prediction, now you are not. When you meet one of Madam Z's trade rivals—a Mr. E (yes, he is a Mr. E)—at a party, he predicts that you will actually lose all of your money next year. But you scoff at his claims, reasoning as follows:

> *I am justified in believing Madam Z. I have evidence—readily available evidence—supporting her prediction. Hence, I am justified in dismissing any claim inconsistent with what she says. Mr. E's claim that I will become poor is inconsistent with her claim that I will become rich. So, I am justified in dismissing what Mr. E says.*

And, over the next year, whenever someone expresses a doubt as to the truth of Madam Z's prediction, you airily dismiss the doubter from your presence (anticipating your riches with a flick of your hand): "Away. Begone."

The simplest reading of internalism implies that, for your belief to be justified, you must have appropriate reasons or evidence in your mind (easily discoverable by introspection). The irony in the present case is that having such evidence might be blinding you to alternative evidence. Are you being tempted to ignore evidence for competing views? Because you have what are apparently good reasons for believing Madam Z, you might not take competing evidence (such as Mr. E's) seriously enough. Having reasons for a belief might henceforth make you hold the belief too dogmatically. You might not fall into this trap, of course. But you might. And the immediately pertinent question is whether IN leaves you vulnerable to acting like that. If it does, then internalism can succumb to dogmatism in much the same way externalism can (section 14.2). So, does it? Should an internalist worry about this possibility?

15.3 Internalism and Being Too Open-Minded

Isn't there a simple way to avoid dogmatism? In section 15.2, you were portrayed as having reasons readily available in your mind for your belief that Madam Z's prediction is correct—and as then closing your mind to further, competing evidence. So, perhaps an internalist would ask you to use your evidence, not to form a belief that Madam Z is right, but in a way that would permit you to maintain an *open mind* about the truth of her prediction. If there is an open-minded way of really believing her, should you adopt it? Should the evidence or reasons that the internalist wants you to possess be used open-mindedly? Would this open-mindedness prevent you from ignoring Mr. E just because (1) he disagrees with Madam Z and (2) you have already (albeit by using evidence) made up your mind in her favor? Would you now think "If Madam Z is right, Mr. E is wrong. But maybe he is right. Possibly I should not yet accept what she says, in spite of the evidence in her favor"?

If you are tempted by that suggestion, though, here is another puzzle—this time about open-mindedness. Is it possible to be too open-minded? Is it possible to inquire so much that one loses justification? (Be careful. Don't think about this too much!)

You have a lot of evidence in favor of Madam Z. Instead of accepting that evidence over any conflicting evidence (such as that which is furnished by Mr. E), let's say that you resolve to be open-minded. ("I will take all evidence seriously, regardless of whether it supports what I want to believe.") Presumably, you now begin to accumulate reasons for, and reasons against, believing Madam Z. So far, so good; this approach sounds eminently reasonable. But when will your efforts stop? They have to stop at some point, don't they? If you were to never cease gathering evidence, your mind could become too cluttered. There might be so much evidence that you could never use all of it properly. ("Data jam. Clear it now!") How could you ever do justice to all of it?

Suppose, then, that at some point you do stop gathering evidence on the issue. Why wouldn't the worry about dogmatism now return? Let us assume that, after a while, you still see the evidence as favoring Madam Z. Consequently, you accept her prediction as true. Does this decision leave you open, once again, to the danger of ignoring important competing evidence—evidence that might come to light only in the future? (If Mr. E renews his objections, will you be listening?) Moreover, since you have ended up believing what you originally believed (i.e., that Madam Z is to be believed), is it possible that your recognition of opposing views has been nothing more than *token* during the time when you were apparently being open-minded? After all, in the end you have not changed your mind about Madam Z. And if you were giving only token attention to opposing views, you were not being open-minded. Hence, you would not really have escaped the dogmatism worry. Is there also the possibility that you have selected the wrong moment for making up your mind? Maybe the vital piece of evidence that would have convinced you not to believe Madam Z is about to appear. But you will not recognize it for the important evidence it is because you have already committed yourself to accepting Madam Z's claim.

Or suppose that when you make up your mind, it is not in favor of Madam Z. At some stage, your apparently open-minded inquiries lead you to decide against Madam Z and to believe that her prediction is false. You change your mind about her. This decision would avoid the dogmatism worry. Since you have changed your mind, apparently as a result of considering lots of evidence, you cannot justly be accused of only having pretended to consider opposing evidence and to seriously question Madam Z's claim. By now disbelieving her, you are seriously questioning her claim. Nevertheless, is there still no guarantee that your belief is justified? How clear can it be (even to yourself) that you have formed your belief as a sincere, perhaps involuntary, reaction to nothing more than the evidence before you? Perhaps you are merely trying to avoid *looking* dogmatic. Perhaps you are so worried about being, or at least looking, dogmatic that this worry tempted you (perhaps unconsciously) to disbelieve Madam Z, changing your mind about her. To form a belief on such a basis would presumably be no way to gain justification. By inquiring, and then changing your mind, you believe that you have achieved genuine open-mindedness. But how do you *know* that you have been open-minded?

15.4 Internalism and Good Inquiry

Evidence can look like a mighty fine thing to have. But, like so much else of potential value, it has to be used carefully. Consider the following line of reasoning.

1. If you use evidence dogmatically, you close your mind to future, competing evidence. Justification departs (in the way explained in section 15.2).

2. So, open-mindedness is advisable if you are to gain justified beliefs by way of evidence. But even open-mindedness needs care—for the following reasons (from section 15.3).

2a. If you never close your mind on a given topic, you will always be seeking and/or accumulating new evidence. You will never "close the book" on the topic. Won't this method clutter your mind with more details than it can handle? (Or else you will be continually indecisive on the topic at hand. "I can't decide yet. More evidence, please.")

2b. If you do close your mind at some stage of your inquiry, you avoid the problem in (2a). But won't you face the possibility of dogmatism again?

3. The way to avoid the dangers put forth in (1) and (2) is to find a midpoint between the extremes of regrettable dogmatism and hopeless open-mindedness. Inquire in a way that considers all of the available evidence, and hence is not dogmatic. At some point, though, halt the inquiry decisively. Decisiveness without dogmatism, open-mindedness without mental overload—these sound like admirable aims for an inquirer. Is this the moral to be learned from our discussions of externalism and internalism?

This moral is not very precise, though. How are those fine aims to be achieved? Where, in practice, is the dividing line between being too dogmatic and being sensibly decisive? When does an open mind become an undiscerning, all-accepting, useless mind? When does a decisive mind become a closed mind? In short, how much inquiry is the right amount? How much evidence is enough without being dogmatic? How open is a usefully open mind? Such questions catapult us into Chapter 16.

Those questions arise even if, over time, your evidence points in one direction, supporting one proposition. Imagine that you keep on investigating Madam Z's predictive record and that the evidence continues to favor her. Would this uniformly and sustainedly supportive evidence settle the issue? The following options suggest that it might not.

1. If you stop your inquiries at some point by thinking "Surely now, at long last, I have enough justification," do you fall prey to the dogmatism worry?

2. Even if the evidence points in one direction, must you follow it? Can you still be legitimately hesitant about what conclusion to draw from your evidence? Have you no choice in the matter? (Chapter 20 considers this kind of question.)

3. Yet if you stop your inquiries at some point by just ceasing to rely on evidence or reasons ("I can't take any more of this. I can't spend my whole life chasing, or sifting among, pieces of evidence"), internalism no longer applies to you. By ceasing to form beliefs in response to, or which happen to be supported by, reasons that are within (and that can be easily found there by) your mind, you no longer satisfy IN(2). At best, you have justification in an externalist way. Clause (1) of EX and of IN might apply to you—but it would be clause (2) of EX, not of IN, that you would also satisfy. If this externalist option sounds plausible, pay a return visit to Chapter 14. Tired of searching for evidence, but too worried about dogmatism to stop, you might say, "But isn't there another option? Can't there be a compromise between externalism and internalism? After all, can't love be sometimes unreasoned, sometimes reasoned? By analogy, could justification be sometimes externalist, sometimes internalist? Could it contain elements of either basic approach?" Well, that option would require some rewriting of EX and IN. Can you think of a good way to do this?

In early summer, Huck and Tom both sweat through a mutiple-choice exam. They provide all the same answers to the same questions (answer (a) for question 1, (c) for 2, (b) for 3, (a) for 4, and so on). They both finish early. But while Tom leaves the exam room (to go fishing and kidnapping), Huck stays on. Beside each question, he briefly writes his reason for his answer. So when he turns in his exam, each of his answers is accompanied by a short explanation of why he has chosen it. Of course, in a multiple-choice exam, that is seemingly a pointless thing to do. It does not make his answers more justified. Or does it? Should Huck receive a higher mark than Tom? How much of life is like a multiple-choice exam? In general, when (and why) should you have explanations or reasons ready to hand?

FURTHER READING

Alston 1989, Chapter 8. (On different conceptions of the internalism/externalism distinction.)

Plantinga 1993, Chapter 1. (On the basic idea of internalism, in section 15.1.)

Feldman 1988. (On having evidence in mind, a central internalist concept, in section 15.1.)

Alston 1989, Chapter 9. (On the possibility, at the end of section 15.4, of combining externalism and internalism.)

16

Vagueness

A tide can ebb slowly, leaving water in rock pools and the sand. Does this muddy the distinction between the ocean and the land—between where one ends and the other begins? Is there a real boundary between them? If so, then where, exactly, is it? Or is the distinction arbitrary—invented by us, not really part of nature? Is the shoreline more like a disputed border between two countries than the physical discontinuity between two people? Are the ocean and the land somehow one and the same?

16.1 Is Knowledge Understandable?

Our aim (from Chapter 1) has been to understand knowledge. This quest has led (via Chapter 4) to an attempt to understand justification. Have we succeeded? (Have we even begun to succeed?)

We have succeeded only if at least one of the suggestions offered thus far captures what it is to know or to have justification. And is it clear that any one of them does that? If not, is that because we still have not found the right account? (Is the fault ours?) Do we just need to keep on searching? Must the right account be "out there," awaiting discovery? Have we not looked hard enough for it?

Or is there a deeper reason why we have not yet fully understood knowledge? Perhaps, no matter how long and hard we look, we will never find an adequate account of knowledge because no such account is even possible, at least not for us. Any account is either externalist (Chapter 14) or internalist (Chapter 15); yet both externalism and internalism seemed puzzling. Maybe both of them fail. If they do, is that because U is false?

U *Knowledge is in principle understandable by us. (If we think hard enough and long enough, we can find out what it is to know, and what it is to not know. If we do not understand knowledge, this is because we have not yet thought long enough and hard enough about it.)*

All of the suggestions proposed thus far apparently presuppose U. (Has U, in fact, guided those efforts? If you think that U is not true, will you cease trying to understand knowledge? Do you seek only what you think exists?) So, is U true? Is knowledge understandable?

16.2 Vagueness and Knowledge

One possible way to deny U is to argue that knowledge is too *vague* a concept to be understood. A vague concept is one with borderline cases. For instance, take the concept of baldness. To have literally no hair on one's head is to be bald. That seems clear. It is equally clear that having a thick, matted clump of hair on one's head is to not be bald. But what about all of the possible cases in between? To have 128 hairs on one's head . . . does that make one bald? Does it depend on how thick the hairs are? Does it matter how long they are? Does it depend on how evenly they are distributed across the scalp? What about 129 hairs? Is that a substantially different case compared to 128 hairs? Could someone with 128 hairs be bald, and someone with 129 not be bald? What about having only five hairs? Surely that is bald, isn't it? However, it is not as bald as having no hair. What about having one hair less than you had yesterday (when you had enough hair to fill a pillow)? Where is the dividing line between being bald and not being bald? Perhaps there is no objective answer to these questions—and no determinate boundary between being bald and not being bald. If so, then the concept of baldness has borderline cases—that is, cases where it is not clear whether we have an example of the concept in question (in this instance, an example of baldness).

But then it is not surprising that, beyond agreeing that having no hair at all makes one bald, different people use "bald" differently. (David thinks John is bald because John has little hair. John does not call himself bald.) Might some of those varying uses be false, though? (Might all of them be false?) Perhaps the term is used loosely, inaccurately. Yet maybe that is inevitable when a term is inherently vague. Is it impossible to nonarbitrarily determine a boundary between being bald and not being bald? Perhaps we could agree on a boundary at an Anti-Vagueness Convention held in Texarkana—"Item 16: Baldness." But would our choice be arbitrary?

And worryingly, perhaps knowledge is like baldness in these respects. Consider the following story.

Suppose that, on a really good day, your eyes are 100 percent reliable over a distance of, say, 200 yards. If your eyes are ever to give you knowledge, it is presumably on such days. Suppose, too, that on a really bad day, your eyes are only 1 percent reliable over that distance. (On such a day, you may as well be asleep. That is how hopeless your eyes are on days like that.) If your eyes are ever to not give you knowledge, it is presumably on such days.

What kind of day are your eyes having today? Really good? Really bad? Somewhere in between? The answer matters. Too far in one direction, and your eyes are not giving you observational knowledge; too far in the other direction, and your eyes are giving you such knowledge (if they are ever to do so). Where, along this spectrum of possible degrees of reliability, is your vision located today? What if your eyes are 51 percent reliable today? Is that good enough to give you observational knowledge? What if they are functioning at 52 percent reliability? What about 53 percent? And so on. Where is the line between the kind of vision that gives knowledge and the kind that does not?

Perhaps there is no such line. Maybe the concept of knowledge is like the concept of baldness. Many concepts are like that; is knowledge one of them? Here are some other possible examples of vague concepts. (1) A country's being overpopulated; where is the precise boundary between overpopulation and underpopulation? (2) Using an appropriate amount of force in self-defense; where is the precise boundary between the right amount of force and too much force?

16.3 Slippery Slopes and Reliability

Can we answer these questions about knowledge by focusing on the easiest cases—100 percent reliability and 1 percent reliability—and working our way carefully from them to the less clear cases in between? Maybe we can reason like this:

> *(1) If your eyes, when operating at 100 percent reliability, give you observational knowledge (leaving aside the Gettier problem in Chapter 5), won't they do likewise when operating at 99.999 percent? After all, the difference between 100 percent and 99.999 percent is trivial. A belief gained via eyes that are 100 percent reliable is insignificantly more reliable than one gained via eyes that are 99.999 percent reliable. (2) Doesn't the same reasoning apply to the difference between 99.999 percent and 99.998 percent reliability? If 99.999 percent reliability gives you observational knowledge, won't 99.998 percent do likewise? (3) In each of these cases, the difference is trivial. And surely trivial differences cannot take you from knowing to not knowing.*

However, such reasoning quickly becomes puzzling. If the difference between 99.999 percent and 99.998 percent reliability is too trivial to turn you from someone who is gaining observational knowledge into someone who is not doing so, isn't that also true of each of the following transitions?

> *99.998 percent to 99.997 percent, 99.997 percent to 99.996 percent, 99.996 percent to . . . to 1.002 percent, 1.002 percent to 1.001 percent, 1.001 percent to 1 percent*

Such reasoning blurs what was formerly, and intuitively, a clear difference between knowing and not knowing. It commits us to saying that each of these transitions is from a degree of reliability that gives you knowledge to a lesser degree of reliability—which nevertheless still gives you knowledge. In each case, the transition is trivial (a difference of a mere 0.001 percent each time), and it seems true that a trivial difference cannot turn knowledge into nonknowledge. The blurring occurs like this:

100 percent reliability gives knowledge (we are assuming, for argument's sake). So, since a mere 0.001 percent less reliability cannot deprive you of knowledge, 99.999 percent also gives knowledge. So, since a mere 0.001 percent less reliability cannot deprive you of knowledge, 99.998 percent gives knowledge. So, since a mere 0.001 percent less reliability cannot deprive you of knowledge, . . . 1.002 percent gives knowledge. So, since a mere 0.001 percent less reliability cannot deprive you of knowledge, 1.001 percent gives knowledge. So, since a mere 0.001 percent less reliability cannot deprive you of knowledge, 1 percent gives knowledge. We end up saying that your eyes give you knowledge even on days when they are only 1 percent reliable.

That conclusion sounds odd, though. It is also inconsistent with our earlier assumption that, if ever your eyes can be said to be not giving you knowledge, it is on days when they are as unreliable as 1 percent.

This puzzle can become even more perplexing. Let's reverse the above reasoning, this time starting at the other end of the reliability spectrum. We begin by noting that since 1 percent reliability does not give you knowledge, 1.001 percent is similarly ineffective. After all, the 0.001 percent difference between 1 percent and 1.001 percent is trivial. A belief gained via eyes that are 1.001 percent reliable is insignificantly more reliable than one gained via eyes that are 1 percent reliable. We then repeat this reasoning, time and again, all the way up to 100 percent. Each transition is a trivial move from a degree of reliability that is too low to give you observational knowledge. If we continue to say that a trivial difference in reliability cannot make the difference between knowing and not knowing, mustn't we eventually say that even 100 percent reliability does not give you observational knowledge?

Not only does this new conclusion sound intuitively odd; it is inconsistent with our earlier assumption that if ever you are to have observational knowledge, it is on days when your eyes are working perfectly. So we have blurred the line between what is knowledge and what is not knowledge. How can we nonarbitrarily make that line clear again (if, indeed, it ever was clear)?

This kind of puzzle uses what is called *slippery slope* reasoning. We begin with what we think is a clear understanding of some cases of what is, plus some cases of what is not, knowledge—and we blur the distinction between those cases by finding many intermediate, and only trivially different, possibilities.

Try repeating the above reasoning on the following example. (1) Maybe every day of your life, your mind plays tricks on you—so much so that on no day do you know anything. You never realize at the time that you are being tricked. (2) Maybe on no day of your life does your mind play even a single trick on you. Other things being equal, such a mind is well placed to gain knowledge. (3) But aren't there many possibilities between these two? Where do you draw the line between an acceptable number of "trick days" in a life (a number that allows your life to be one in which you gain knowledge) and an unacceptable number of them (a number that does not allow your life to be one in which you gain knowledge)?

16.4 Generalizing the Puzzle

Don't presume that the puzzle arises only for attempts to understand knowledge in terms of reliability. Section 16.3 provides one example of how the worry might apply to the attempt to understand knowledge. But it also applies to other attempts.

For instance, we asked (in Chapter 8) whether the key to having knowledge is being causally linked to an appropriate fact. Perhaps you know that you are hot, for example, because (in part) you are being acted on by the heat. But aren't there standard, and nonstandard, ways to be acted on by the heat? Where should we draw the line between the two kinds? Do you know that it is hot, if (1) you have been inside an industrial refrigerator all day (as part of an attempt to break the world record for the number of days spent in a refrigerator), but (2) a friend joins you for a few minutes each day in order to give you a news and weather report? What if the friend is only 99 percent trustworthy as a source of information? What if he is only 98 percent trustworthy? What if . . . ?

Such questioning can be repeated for the other concepts we have discussed. Try it for yourself. Test this worrying claim. Then test it again to make sure of your previous thinking. Test it once more. Then again. How many times should you test it in order to know that your conclusion is true? Is there a clear answer to this question? Or does slippery slope reasoning apply here, too? Where doesn't it apply? (Have we let loose a monster?)

16.5 Escaping the Slippery Slope

Is it hopeless to try to understand knowledge? Well, we might think that the slippery slope puzzle helps us to understand knowledge by telling us this much about it: There are clear cases of having knowledge, clear cases of lacking it—and unclear cases in between (the puzzle's distinctive contribution being to reveal the existence of the unclear cases). Yet is even that much understanding possible in the face of the slippery slope puzzle? It is, so long as we can draw a line between the clear cases and the unclear ones. But can we do even that? *Is* there a clear border between clear cases and unclear ones? Consider the following possibilities.

1. You might insist that there are clear cases of having knowledge, clear cases of lacking it, and other cases—unclear ones, borderline ones. But is even that claim so clear? Can't there be clear borderline cases and borderline borderline cases? Maybe a belief formed by a method that is 50 percent reliable is a clear borderline case (between knowing and not knowing). Equally, though, might a belief formed by a method that is 60 percent reliable be a borderline borderline case? Is it on the borderline between (i) being on the borderline between knowing and not knowing, and (ii) knowing?

If you claim that there is a difference between knowing and not knowing, the challenge is to find it. Probably all of us believe that there is a difference between knowing and not knowing (and that we can recognize cases of each). But *where* is that difference? If we cannot find it, what is our justification for thinking that there is one? Of course, as with baldness, we could stipulate a precise boundary between what we would henceforth call "knowing" and "not knowing." But might any such boundary be too artificial and arbitrary? Go on. Decide how many hairs it takes for someone to not be bald. How nonarbitrary is your decision?

2. Or, if there is no objective border between knowing and not knowing, is the distinction between knowing and not knowing threatened? If we give up that distinction, do we admit that we cannot understand knowledge? Do we give up our whole epistemological project?

3. Should we see the distinction between knowing and not knowing as flexible, as something that depends on the believer's context? Perhaps no single degree of reliability, for example, distinguishes knowing from not knowing. Maybe on some occasions (e.g., in medical testing) you have to be especially reliable in your thinking if you are to gain knowledge. (Would knowledge of a God's existence be like that?) Possibly at other times you can gain knowledge by meeting a looser standard. Can you think of situations like that? Nevertheless, isn't there still something in common to these occasions? Even if we set high standards in one context and lower ones in another, isn't there something shared by the two contexts—namely, knowledge? But, once again, what distinguishes it from nonknowledge? And as soon as you try to answer this question, don't you again encounter a slippery slope? Even if there is no single degree of reliability, say, common to all situations in which knowledge is present, is there a specific *range* of degrees of reliability that distinguishes knowledge-situations from those in which knowledge is absent? And where are the borders of that range? If there are none, we return to (2). Does "knowledge" become a meaningless term?

Pick a topic about which you care passionately and have thought long and hard. Couldn't you give it one more minute's thought? Wouldn't that improve your thinking about the issue? Fine, but why stop there? Wouldn't a further minute's thinking about the issue help even more? Then wouldn't another minute's thinking help still more? And so on. Hey, maybe you need to do a lot more thinking! Do you? (Think—for at least a minute—before answering.)

FURTHER READING

Fogelin 1987, pp. 72–77. (On slippery slope reasoning in general.)
Sainsbury 1988, Chapter 2. (On responses to slippery slope reasoning in general.)
Lewis 1979, pp. 339–347, 351–354. (On vagueness and context, as in section 16.5(3).)
Sorenson 1987. (On some further implications of the vagueness of "know.")

17

Fallibilism

When you buy a lottery ticket, do you know that you will win? "No, but I don't know that I won't win. For all that I know to the contrary, I might do so!" Is that why you have bought a ticket for today's lottery? Do you often act on the basis of what you don't know?

17.1 Fallibilism and the Slippery Slope

We began (in section 1.1) with two questions—A (What is knowledge?) and B (Is there any knowledge?). But the slippery slope puzzle in Chapter 16 threatens to make these questions unanswerable. It might even make us discard the concept of knowledge—and hence answer B with no. Are these acceptable outcomes? If not, maybe we should think about what fuels the slippery slope puzzle.

Suppose that a teacher sets a due date for an essay and tells the class that no late essays will be accepted. She thereby sets a very high, or strict, standard. There is only one way to satisfy her: Hand your essay in on time!

But suppose, too, that because you are sick for the three days before the due date, you do not complete the essay on time. On the due date, you approach the teacher, tell her what happened, and ask for an extension. She refuses. You curse inwardly: "Why can't she give me an extra few days? Would it hurt her terribly to do so?" She, too, curses inwardly: "Why can't I give him an extra few days? Would it hurt me terribly to do so?" Well, would it?

Maybe, maybe not. Can we answer this question without returning to the slippery slope puzzle? The teacher is concerned about that puzzle. That is why she gives you no extension. She is worried that if she permits you to hand in your paper a few days late, it will become hard for her to refuse requests from everyone else. Wouldn't almost everyone want an extension? And although she believes your claim that you were sick, she might think that some students will not tell her the truth and that she will not know how to distinguish those who are being truthful from those who are not. Moreover, she does not want to rank, in order of seriousness and merit, all of the excuses students might offer. How could she do it nonarbitrarily? How should she compare (1) three days in bed with a virus, looked after by one's parents, with (2) suddenly being required by one's boss to work on the two days one had allocated to writing the essay? What about a student who felt sick but managed to hand in her essay? Maybe her essay was poorer than it would have been if she had been healthy. Yet, since the teacher had said that there would be no extensions, the student preferred to hand in a lesser essay than no essay at all. If you were to be given an extension, should the teacher then talk to every other student, in order to find out whether they needed extensions? Could she ever nonarbitrarily "even up" the conditions for everyone in the class?

A simple way for the teacher to avoid such problems is to not allow them to get started. Accordingly, she says that she will accept no late papers. She sets a strict standard.

Should we do something analogous for knowledge? Should we set so high a standard for knowledge that no slippery slope problem ever develops? Should we deny that eyes that are 96 percent reliable, for instance, can give knowledge? (Is this like saying that a student who is sick, but not desperately so, merits no extension?) For once we allow 96 percent reliability to be appropriate for knowledge, where do we draw the line? The slippery slope puzzle poses this question: If 96 percent reliability is good enough for knowledge, is 95.999 percent good enough too? Then the puzzle continues: "I guess it must be good enough. There is only a trivial difference between them. And trivial differences are . . . well, trivial." Once we begin talking in this way, we face the puzzle.

So should we avoid that way of talking? Perhaps we should cultivate hard stares and jutting chins when thinking about knowledge and accept nothing less than 100 percent reliability. More generally (in case reliabilism is a mistaken account of justification), perhaps we should say that nothing less than the best will do for knowledge—and demand that, in order to be knowledge, a belief not only has to be true but also has to be perfectly justified. In other words, your justification must guarantee the truth of the belief. Gone would be justification that makes a belief even quite probable; the justification would need to guarantee truth.

The apparent problem with this approach, though, is that it could end up denying knowledge to (at least) almost all of us. Just as no late essays would be accepted for marking, nothing less than conclusive justification would be accepted for knowledge. But then knowledge would be well-nigh unattainable. And such exclusivity may be too harsh, unpalatable. Must we go to such extremes if we are to avoid the slippery slope?

Well, consider the alternative. How cogent is a more generous approach to knowledge? Teachers rarely want to look, or be, noteworthily strict and apparently unsympathetic. A teacher might feel like she is being fair to you if she gives you an extension. But might she actually be failing to be fair, all things considered? Is she making her treatment of the class as a whole unfair by not treating everyone equally? A more generous policy on attributing knowledge could be just as worrisome. Is it too hard for us to treat all claims to knowledge equally once we become generous in our approach? A given belief might appear to us to be knowledge, for example, only because we are not taking into account enough other beliefs—perhaps competing ones, along with *their* claims to being knowledge. The "bigger picture" might make us less generous about attributing knowledge.

More generous approaches to knowledge fall under the category of *fallibilism*. This concept is most easily presented as a general thesis about the justification component of knowledge (or whatever else knowledge requires in addition to true belief):

FJ (1) *A given belief of yours is fallibly justified = df. (i) Your belief is justified (in a way that might be described by some other, more specific, account of justification). (ii) A belief's being justified in the way referred to in (i) is compatible with its being false. (2) At least some of your justification is fallibilist, as defined in (1).*

For example, suppose that your belief in your best friend's good character is not 100 percent reliable. Even if some version of reliabilism (as presented in Chapters 6 and 7) is true, your belief is justified only fallibly at best. Thus, your justification does not entail that your belief is true.

Similarly, suppose you believe that you are wearing a hat. You seem to remember putting on a hat this morning, and it feels to you as if you are still wearing one. This evidence might make the belief undefeatedly justified (as described in Chapters 9 and 10). But does it guarantee the truth of the belief? If not, then the belief, even if justified in this way, is only fallibly justified.

FJ thus captures a "loose" approach to justification. Having fallibilist justification is compatible with believing falsehoods; to have fallibilist justification for a belief does not entail the belief's being true. By FJ(1), therefore, such justification is not perfect. A fallibilist is generous, trying to make justification more accessible for imperfect beings—such as you and me.

But if fallibilist justification is not perfect, and if—as FJ(2) claims—you have some such justification, it is natural to say that within your body of justification, there is better and worse justification. (Maybe you have fallibilist justification for the belief that the weather is hot today, and fallibilist justification for thinking that yesterday was also hot. But perhaps your sensing of today's heat is more trustworthy than your memory of yesterday's heat. That makes the former belief the firmer belief—the better justified of the two.) So, to test FJ(2) is to test the slippery slope puzzle about justification. For that puzzle relies on distinguishing between degrees of justification—that is, better and worse cases of justification. And to reject FJ(2) would be to say that justification has to be perfect. We would thereby confess ourselves unable to distinguish a better case of justification from a poorer one. Each case of it would be perfect—in which case, no slippery slope puzzle would arise for the concept of justification.

17.2 Fallibilism and the Lottery Paradox

One way to test FJ(2) is to ask whether it is too generous. In allowing that a belief can be justified in a way that does not guarantee the belief's truth, does fallibilism open the epistemic floodgates? If we accept good but imperfect justification, does our generosity lead us astray?

Perhaps we can answer that question via a version of the *lottery paradox*. Suppose that you buy a ticket in a 100-ticket lottery. You never look at the number on the ticket. You know only that it is a ticket in a lottery. But the lottery, you believe, is fair. This allows you to reason in the following manner:

> *In a fair lottery, all tickets have an equal chance of winning. Hence, I can have no evidence, prior to the drawing of the winning ticket, that ticket number 1, rather than ticket number 2 (or number 3, or number 4, and so on), will win. I cannot rationally favor any one ticket over another. But this is not good news. For doesn't each ticket have almost no chance of winning? With each ticket, chosen arbitrarily, I have excellent evidence for thinking that it will lose. It is 99 percent likely to lose and I am aware of this. Don't I therefore have good (fallibilist) justification for thinking, of each ticket, that it will lose?*

If you are right, though, you have (1) no justification for favoring one ticket over another, and (2) good (fallibilist) justification for thinking, of any given ticket, that it will lose. And, given (1), doesn't (2) imply that you have good justification for thinking that no ticket will win? (Imagine buying every ticket in the lottery. Shuffle them; lay them face downward. Point at each in turn; realize that it has almost no chance of winning. When you have done this with each ticket, aren't you committed to thinking that none of them will win?)

Yet isn't that line of reasoning inconsistent with what you are no less justified in believing—namely, that there will be a winning ticket? Unless the lottery is not fair, or is never drawn, one ticket will win. You are at least as justified in believing that one ticket will win as you are in believing, for any given ticket, that it will not win. Once more, isn't there an inconsistency in all of this? How can you be justified in thinking that no ticket will win and no less justified in thinking that some ticket will win? Can you rid yourself of such unwanted inconsistency?

Perhaps you think that you can do so in this way:

> *I am perfectly justified in thinking that some ticket will win, and only imperfectly (albeit very well) justified in thinking that no ticket will win. But, when I can, I choose between possible beliefs on the basis of how justified they are. So, I believe that some ticket will win; I do not believe that none will win.*

This reasoning, however, might indicate only your determination to *reject* FJ(2)—by not really accepting (as you would presumably do, were you to think of it as being justified) the imperfectly justified belief. If it does, the lottery paradox has succeeded, after all, in questioning FJ(2). (Hurry, then, to section 17.3!)

You might object that the puzzle plays on the peculiarities of lotteries, and that a lottery is not a situation where we expect to gain justified beliefs. "Give me a more straightforward context. That's where I can gain fallibly justified beliefs. So, FJ(2) remains true." But where is the boundary between the odd situations and the normal ones, those in which fallibilism cannot be applied safely and those in which it can? If you think there is such a boundary, visit Chapter 16. When do you, and when don't you, need to avoid fallibility if you are to attain justification? Where is the boundary between those kinds of situations? Maybe there is none. Might your life be one large lottery paradox?

17.3 Rejecting Fallibilism

The lottery paradox casts doubt on FJ—specifically, on FJ(2). Do problems ensue when you claim justification for beliefs for which you have good, but inconclusive, evidence? Is justification always infallible instead? Should we discard FJ for IJ?

> IJ (1) A given belief of yours is infallibly justified = df. (i) Your belief is justified (in a way that might be described by some other, more specific, account of justification). (ii) A belief's being justified in the way referred to in (i) is incompatible with its being false. (2) All of your justification (if you have any) is infallibilist, as defined in (1). (None is fallibilist.)

That is, should we approach justification much as the teacher approached essay extensions? If so, we would accept as justification only evidence, say, that met the strictest of standards. We would make it difficult to have a justified belief. (Note that IJ does not entail what would be the unwelcome result that all beliefs in necessary truths—truths that logically must be true, as section 13.2 explained—are infallibly justified. Suppose that you believe that $53 + 139 = 192$. Your belief cannot be false. But it is not therefore infallibly justified. If you are bad at addition, and you are merely guessing that $53 + 139 = 192$, your belief is not justified at all. IJ(1)(i) undoubtedly combines with any of the theories of justification described in earlier chapters to deny justification for your belief.)

Anyway, if we were to accept—as required by IJ(2)—that only infallibly justified beliefs are justified, maybe we can defuse at least some of our previous puzzles (as follows).

First, if justification has to be as good as IJ(2) demands, you are not justified in believing that no ticket will win the lottery. Your evidence, for each ticket in turn, for believing that it will not win is at best 99 percent conclusive. The lottery paradox followed FJ(2) in saying that you were thereby justified in the belief that the ticket would not win. But justification that puts the probability of your belief being true at only 99 percent is not conclusive justification. The ticket could still win. So, by IJ(1), your belief is not infallibly justified—and hence, by IJ(2), it is not justified at all. Thus, on IJ, the lottery paradox apparently fails to arise.

Something similar is true of the slippery slope puzzle that we met in section 16.3. Suppose we agree with IJ(2) that a belief is justified only if it is infallibly justified. Then we will insist that only 100 percent reliability, for instance, is good enough for justification. We have no need to distinguish between, say, 51 percent reliability and 50 percent reliability (asking whether one, but not the other, makes a belief justified). Neither is justified, according to IJ. By IJ(1), neither is infallibly justified—and hence, by IJ(2), neither is at all justified.

Recall the Gettier problem, too (from section 5.1). Your perceptual evidence for thinking that you were looking at a sheep was good but not logically watertight. Although the animal looked like a sheep, looking like one does not logically entail being one. (How could it do so? You were actually looking at a dog!) Does IJ close the loophole that allows the Gettier problem to exist? IJ would not class your belief as justified. It would therefore not accord you a justified true belief that nevertheless fails to be knowledge.

So, can we use IJ in proposing a simple account of knowledge? Is knowledge an *infallibly* justified true belief? Let's try IK:

> IK   *A given belief of yours is knowledge if and only if it is true and it is infallibly justified (as defined by IJ(1)).*

When did you last satisfy IK, though? Have you ever satisfied it? Does IK place knowledge beyond us all, by asking too much of us imperfect thinkers? (Yes? Then go back to FJ and the chapters that led up to it. No? Then proceed to Chapter 18.)

> *For any given day of the year, it is overwhelmingly probable that the person sitting next to you was not born on that day. So, are you justified in thinking that he or she was not born on that day? But doesn't such thinking justify you in inferring that there is no day of the year on which he or she was born?*

FURTHER READING

Kyburg 1961, pp. 196–197. (For the original version of the lottery paradox, in section 17.2.)

Levi 1967, pp. 38–42. (For a simpler version of the lottery paradox.)

BonJour 1985, pp. 53–55. (On the link, in section 17.2, between the lottery paradox and fallibilist justification.)

Dretske 1971. (On the idea, in section 17.3, of conclusive, or infallibilist, justification.)

18

Infallibility Skepticism

Does it make sense to say, "I know that I know nothing"? (The Greek philoso-
pher Socrates described himself in such terms.) Or is it self-contradictory, and
hence a statement you know cannot be true? If so, do you know that you cannot
know that you know nothing? Is it therefore impossible to lack all knowledge?
Must you at least know that you have some knowledge?

18.1 The Basic Idea of Skepticism

If we set a very high standard for knowledge, we take the risk that few (if any)
people will have any knowledge. Knowledge would be like a college with such
high admission standards that no one is ever accepted. ("No, Professor, once
again we have admitted no students." "But one of these days, Dean, wouldn't it
be nice for the college to finally find someone who satisfies its standards?") Do
we run that risk with the account of infallibilism proposed in section 17.3?
Perhaps infallibility is an unsatisfiable standard. If that is what it takes to have
knowledge, maybe no one has any.

That suggestion is what we begin to discuss in this chapter. A person who en-
dorses the suggestion that no one has any knowledge is called a *skeptic* about
knowledge. Many of the most famous arguments in the history of philosophy are
skeptical about one form or other of knowledge. We will review some of those arguments because they provide provocative reasons for denying people knowledge.

At least to most people, though, skepticism seems like a puzzling way to think.
("How can skeptics really think that no one knows anything? Isn't it human to
know?") Skeptics insist that it is more human to err than to know. A skeptic
would approve of a college setting admission standards that no one could meet.
("We're sorry, Mr. Einstein. You just don't meet our standards for admission.
Keep trying. You did well, but not quite well enough. Cheer up. Yours was the
best application since Plato's. Oh, Kant's was pretty good, too." The skeptic ap-
plauds.) You might say that unrealistically high standards would defeat the point

of the college's existence. Nevertheless, skeptics typically set standards that, they think, no one ever meets. Does their approach sound as unrealistic as that of the college with impossibly high standards? In considering how to answer that question, we will find it helpful to summarize the general form taken by skeptical arguments:

> S1   *For any given person, the person's having knowledge requires his or her being thus-and-so.*
> S2   *But no one ever is thus-and-so.*
> S3   *So, no one ever has knowledge. [From S1 and S2.]*

Let's call this form of reasoning the *skeptical template*. Premise S1 is an answer to question A in section 1.1—What is knowledge? S1 makes a claim as to what, at least in part, knowledge is like. And conclusion S3 is an answer to question B—namely, Is there any knowledge? The answer, according to S3, is no.

There are many possible instantiations of S1, some of which we have discussed. For example, suppose you like the idea (introduced in Chapter 11) that knowledge is a true belief based on evidence, none of which is false. A skeptic might agree (perhaps for argument's sake) that if there is knowledge, it is as you describe. He would replace "thus-and-so" in S1 with details from your account of knowledge.

He would then argue (per S2) that no one ever satisfies S1's account of knowledge. For example, he would argue that no one ever manages to remove all falsity from her reasoning.

From these two premises, he would then infer (by logically valid reasoning) that no one ever knows anything. That is, he would have conceded that knowing requires people to use evidence that contains no false reasons, but he would have proceeded to argue that people's evidence always manages to contain something false; then, he would have concluded, it logically follows that no one ever has knowledge.

18.2 Skepticism and Infallibility

One high standard for knowledge often called upon by skeptics is the requirement of infallibility (see section 17.3). This concept is well suited to skepticism, for infallibilism seemingly asks a great deal of us if we are ever to have knowledge. It makes knowing-that-p depend on being infallible about p—a lot to expect. Mightn't it even set an impossibly high standard—one that no one ever meets?

Here is how the skeptical template applies to this case:

> S1$_{if}$ *Knowing-that-p requires being infallible as regards p.*
> S2$_{if}$ *But no one ever is infallible.*

$S3_{if}$ *So, no one ever has knowledge. [From $S1_{if}$ and $S2_{if}$.]*

You will accept $S1_{if}$ only if you accept an infallibilist account of knowledge, such as IK (proposed in section 17.3). (And do you? Need knowledge be infallible? If you do not think so, go back to Chapter 17. If you do think so, hold on tight for the skeptical ride.) Suppose for now that you do accept it. Nevertheless, you might resist becoming a skeptic. You might say, "Yes, knowledge requires infallibility. But aren't our beliefs often like that?" The skeptic responds, "No, they are never like that." He thereby insists on $S2_{if}$.

How does he support $S2_{if}$, though? Perhaps the simplest way to try to do so is to argue that no justification is ever strong enough, or sufficiently exhaustive, to guarantee the truth of any belief. An example of just such an argument appears in section 18.3. (But will the skeptic's argument supply sufficiently strong and exhaustive evidence for its own conclusion? If it does not, will the skeptic fail his own standard? Should this possibility worry him?)

18.3 The Evil Demon

You are human. And, whether or not 'tis more human to err than to know, 'tis probably human to think that one knows. So, in order to counteract that tendency, a skeptic might seek not only a reason for thinking that you lack knowledge but also a memorable such reason. This is what the French philosopher René Descartes did in his *Meditations on First Philosophy* (1641). He realized how natural it is to continually fall into the smug, unreflective assumption that one has knowledge (and lots of it!). Therefore, he proposed a rather *dramatic* skeptical possibility. It is a particularly famous skeptical puzzle, and if it succeeds it undermines all of your efforts to acquire knowledge.

Descartes suggested the possibility that there is an evil demon, or evil genius, who can put any thought at all into your mind and mislead you on any subject whatsoever. (Here is an analogy. The demon functions much as deeply unconscious motivations, desires, fears, and the like could. These, too, might lead you badly astray in your beliefs—leading you to believe that p is true, just because you hope that p is true, for example. But let's concentrate on Descartes's specific worry.) Wouldn't such a creature prevent you from ever having knowledge? Whenever you looked around you, no matter how carefully you did so, the evil demon would be watching you—playing with your perceptions and misleading you about the nature of the world. Whenever you sat down to work out a problem in geometry or mathematics, the evil demon would be present. He would give you false thoughts, cause you to think confusedly, and make your thinking completely unreliable. If there was such a demon, you would lack all knowledge.

Descartes's challenge is this: Rule out there being any such demon! If you cannot do so, are all of your efforts at knowing tainted? How can you, in good conscience, think that you know that 2 + 2 = 4, if you cannot know that this mathematical thought has not simply been planted in your mind by the evil demon? Maybe 2 + 2 is not equal to 4; perhaps the evil demon merely makes us all think that it is. So, even a priori knowledge (see Chapter 13) is under threat. If you cannot know that this mathematical belief has not been put into your mind by the evil demon (says the skeptic), you cannot know that the belief is true. Such thinking gives the skeptic his premise S1$_{ed}$:

> S1$_{ed}$ *Your knowing-that-p requires your knowing that there is no evil demon causing your belief that p.*

S1$_{ed}$ is apparently an instance of S1$_{if}$ (from section 18.2). If you cannot know that there is no evil demon messing with your mind, presumably your beliefs are not infallible. An evil demon does not seem conducive to infallibility. On the contrary; it fosters fallibility.

And, continues the skeptic, you can never know that there is no evil demon lurking behind your thoughts, causing them, shaping them. The reason why you can never catch the evil demon out in his deceitful deeds is that he does his work while giving you no hint that he is doing it. It is not as if you could find a "calling card" left by the demon. He is not like a computer virus that makes its presence felt when upsetting your files by inserting a message in them or by clearly messing with their content. He is more like a computer virus that upsets your files— your thinking—without your realizing that it is doing so. If this evil demon could exist, not only is S1$_{ed}$ true, but S2$_{ed}$ is, too:

> S2$_{ed}$ *But you never know that there is no evil demon causing your belief that p.*

The skeptic is not saying that there is a demon, of course. He is saying that you cannot know that there is no demon. Nor can you know that there is one. You cannot know about the demon either way. Our skeptic says that you lack both of these pieces of knowledge.

Well, is S2$_{ed}$ true? Try to disprove it. Tell us how you know that there is no evil demon playing with your mind.

According to the skeptic, any such attempt is doomed to fail. For any such attempt involves you in doing some thinking. ("If I concentrate really hard, I can look for inconsistencies in the thinking left behind by the demon. Surely he will make some mistake like that.") And, according to the skeptical hypothesis, the demon will be playing with that thinking as well. Therefore, even the attempt to confront the skeptic's worry is susceptible to the worry. (So says the skeptic, at any rate. Is he right?)

Could you try to "correct for" the demon's meddling, though? Could you reason as follows?

> *I cannot know that the demon is not always misleading me. But so what? If he is, I need only believe the opposite of what I would otherwise believe. Hence, I could still have a stable set of beliefs. And that will satisfy me. What more could I ask of my beliefs?*

But once you attempt to carry out this plan, don't you quickly fall into the following mental morass?

> *I think that this thing in front of me is a dog. But wait a moment; should I trust that thought? Maybe not. For it could have been placed in me by the demon—and if it has been, it is false. But if it is false, I should believe its opposite: I should believe that there is no dog in front of me. Hold on a moment, though; is even that so? If the demon is as powerful and as troublesome as Descartes says, the thought that I should believe the opposite of the first belief would also be the work of the demon. Hence, I should believe its opposite: I should revert to my original belief. I should think that there is a dog in front of me after all. No, that would be too hasty. The demon could still be doing what he does best. So, I should again disbelieve what I would otherwise believe. That is, I should again think that there is no dog in front of me. But this thought, too, will be the demon's doing—and therefore will be false. Consequently, should I once again think that there is a dog in front of me? . . . But . . . But . . . When will this end?*

The skeptic says that it never ends. (Could this parable of the dog and the demon forever hound your thoughts?) If this demonic skeptic is right, you become disturbingly like the man wearing the puzzling T-shirt in section 2.3. (Its front said "BACK is true." Its back said "FRONT is false.") You are willing to suppose that your belief about the dog (call the belief b) is false because of the demon. But then, also due to the demon, you "correct" yourself, deciding that b is true after all. Next, still because of the demon, you "correct" this move—now saying that b is false. However, "correcting" that move in turn leads you to think that b is true. But . . . This process continues without end, says the skeptic. You can never assign one stable truth-value to a given proposition. So, to the extent that you believe only what you take to be true, you will lack a stable of stable beliefs. (You might retort, "And yet I do have stable beliefs. Does it therefore follow that I can reject the supposition of an evil demon who would deny me such stability?" Then what of an evil demon who deceives you when he wants to do so—but not all of the time? His trickery would be unpredictable. How would you cope with him?)

The demonic skeptic condemns your beliefs to unremitting fallibility. Since on no occasion do you know that you are not being deceived by an evil demon, each of your beliefs is fallible. Hence, by $S1_{ed}$ and $S2_{ed}$ (perhaps functioning as instances of S1$_{if}$ and S2$_{if}$), it logically follows that none of your beliefs are ever knowledge. You know nothing. You have neither a posteriori knowledge nor a priori knowledge. You do not even know that 2 + 2 = 4. The evil demon—or, rather, the skeptic—has spoken! Do you believe him? If not, why is he wrong? How would you rule out the demon possibility? Descartes thought that he had a way of doing so. We consider his idea in Chapter 19.

> *At any given moment of your life, do you know that you are not being Gettiered? (As Chapter 5 explained, to be Gettiered is to have a justified true belief that nevertheless fails to be knowledge.) Might the evil demon be behind your being relentlessly Gettiered? Do you know that he is not? You believe—correctly—that you are sitting on a chair. This is apparently no guess, since you looked at the chair before settling down onto it. But how do you know that there was no evil demon about to manipulate your eyes, deceiving you into seeing the chair as a pony—only to suddenly change his mind on a whim, leaving your eyes alone, leaving you free to see the chair as a chair? If you do not know that there is no such demon, do you really know that you are on a chair?*

FURTHER READING

Pappas 1978. (On the basic idea of skepticism, in section 18.1.)
Unger 1971. (On the idea, in section 18.2, that knowledge must satisfy a particularly high standard.)
Descartes 1641, Meditation 1. (For the evil demon worry, in section 18.3.)
Lehrer 1971. (For further development of the evil demon worry.)

19

External World Skepticism

Dexter had never heard of a city called "Calcutta." Yet lately he has been dream-
ing of being in such a city. Moreover, his dreams do accurately portray Calcutta.
Do they give him knowledge of what Calcutta is like? Miranda, in contrast, has
been to Calcutta. But her perceptions of it at the time were less accurate than
Dexter's dreams, and her memories are even foggier. Strange, but true; some of
Dexter's dreams even portray Miranda's being there! Which, if either, of them
knows more about Calcutta? Can dreams give knowledge? If you dream a solu-
tion to a problem, has the dream given you knowledge? Or has it provided only
a true belief?

19.1 The Cogito

Supposedly, there are no limits to the powers of deception possessed by
Descartes's evil demon (from section 18.3). Any belief of yours might be his doing. And (say skeptics) this is your undoing, insofar as you seek knowledge. You
know nothing—zilch, zero, zip.

Now, you might have thought you knew quite a lot; it might be important to
you to think of yourself in that way. But the evil demon cares nothing for your
feelings. His job is to deprive you of knowledge. And, amazingly, he does not
even have to exist in order to accomplish this objective. According to the skeptic,
it is enough if you cannot rule out there being any such evil demon. If you cannot, you lack all knowledge. You lack it as much as if the demon really did exist.
Such is the skeptic's subtlety. Is he not only subtle, though? Is he also powerful?
Can he be defeated?

Descartes thought that it could be done. He was no skeptic himself. Although
he took skeptical arguments seriously, he thought that he could answer them. In
his opinion, no demon could be as powerful as the skeptical argument requires.
Why is that?

The demon can deceive you only by giving you false thoughts. Suppose you have a thought that you take to be true. Nevertheless, it is false; this is the demon's doing. Say, for example, that you think there is fog around you—but in fact there is none. You have been given a false thought by the demon. Even so, to give you a false thought is to give you a thought. (A false thought is still a thought.) And a thought cannot be given to, or thought by, something that does not exist. Thoughts are thought by existing entities. Hence, even if you are thinking false thoughts (thanks to the demon), it remains true that you can know of the thoughts and their existence. You can know that you are thinking, hence that you exist. You can know of your existence as a thinker of those thoughts. Thus, said Descartes, "Cogito, ergo sum": "I think, therefore I am." (This statement is generally referred to as *the Cogito*.) More fully: You know that you are thinking; therefore you know that you exist. No demon can spirit away that knowledge. Thus, you have some knowledge.

So thought Descartes. Was he right? Or could a nonexistent being think the Cogito to herself? Imagine Winnie-the-Pooh telling himself that he Might not know Much, but he knows that he Is Thinking, and hence that he Exists. Wouldn't he be wrong? (He does not exist. He is fictional.) Did (or does?) Macbeth know that he exists? He is, we may presume, a fictional character. But couldn't Shakespeare have described him as being deceived by an evil demon (spurred on by those three witches)? After all, Macbeth is described as thinking, falsely, that he sees a dagger suspended in the air, and later on as being confronted by Banquo's ghost. (Even Macbeth does not purport to see Descartes's evil demon, though!) Yet couldn't Macbeth think the Cogito to himself? "I, Macbeth, am thinking. So, I exist." If he can, something that does not exist can think that it exists. Run through the Cogito on your own: "I think . . . yes. So, I exist. Phew." Like Descartes (but also like Pooh and Macbeth?), you are confident that, as a thinker, you exist. Might you be fictional, though? Could your thoughts be fictional ones being thought by a fictional being? Or can only something real really think?

19.2 A Less Powerful Evil Demon

Descartes saw the Cogito as a victory over the evil specter of the evil demon. An evil demon can try to deceive you about everything. But, says Descartes, he cannot deceive you about your existence as a thinker. So, he cannot deceive you about everything. Let's suppose, for argument's sake, that Descartes is right about this. Is it a victory worth having? How much knowledge does it give you?

One response would be to say that the Cogito gives you very little knowledge. In particular, it does not help you to know of a world outside your own mind. It tells you that there is one kind of knowledge of which no evil demon can deprive you—knowledge of your own thinking, knowledge of yourself as a thinker. But this bit of knowledge is all that the Cogito apparently promises to restore to you.

If the evil demon argument succeeds, all of what you took to be your knowledge is wrenched away from you. If the Cogito succeeds, some—but seemingly not much—of that knowledge is restored to you.

Does it restore your knowledge of having hands? No, it does not. What about knowledge of birds nearby? Not at all. Knowledge of your feet? Forget it. Knowledge of other people? No way. Even if the Cogito undermines a skeptic who uses the threat of the evil demon to argue that you know nothing, it leaves you with knowledge of nothing other than your own thinking. Is it therefore restoring almost none of your putative knowledge? Aren't you still in quite a predicament even if the Cogito is to be trusted?

Even if no demon, no matter how hard he tries, can falsify your thought that you are thinking, he still could falsify all of your *other* thoughts. Crucially, then, isn't the Cogito compatible with the idea that all of your thoughts about an *external world* are false ones implanted in you by an evil demon to mislead you into thinking that you are a creature existing in a physical world—when really there is no such world at all? In short, the Cogito might give you some knowledge of your own mind; but could you then be stuck with no knowledge of a world outside that mind? Might you only think that there is an external world at all because the evil demon can deceive you about such things? In other words, even if he cannot deceive you about your being a thing that thinks, couldn't he deceive you about there being a world external to your thinking mind?

"No," you might say. "Those thoughts are a *response* to that external, larger world. It is only because there is an external world, a world of bodies and substance, that I think there is one. My body, for example, is part of that world. So is yours." Of course that is what you say; it is what almost all of us would say. But does that general agreement help to justify your response? (If you think that it does, go back to Chapter 10.) Might the evil demon—and not an external world—be what causes you to think that such a world exists around you? Might there be no outer world? (You would be all outa outer world, knowing only of being inna inner world.) For all that you know to the contrary, might there be your mind (thinking that it is not alone in the world!) and a quite—although not supremely—powerful evil demon (making you think whatever you think about a supposedly external world)?

The thesis that your mind does not know about anything outside itself (not even the demon) is a specific—and especially famous—kind of skepticism. It is called *external world skepticism*. This form of skepticism denies that there is any knowledge of an external world—a world external to a mind. When applied to you, it denies that you know anything about a world external to your own mind.

Does this thesis sound plausible? Even if it does not, does it sound possible? (A skeptic will probably not expect you to find it plausible. He will ask only that you concede that it is possible.) If it is possible, should you become more cautious in thinking of yourself as having knowledge of a world around you? What forms could such caution take? Should you decide that you do not know of the existence of any of your friends, say? (Would you try to break the news to them? "I'm sorry. I don't know that you exist. True, I don't know that you don't exist. But I do not know that you do exist, either.") What practical implications might such skepticism have? Would it show that, previously, whenever you claimed to have knowledge of the world around you, you spoke without sufficient thought? Would it show that you never really understood what knowledge is?

19.3 The Dreaming Argument

Descartes himself used a somewhat different argument in order to motivate external world skepticism. He gave us what has come to be termed the *dreaming argument*. It proceeds as follows.

Right now, it seems clear to you that you are reading a page in a book (this one, right?). Your eyes are working well enough, and they tell you that your hands are holding a book. Your hands confirm this. The thing you are holding also smells like a book. Doesn't it sound like one, too, as you flip the pages? (That's enough. You need not bother to taste the book.) Don't your senses conspire to tell you one thing—namely, This Is A Book? What could be clearer than that? If you are to know anything about the external world, isn't this as straightforward a case of knowledge as any?

But (as Descartes asked) isn't there always a possibility that you are merely dreaming these experiences? You think that you see the book. Might that apparent sighting be part of a dream in which you read the book? It feels to you as if your hands are holding a book. Might that, too, be nothing more than a dreamt feeling? The same applies to the other senses. Each time, isn't it possible that, although you seem to be experiencing an external world, you are only dreaming about doing so? (A more modern version of Descartes's puzzle—one with elements of the evil demon puzzle, too—ponders the possibility that you are a disembodied brain floating in a vat of appropriate chemicals. The vat is connected to a machine being operated by a scientist so as to mislead you in an apparently realistic way. It seems to you that you are experiencing the world in a standard way. But those experiences are, in effect, just the scientist's doing.)

If you might be dreaming about being in an external world instead of really experiencing one, can you have knowledge of the world? After all, isn't dreaming unlikely to give you knowledge? Intuitively, there seems to be something inadequate about dreaming. (But what, exactly, is wrong with it? Is it too unreliable a way of forming beliefs? Recall, from Chapter 7, that there might be better and worse methods of forming beliefs. Do you need to be in closer causal "contact" with the world in order to have knowledge? On that suggestion, reconsider Chapter 8. Which, if any, of the ideas presented in earlier chapters explain why dreaming is not a way to gain knowledge of the external world?)

Moreover, say skeptics, there is no way for you to know that you are not simply dreaming your apparent experience of reading the book. Not only might you be dreaming, but you can never eliminate this possibility. Thus, the possibility is a worry. The following reasoning explains why.

1. The only kind of evidence you can have for the claim that you are really reading the book is sensory evidence. You look, listen, touch, smell (and taste, if you insist). Then you might look up in surprise—the book that you are sensing asks you whether such evidence is good enough. (How can a book seriously ask you to doubt that you know of its existence? Do you have to know that it exists, in order to use it in the first place? Or can you use it without knowing that it exists?) "Of course such evidence is good enough," you think. "Besides, what other evidence could I have for thinking that I am reading a book? Obviously, I must use my senses."

2. But mightn't you be dreaming those sensory experiences described in (1)? Even as you stop and think, gathering together your sensory evidence for thinking that you are reading a book, might you be asleep, dreaming? If you were asleep and dreaming, you would not realize it. If you were having the "realistic" kind of dream that so worried Descartes, you would think that you were awake. Yet you would be wrong about this. You would be dreaming being awake; you would be dreaming that you were not dreaming.

Right now you probably think that you are awake and not dreaming. But thinking that you are awake does not prove that you are. That optimistic thought could be part of your dream. If so, how are you ever to have knowledge of an external world—a world external to your dreams? Here is how this skeptical argument fits the skeptical template outlined in section 18.1:

$S1_{dr}$ *Let p be any given proposition about an external world. In order to know that p, you have to know that you are not merely dreaming p's being true.*

$S2_{dr}$ *But you never know that you are not merely dreaming p's being true.*

$S3_{dr}$ *So, you never know that p. (You know nothing about the external world. You do not even know that there is an external world.) [From $S1_{dr}$ and $S2_{dr}$.]*

$S1_{dr}$ entails that, in order to know that you have a hand, you must know that you are not dreaming that you have one. But how can you know that? Any evidence you think shows that you have a hand might be part of a dream you are having. So (as $S2_{dr}$ implies), you do not know that you are not dreaming about having a hand. Hence, as $S3_{dr}$ tells us, you do not know that you have a hand. If you think you have such knowledge, you are Just Plain Wrong.

19.4 Possible Responses to the Dreaming Argument

Descartes was an internalist (a notion defined in Chapter 15), and his skeptical arguments reflect this preference. For instance, he worries about a kind of dreaming that fools you into thinking that you are having normal experiences and hence into thinking that you have good reasons for believing that there is an external world. His skeptical question is whether, even if you are actually having normal experiences, you can eliminate the possibility that they are not normal. Perhaps you are only dreaming them; how can you know that you are not doing so? You cannot (says the Cartesian skeptic). Any relevant reasons you have might be the result of dreaming—and therefore inadequate. If you rely on reasons (as internalism requires you to do), you will not gain knowledge.

But maybe, as externalism would claim (see Chapter 14), your knowledge of an external world does not depend so heavily on your mental perspective and reasons. Can externalism evade the dreaming argument? For example, perhaps the reliabilist from Chapter 7 would say this:

> *When awake, you might happen to be well enough attuned to your environ-ment to form mostly true beliefs about it. If so, you can know about the world. It doesn't matter that your mental perspective (containing your reasons or evi-dence) is inconclusive. (It is inconclusive because, as Descartes noticed, it could have been produced in a dream.) To an externalist reliabilist, what matters is whether in fact you produce your beliefs in a reliable way, not whether you have conclusive reasons or evidence in mind for the beliefs.*

Does that reasoning sound plausible? Or is externalism too high a price to pay for escaping the dreaming argument? Consult Chapter 14 if you wish to reflect on externalism's merits. (And if they are insufficient, come back here!)

Suppose that you do not accept externalism. There are other ways to try to re-fute the dreaming argument. You could say, for example, "Even from within, I can tell the difference between dreaming and being awake. One is chaotic; the other is orderly." But is that so? When you think you are aware of that difference, mightn't you be dreaming? Dreaming might make you think that you are awake, when you are not. Might you be wrong about there even being a difference?

"Of course there is a difference," you continue. "I dream only when asleep. That's why we call it a dream. And I do it very little, since I am awake most of the time. So, the kind of experience that I most frequently am having does not in-volve dreaming. I can distinguish dreaming from waking experience because one kind of experience is more usual. I gain knowledge from the more common kind of experience!" But how do you know that you are not daydreaming? And is daydreaming any more likely than dreaming to give you knowledge?

"There must be a difference between dreaming and being awake. Otherwise, we wouldn't have different words for the two states," you insist. Is that so? Are all of our uses of words correct? Can't we alter our language if we find it to be inadequate? (We contemplated this kind of possibility in section 12.4.) Perhaps we should refine our language now, in response to external world skeptics, and no longer say that there are states in which we know (e.g., being awake and alert) and states in which we do not know (e.g., being asleep and dreaming). Is it possible that, even if there is a difference between being awake and being asleep, it is not a difference between a state that gives us knowledge and one that does not? Maybe neither state gives us knowledge.

Look at yourself in a mirror. Think to yourself, "That person looks so fine." But do you really know, on the basis of what you see, that you are thinking? You see a face staring back at you. How do you know that it is thinking, let alone that it is thinking what you are thinking? "Ah, but I know 'from within' that I am thinking," you might say. Nevertheless, do you know that the face you see is a reflection of yours? Maybe yours is quite different. Have you ever seen your face other than by using something reflective, like a mirror? How do you know that mirrors do not seriously distort? Is this a way in which you can fail to know that you are thinking?

FURTHER READING

Descartes 1641, Meditation 2. (For the Cogito, in section 19.1.)

Nozick 1981. (On fiction and the Cogito, in section 19.1.)

Descartes 1641, Meditation 1. (For the dreaming argument, in section 19.3.)

Putnam 1981, Chapter 1. (On the brain-in-a-vat worry, noted in section 19.3.)

Stroud 1984, Chapter 1. (On Descartes's dreaming argument and responses to it, in sections 19.3 and 19.4.)

20

Inductive Skepticism

Josh has a coin that has always come up heads when tossed. What should he expect to happen on the next toss? Should he think that heads will continue? Should he assume that tails is due? Or should he think that there is an equal chance each way? "There is an equal chance, because the coin is fair," says Josh. But how does he know that the coin is fair? Is its unbroken history of heads evidence against the notion that it is fair?

20.1 The Basic Idea of Inductive Skepticism

Different types of skepticism have different targets. Even if you escape one type, another one might be lying in wait for you:

Threat: Infallibility skepticism. (The evil demon.) Escape? (The Cogito)
New threat: External world skepticism. (Dreaming.) Escape? (Externalism?)
New threat: Inductive skepticism.

Infallibility skepticism (Chapter 18) denies that there is any knowledge. Descartes's Cogito (section 19.1) denied that denial, claiming that there is some knowledge. (You know that you are thinking. You know that you exist as a thinker.)

Still, the Cogito left itself open to the skeptical reply that it gives us only a very small amount of knowledge. Even if there is the knowledge described by the Cogito, it is only knowledge of one's own mind (section 19.2). The world beyond might still be unknown. Indeed, external world skeptics claim that no such world is known (section 19.3). You do not know that you have a hand. Even if you know that you are thinking that you have a hand, you do not know that you do have a hand. But does externalism provide an escape from that skeptical cave (section 19.4)?

In any event, inductive skepticism now enters the story. Even if you have some knowledge of an external world, this does not ensure that you have very much knowledge of it. You might know that you have a hand, for example, without knowing how that hand will react to internal stimuli (such as your desire to move it) or external stimuli (such as a hot flame). That is what an *inductive* skeptic says, at any rate. In his view, you never have inductive knowledge. You do not know that the sun will rise tomorrow. You do not know that a hand that is put in a flame will feel pain. You do not know that a dropped brick will fall earthward. You do not know . . . much at all.

20.2 The Humean Skeptical Argument

Suppose that the external world skeptic, with his talk of dreaming (section 19.3), has been defeated. "Hello, real world," you say. There are objects to the left of you, objects to the right of you—all awaiting your knowing about them: chairs, carpet, walls, windows, books, pens, . . .

What will those objects do? How will they act? If you step onto a carpet, don't its threads flatten, then rebound? If you sit on a chair, doesn't it support you? Don't objects "react" in characteristic ways? Don't we generally know what those ways are?

Not according to the new skeptic in town—the inductive skeptic. Drawing his inspiration from David Hume, the eighteenth-century Scottish philosopher, this skeptic argues as follows.

Say that you are holding an apple in your hand. Do you know what that apple will taste like? Are you justified in predicting its taste? Or should you hesitate, not committing yourself as to the apple's taste, reluctant to eat it?

Well, if you think you know how the apple will taste, how would you justify such a prediction? Would you rely on your relevant experiences? Will you recall other apples you have known and loved (or at least eaten)? That would give you a sense of this apple's likely taste. If you have tasted enough apples, can you make a justified prediction as to this one's likely taste? You might not bet your life's savings on the prediction. Apples vary in taste, and there are such things as worms. But even allowing for such variables, isn't your prediction likely to be true? If so, is it justified? If it is, and if it turns out to be true, can you look back, later on, and—the Gettier problem (section 5.1) aside—say that you knew what the apple would taste like?

"No," says a Humean skeptic, reasoning in the following way.

Your prediction takes for granted that the world is not about to radically change in character. Apples could suddenly start having no taste at all. They might start tasting like plums. Or like vanilla ice cream. Or sawdust. Or . . . Can you know that this is not about to happen? If you cannot, don't your past experiences count for nothing? If you do not know that there is to be no change, you do not know that your experiences should be relied on.

"What could be easier to know, though? Of course the world isn't about to change dramatically. We can test this. Just wait a moment: . . . There. Nothing much changed. Stop worrying."

But, says the skeptic, maybe you were simply lucky just now. The world could have changed. It did not, but it could have. You predicted that it would not do so, and you turned out to be right. What does that prove? It shows that your belief was true. (You said there would be no sudden upheaval. You were right.) Nevertheless, didn't you need to know that you could rely on your past experiences? Didn't you need to know that the world was not about to fundamentally alter? And haven't we already seen (in Chapter 4) that a true belief is not clearly enough for knowledge? What is also needed is justification. What can justify you in believing that the world is not about to change?

According to a skeptic, nothing can provide justification for that belief. You can only wait (your head edging ever closer to the apple, your mouth opening ever wider), thinking that all the apples you have eaten so far in your life have tasted a certain way. In your experience, the world has been well behaved (at least as regards apples). Even so, says the skeptic, the observation that the world has been stable up to now cannot help you here. For it is just more inductive evidence. You would be inferring 2 from 1:

1   *Up to now, apples like this have generally had taste T.*
2   *So, this one will probably have taste T.*

Yet your inference would rely on 3:

3   *The world is not about to change dramatically, as regards the taste of apples like this one. (Whatever taste such apples have generally had in the past is the taste they will generally have in the immediate future.)*

And what is your justification for 3? Isn't it something like 4?

4   *Up to now, the world has never changed dramatically, as regards the taste of apples like this one.*

But today might be the day that the world does change! (If it does not, maybe tomorrow will be the day. If tomorrow is not the day, maybe the next day. . . .) Isn't the inference from 4 to 3 subject to the same skeptical worry as the inference from 1 to 2? Yet weren't you relying on the former inference to eliminate that worry from the latter inference? Indeed you were, says the skeptic. Thus, you have failed. The worry persists.

The skeptic's point is that you never know that sudden change is not around the corner. Whenever you make an inductive prediction, there is risk involved. Part of that risk is something we noted earlier (section 12.1)—since inductive reasoning is not deductive, inductive evidence always leaves open the possibility that the inductive conclusion is false. Inductive justification is fallibilist. (Inductive justification is a paradigm of fallibilist justification; on the latter notion, see section 17.1.) If you were already reluctant, when reading Chapter 17, to embrace fallibilism, you will feel similar coolness toward inductive thinking. But the current argument raises a new puzzle: Hume is not saying that, just because inductive thinking is not infallible, it is no good at all. He is saying that it is good, relative to whatever fallibilist standard you like, only if you can justify the presumption that the world is not about to suddenly change. For if it were about to change, your past inductive evidence would no longer be a guide *at all* to the future, even relative to a good but lower standard of justification! All bets would be off. You would flounder. Whatever had formerly seemed like inductive evidence would be nothing of the sort. So, if you do not know that the world is not about to change radically, you do not know that what seems like inductive evidence really is evidence—even inconclusive evidence!

The inductive skeptic's talk of the world undergoing a sudden and radical change thus parallels the earlier skeptical ideas—the evil demon (section 18.3) and dreaming (section 19.3). Each time, a skeptic describes something unexpected that you need to know is not affecting you (by denying you knowledge). In none of these cases, though, can you eliminate that striking possibility, say the skeptics. Thus, inductive skepticism, too, fits the skeptical template in section 18.1:

S1$_{is}$ *Let p be any given inductive proposition (e.g., the proposition that the apple in your hand will taste sweet). In order to know that p, you have to know that the world is not about to change dramatically, rendering p (surprisingly) false.*

S2$_{is}$ *But you never know that the world is not about to change dramatically, rendering p (surprisingly) false.*

S3$_{is}$ *So, you never know that p. (That is, you have no inductive knowledge. None of your predictions are even justified.) [From S1$_{is}$ and S2$_{is}$.]*

20.3 The Humean Skeptical Solution

Do you accept the skeptical argument? If you do not, which of its premises (S1$_{is}$ and S2$_{is}$) do you reject? (The argument is logically valid. Its conclusion is entailed by its premises. If you accept the premises, you should accept the conclusion.) Can you reject S2$_{is}$, say, by saying that some people can know the future? Need we look no further than Madam Zelda (in section 6.4)? Her livelihood depends on her supposed accuracy in foretelling the future; can *she* know whether there is to be sudden and dramatic change in the world?

It depends on whether she indeed has a gift for knowing the future. Suppose that her mind can travel to the future, observe what is happening, and return to the present time. Then she tells us what is about to occur. Would her gift enable us to overcome the limitations of induction? Well, her claims about the future would be more like observations than predictions. (She has already observed what is to happen in the future. She was there, experiencing it.) So she would not really be using induction. Her success would not be a triumph for inductive thinking. And even if her mind could go to the future, escaping the restriction of relying on induction, how does this help us? How could we know that she really has traveled to the future? (And if—like the rest of us—she has to rely on experience of how the world has been, then she has no advantage over us. She, too, has to know that the world is not about to radically alter. If Hume is right, she cannot do this.)

If Madam Zelda is of no help to us, should we accept the Humean skeptical argument and say that no predictions are justified? What would this concession mean to your life? Here are two possible ways to "live" that acceptance.

Ceasing to Predict. One possible response to a Humean skeptic is to stop making any inductive claims. Should you no longer predict that the sun will rise, or that apples will taste different from pears, or that your hand will hurt when it touches flames, and so on? Or is this easier said than done? Is it even possible to relinquish such thoughts—and to stop using your experiences as guides to what you think will happen? (Go ahead; try it. Cease having any expectations as to how food will taste. Choose recipes at random from your cookbooks. Don't even expect the food to cook when heated!)

Hume apparently did not think that people could play fast and loose with their thoughts in that way. This is part of what generated what he called his *skeptical solution* to the skeptical argument. The supposed solution has two parts.

1. It is skeptical, in that Hume accepts the skeptical argument. He thinks that there is no internal problem with the skeptical argument itself. Its premises are true; its logic is impeccable. If we accept the premises, we are committed to the conclusion. He does—and hence he is.

2. Nevertheless, Hume tries to lessen the impact of the skeptical argument by acknowledging a sense in which you need not change your life in response to the argument. You need not stop using induction—because you have no choice about using it. You need not discard your inductive beliefs—because you cannot do so. You cannot stop thinking that the sun will rise tomorrow. You cannot stop expecting apples to taste different from beef. (By analogy, does the fact that you cannot become nine feet tall relieve you of any need to try to become so tall?)

Why is this so? You cannot cease being inductive, says Hume, because it is such a strong habit in us to think inductively. You think that mandarins will have one taste and pineapples another. All of your relevant experience supports this thought. And how can you really ignore such evidence? According to Hume, it is not justified, but it is natural, to use one's experience of the world as a guide to how the world is. If your experience says that apples have always fallen when dropped, can you seriously doubt that they will do so in the future?

How good is this solution of Hume's? Is he saying that, to the extent that your inductive thinking is a reflex, a habit, you need not change anything in the light of his skeptical argument? Or are there good habits and bad ones? Shouldn't we try to change a bad one, even when it seems natural? And isn't one that provides no knowledge a bad one?

Moreover, can we know which habits are natural? Might induction be merely a social, arbitrary custom? Indeed, can Hume know that you do have a given habit? To say that you have the habit of believing that the sun will rise is, in part, to say that you will continue to have that belief, isn't it? By his own skeptical argument, though, Hume cannot know that your practice is not about to radically change—and hence that your practice is a real habit. Could you alter overnight, from someone who confidently and continually makes predictions to someone who humbly makes none?

Viewing One's Predictions More Humbly. But even if you continue thinking inductively, might you at least change your self-image when doing so? Maybe you will not stop making predictions on the basis of experience. However, should you at least cease thinking of yourself as being rational in so doing? Perhaps Hume is not trying to remove induction from the world. But he is questioning whether inductive beliefs are justified, and hence whether they are knowledge. If so, then even if you have no choice about having such beliefs, can't you at least view them more humbly than before? Being human, maybe we are fated to have inductive beliefs. But should such fated beliefs also be so feted? Must we credit ourselves with thereby having knowledge? Could it be that we form our beliefs inductively (following our past experiences) only because we know no better? (But now you do know better, don't you? Is this self-understanding what the skeptic's argument can give you?)

So, should you henceforth cease thinking that experience gives you knowledge of how things will proceed? It gives you beliefs—but not knowledge, says the skeptic. Could we be wrong, even as a society, when assuming that prediction can give us knowledge? (If so, should you tell other people of this news? How do you think they would react? With disbelief? But can you know this? Such knowledge would be inductive. Hence, if the skeptical argument is to be believed, you do not know how people would react to being cautioned to be more cautious in their thinking. Does this make you more willing to try cautioning them?)

Scientists have made many attempts to understand the physical world. Yet one scientific theory after another has failed to be the final word on the world. Should we therefore predict that scientists will never find that final word? (This prediction would be skeptical, denying science fundamental knowledge. But it would be inductive in method, extrapolating from inductive data about past scientific failures.) Or, ironically, does inductive skepticism give science hope, by blocking that skeptical use of induction? For does it deny that an inductive prediction of ultimate scientific failure is justified?

FURTHER READING

Hume 1748, sections I–VII. (For the skeptical argument, in section 20.2, and the skeptical solution, in section 20.3.)

Strawson 1985, Chapter 1. (On the skeptical solution, in section 20.3.)

BonJour 1986. (On other possible solutions to Hume's skeptical argument.)

21

Rule Skepticism

Might it be that no one ever chooses quite the right word to capture his intended thought—but that we are rarely aware of this problem? When we are aware of it, we might say, "I can't quite think of the right word. Give me a moment." Maybe we are rarely aware of it, though, because when a lot of slightly wrong words are used, they usually combine—one mistake compensating for another—to make a coherent thought. It just wouldn't in fact be the correct thought! One could object to this notion by saying, for example, "No, I use 'It's Sunday' to mean that it is Sunday." But couldn't you still be using words—without realizing it—as parts of a code, where each letter or pair of letters, say, represented something other than what you thought it represented? Here is a challenge for you: Crack the code of your own thinking!

21.1 Knowing One's Own Mind

Regardless of whether you know of a world outside your mind (a worry raised in section 19.3), can you at least know what is in your mind? Descartes would have said that you can (section 19.1). As his Cogito exemplifies, you know that (and what) you are thinking. Similarly, regardless of whether you never know that your predictions as to what will happen in the world are true (as suggested in section 20.2), can you at least know what your predictions *are*?

After all, your predictions and thoughts about an external world seem to have meaning (content). And can you at least know what those thoughts mean—even if, as external world skeptics claim, you do not know that the thoughts are true? Even when a thought is false, it has meaning. Its meaning is what makes it the thought it is. So, can you know what it is that you are thinking, regardless of whether or not you know that what you are thinking is true? Can you know what your thoughts *are*? (If so, can you equally well know what you are *saying*? "Even if what I say is false, can't I still know that I am saying it? I know what it means, even if I do not know that it is true." But is speech so like thought? Or does speech require a mouth? If it does, then—since a mouth is part of your body and hence part of the external world—does external world skepticism in Chapter 19 already deny you such knowledge?)

21.2 The Basic Idea of Rule Skepticism

Some skeptics deny you even knowledge of your own thoughts. *Rule* skeptics do so. Their way of thinking is associated with the Austrian philosopher Ludwig Wittgenstein. He was not a skeptic himself. But, like Descartes (section 19.1), he took skepticism seriously.

A rule skeptic thinks that it is not at all easy for you to know what your thoughts are. Indeed, he argues, you cannot do so. You try to work with concepts in formulating your thoughts, but how do you know that you have found the right concepts with which to express them? You never do know this, say rule skeptics. There are always—always—mistakes that you might be making. Even when you concentrate on your thinking, being as careful as possible, you will overlook alternative interpretations of your thoughts. (What interpretations are those? Wait until section 21.3.)

In terms of our skeptical template (section 18.1), here is a basic outline of the rule skeptic's argument:

$S1_{rs}$ *In order to know that you are thinking that p, you have to know that your thought cannot equally well be interpreted as meaning something other than p.*

$S2_{rs}$ *But you never know that your thought cannot equally well be intepreted as meaning something other than p.*

$S3_{rs}$ *So, you never know that you are thinking that p. [From $S1_{rs}$ and $S2_{rs}$.]*

Why is this called rule skepticism? A rule skeptic says that your thought is the thought it is only if it has a specific meaning (e.g., "It is hot" should mean that it is hot). But "It is hot" has that meaning (and no other) only if it is used standardly—in accord with a standard semantic rule. You mean that it is hot, when thinking "It is hot," because there is a rule making your words mean that it is hot. If your words did not mean this, they would be meaningless or would have a nonstandard meaning. But a nonstandard meaning is still generated by rules— nonstandard rules. For example:

Standard: "It is hot" means that it is hot.
Nonstandard: "It is hot" means that it is snowing.

Rule skeptics contend that you never know that your words are not as easily interpretable by a nonstandard semantic rule as by a standard one. When you seemingly think, "It is hot," do you know that you are not really "getting hold of" the thought that it is snowing rather than the thought that it is hot? You do not know this, says a rule skeptic. If he is right, his argument bodes ill for you. You can never know what thought it is that you are thinking. And that (he thinks?) prevents you from even *thinking* a specific thought.

21.3 The Rule Skeptical Argument

But how can anyone hope to support such a surprising contention? By analogy, consider someone who often says, "I am not a racist. I respect people of all races." For many years, this person seems to be as she claims to be. But one day her son tells her that he plans to marry a woman who, as it happens, has a markedly different skin color from his own. He has no reason to believe that his mother will take this news badly. She has always acted in an apparently non-racist and tolerant way. But she surprises him—and, in fact, herself. Unexpectedly, she finds herself saying, "I don't want someone with that skin color as part of my family." He is flabbergasted; his mother seems to be racist after all.

Should we say that she has suddenly become racist? Or was she racist all along (but no one, including her, realized it)? How do we choose between these two interpretations? Might there be no decisive way of choosing between them?

The woman had never previously been in this situation—or any other situation that could reveal her racism (even to herself). Was she wrong when claiming to know that she thought of color as an irrelevant criterion by which to evaluate a person's acceptability? Should we reinterpret her earlier words, her apparently tolerant remarks, and say that her thoughts never really were tolerant or non-racist? Was she wrong to assume that she knew herself to have tolerant thoughts? In short, is it so easy for a person to know what she is thinking—such as what "tolerant" means, even in her own mind?

The rule skeptic generalizes this kind of worry. For any possible thought (e.g., "I'm no racist"), there are both standard and nonstandard rules for interpreting it. We tend to ignore nonstandard ones, since they do not take a person's words "at face value." But what justifies this tendency? Might it be merely a habit into which we have fallen? (On such habits, see section 20.3.) Should we always be open to other ways of interpreting a person's words? Should you be alert to different ways of interpreting your own words?

Let's take, as an example, the word "vase." Suppose you think to yourself, "At least I know what I think. I know that I think that this object is a vase. It might not be a vase. But I know that I think it is." *Do* you know this? Or might there be other ways to interpret the word "vase," so that although you are using the word, you do not understand it well enough to use it to capture your intended thoughts? The rule skeptic says that this *is* true of you. (Might it even be true for all of your words?)

Obviously, this rule skeptical claim sounds implausible. Nevertheless, might it be true? We can test it by asking what is needed if you are to really understand a word you are using in your thinking.

For a start, do you need to picture (or be able to picture) a vase to yourself? Do you know that you are thinking about vases, only if you do (or can) form a mental picture of a vase? (Go ahead; form one. "That's a vase," you think.)

But isn't your mental picture unavoidably specific? If it looks like a vase, won't it look like an individual vase? How could you form a picture of a generic vase? Even a vase with a label on it that says "Generic Vase" is a specific picture of a specific vase. How can this picture prove that you understand the general concept of a vase? (Analogously, the mother in our example can be apparently nonracist on a given occasion. At a party, she might be friendly toward a person of another skin color. Does that prove that she is nonracist in general? Can a person mean to be nonracist, yet be racist? Can a person mean to be racist, yet be nonracist?)

Should you picture a few vases instead? (Again, please do so.) But how many should you picture? Five? Ten? Twelve? Twenty? Is there a determinate answer to this question? (If you think so, go back to the slippery slope puzzle in Chapter 16. Otherwise, you are on the verge of slipping down a rule skeptical slippery slope.)

Equally, how much variation should there be among your imagined vases? Should they have different colors? If they do not, perhaps you do not understand that having one special color is not part of being a vase. Should they be of different shapes? If they are not, perhaps you do not understand that having one special shape is not part of being a vase. There are more constraints on a vase's shape than on its color, too. How do you capture this limitation in your pictures?

Suppose, then, that you picture ten vases of different colors and shapes. Even then, you might be misunderstanding something about vases. Perhaps you do not realize that two (or even ten) vases can have the same color and shape. If you say that you do not suffer from this misunderstanding, is this because you already take yourself to understand well enough what a vase is? But the skeptic is asking what gives you that understanding in the first place.

The puzzle does not end there. If your imagined vases are empty, could it be that you do not understand that they can contain things? Yet if they are not empty, maybe you do not understand that they can be empty. Could that lack of understanding mislead you into thinking that an empty vase is not what you mean by "vase"? If not, what is to prevent it from doing so? And if you picture some vases as empty, some as not empty, might you be failing to realize that perhaps, at a given moment, all of the vases in the world are empty? In short, is there a problem with your picture no matter what it looks like?

Such thinking can go on forever, according to rule skeptics. (What further aspects of vases might succumb to such questioning?) For don't vases have too many actual or possible characteristics to enable you to picture them all? Hence, how can an image (even a range of images) prove that you understand the concept of a vase? At what point do your images rule out all possible misunderstanding (even by you)? Might you have only managed to picture a sculpture of a vase, for instance, without realizing it?

Can you avoid these problems by using a mental description instead of a mental picture? You might describe a range of shapes the object could take. You might say that it can have any color at all. You might try describing what function a vase performs.

Is this approach really any better, though? Don't descriptions pose perfectly analogous puzzles to those we have just discovered for pictures? How do you know that your description covers all important aspects of what makes something a vase?

Moreover, what if your description contains a mistake? It might say that vases are always less than eight feet tall. But it could in fact be false. Suppose that there is a vase as tall as that, and that you have even seen it, although you did not recognize it as a vase. Your mistaken preconception as to what constitutes a vase prevented you from seeing it as a vase. You thought it was a statue. So your description is wrong. At best, it describes smaller vases, not vases in general. Does this reasoning imply that you never know that you are thinking about vases in general? (If you say no, is this because you can correctly picture vases? If you think so, go back to the discussion above about how you might picture vases. Or do you say it because knowledge—even of what you mean—does not have to be based on a complete absence of falsity in your thinking? If you think this, return to Chapter 11.)

Perhaps, after realizing that you cannot picture or describe vases in general, you find a real vase and point at it, saying, "There, that's a vase. Watch it being a vase!" But couldn't the rule skeptic still barrage you with questions similar to the ones pertaining to pictures and descriptions? For instance, do you know how to generalize from the object in front of you? You might say, "That's a vase, as is anything sufficiently like it." But when is something sufficiently like this thing? Might someone focus on the wrong aspects of this specific vase when trying to understand what vases are in general? (Note that this approach is not available to you if you do not assume that you have external world knowledge and hence if you seek knowledge purely of your own mind without reference to anything external. After all, the real vase is an external object.)

If you cannot get around these problems either, do you merely seem to understand your own thoughts? Maybe you can never succeed in giving your words the meaning you intend. "Of course I can," you might respond. "I just say or think that my intended meaning is thus-and-so. I decide what my thought means." Is that so? Can meaning be so private? And anyway, can't even these words that you are now using—while claiming to be able to decide authoritatively what meaning is in your mind—also be subjected to rule skeptical questioning? Maybe there are always alternative ways of interpreting your mental pictures or descriptions, ways that allocate nonstandard meanings to them. Rule skeptics deny that you can know that you are using words in one, rather than another, way. How do you know that you are following the right semantic rule when you think "vase"—the rule that makes your word mean vase (and not this-specific-vase-with-this-specific-shape)? (Is it enough if other people agree that you understand the word? If you say so, return to Chapter 19: Do you even know that there are other people?)

And might this kind of thing be happening all of the time to all of your words? If it is, do you lack all knowledge? If you cannot know what it is that you are thinking, what hope is there for knowing anything else? (Do you lack even a priori knowledge, as discussed in Chapter 13? How can you know that 2 + 2 = 4, if you cannot know that you have in mind the thought that 2 + 2 = 4?)

Do you understand baseball if you do not know all of its rules? And do you know them all? If you do not know all of them, how do you know that it is baseball you have in mind when you think "Baseball is the greatest!"? Might it really be some sport of which you have never heard—spaceball—whose rules overlap with baseball's? Might the rules that overlap happen to be those which you do know, and which you mistakenly assume are peculiar to baseball? (List the rules you know. These are shared by baseball and spaceball. Couldn't the rest of either sport's rules then be legitimately added to your list? If so, the rules you know need not be rules of baseball rather than of spaceball. So, how do you ever know that you are watching a game of baseball and not of spaceball?)

FURTHER READING

Wittgenstein 1953, paragraphs 1–88, 143–242. (For the seeds of rule skepticism, in sections 21.2 and 21.3.)
Kripke 1982, Chapters 1, 2. (For a more explicit version of rule skepticism.)
McGinn 1984. (For a discussion of Wittgenstein, and of Kripke, on rule skepticism.)

22

Regress Skepticism

What is wisdom? Does it involve understanding, or justifying, in more and more depth, whatever knowledge one has? If so, who among us has any wisdom? Can an eight-year-old child be wise? Can even you ever be wise? If there is no limit in principle to how far understanding or justification can go, can anyone ever really attain wisdom? Or is the wise person the one who knows when to stop *seeking more understanding or justification? Yet how can one know that one has all the understanding or justification one needs? If one cannot, does even understanding or justification fail to make one wise?*

22.1 Inferential Justification

Recall how we introduced the notion of justification (section 4.1). Imagine striking it lucky at the racetrack. You make a wild guess as to the winner of the next race—and lo and behold, your prediction is correct! But do you collect money as a knower? Seemingly, you do not. Since your belief was nothing more than a guess, it would be misleading to say that you knew which horse was going to win. A guess is not knowledge. To guess that Horse will win is not to know that he will win (even if, as it transpires, he does win). What is missing? What more is needed for knowledge?

The usual answer is that you know that Horse will win, only if you have justification (e.g., consciously held evidence) for believing that he will do so. Having a true belief is only part of what it is to have knowledge. You also need justification.

But if a guess is not knowledge (because it is not a justified belief), one way to lack knowledge is to be making guesses. If one of your beliefs (even one of your nearest and dearest beliefs) is nothing but a guess, it fails to be knowledge. At the time, it might seem to you to be knowledge, but this illusion would reflect only your failure to realize that the belief is just a guess. (Is that possible? Or do you always know when you are guessing? Does a guess always "feel" like a guess?)

One way, then, to ask whether you know that p is true is to ask whether you are merely guessing that p is true. You cannot know that you are in London, for example, if you are only guessing that you are there. This way of thinking gives us the following requirement on knowledge:

$S1_{gu}$ *In order to know that p, you must not be merely guessing that p.*

What does it take to satisfy this requirement? Perhaps the clearest way to satisfy $S1_{gu}$ (the no-guessing condition on knowledge) is to call on further beliefs in order to justify your belief that p. (This is at least what the internalist from Chapter 15 would claim. "Find a good reason for your belief. Otherwise, it is unjustified," he would say.) Arguably, a guess is a belief that is not based on any supporting beliefs or experiences. So, perhaps you could satisfy $S1_{gu}$ by having further beliefs or experiences that provide justification for your belief that p. Let's assume that this is how you would try to avoid using mere guesses. This method would render your belief *inferentially* justified (if justified at all). For, by being justified on the basis of other beliefs or experiences, your belief would be (or may as well be) inferred from them. To ask whether you satisfy $S1_{gu}$, therefore, is to ask this: In order to know that p, must you be inferentially justified in believing that p?

22.2 Epistemic Regress and Skepticism

The no-guessing condition, you might think, is not hard to satisfy. In support of 1, say, you adduce 2:

1 *I am in London.*
2 *I see that I am in London.*

In other words, you would say, "Of course I'm not merely guessing that I'm in London. I am looking at London—part of it, at any rate—right now." So 2 is your putative justification for your belief that 1; it is what makes your belief inferentially justified (if justified at all). The presence of 2 seems to raise your belief that 1 above a mere guess. You seem to not be guessing that 1, because you believe 2 and because 2 seems like reasonable evidence for 1. Proposition 2 apparently justifies 1. In using 2 as your justification for 1, then, do you satisfy the no-guessing condition on knowing?

Perhaps it depends on whether 2 is justified itself. Surely saying or thinking 2, in support of 1, is not enough to justify 1. For mightn't 2 be a guess? If you were to be just guessing that your surroundings looked like London, wouldn't it be foolhardy for you to believe that you were in London? At best, you would need to suspend judgment as to where you were. ("Maybe I'm in London. Maybe I'm in Newcastle. Maybe . . .") Meanwhile, you might try to gain better evidence than the mere guess 2. Shouldn't you make your commitment to 2 something better than a mere guess?

Thus, instead of relying on 2 in its current guise (as a mere guess), would you need to call on something like 3?

   3   *I can see the Tower of London.*

"This," you think to yourself, "gives me justification for accepting 2. Only in London can I see the Tower of London. So, no longer is 2 just a guess. Now I have evidence for its being true."

But does 3 really justify 2? What if 3 itself is a mere guess? If it is not, this is because you have justification for 3. For instance, you also believe 4:

   4   *I can see the river Thames just over there, as well as Tower Bridge. (They are exactly where they would be if this building in front of me was the Tower of London.)*

And, with this belief, your evidence for 1 might seem to be gaining strength. No longer is it just 2; now it is 2, 3, and 4. Taken together, do they make a good case for the truth of 1?

They do not, if 4 is a guess. If it is a guess, not only is it unjustified, but 2 and 3 are unjustified (since they are relying on 4 for their own justification)—in which case, so is 1 (which is relying on them for its justification). A pattern of dependence is being revealed. Belief 1 is knowledge only if it is not a guess; it is not a guess only if 2, say, is not a guess; 2 is not a guess only if 3, say, is not a guess; 3 is not a guess only if 4, say, is not a guess.

And is 4 a guess? That depends on whether you have justification for it. In this way, 4 is like 1, 2, and 3. In order to be better than a guess, it must be justified. This seems to take you to yet another belief, one with which to justify 4:

   5   *It is a clear day, my eyes are reliable, and I have consulted a guidebook as to what Tower Bridge looks like and as to where the river Thames is.*

But there is no prize for guessing(!) that the next question is whether 5 is anything more than a mere guess. Is it justified?

Must we find some new justification, 6, for 5 (so that 5 is not a mere guess)? (What could 6 be?) Yet won't 6 cry out for some supporting justification of its own—7? Won't the new support, 7, need to be supported in turn by some further proposition, 8? Otherwise, it will be no better than a mere guess! Won't that new support, 8, need support of its own? And so on . . . and on . . . and on. Where will such questioning stop?

The skeptic says that it can never stop. Or, at any rate, it can never stop in a way that allows what has gone before to really be justification (hence knowledge). You can stop providing new reasons for your beliefs, but you will therefore render all of the previous beliefs in the sequence unjustified—not incompletely justified, but unjustified. Why is that?

It is because of what this sequence (1 through 8 and beyond, to infinity) represents. It is called a *regress*—an infinite regress. It captures a pattern of dependence (as follows).

Your belief in proposition 1 is justified only if 2 is justified. For 2 is what is supposed to justify 1, but a mere guess cannot justify anything. Proposition 2 does not justify 1 if 2 is not justified itself. That is, 2 does not justify 1 unless *and until* 2 is justified. But what justifies 2? Supposedly, 3 does. However, what was true of the relationship between 1 and 2 is also true of that between 2 and 3. Hence, 2's being justified depends on 3's being justified. That is, 2 is not justified unless and until 3 is justified. But the same is true of 3 and 4. Unless and until 4 is justified, 3 is not justified. And this pattern will continue with any other propositions that you may add to the sequence—in other words, with your other pieces of supposed evidence or justification. Each piece depends on the next one being justified; otherwise, it is not justified. To be supported by what is unjustified is not to be justified. (Do character references work on this principle?)

But if this problem arises with every proposition in the sequence, how can the sequence ever end? Do we face the prospect that the pattern of dependency goes on forever? Whatever seems like the final piece of evidence will not really be final; new evidence is needed to justify the previous belief (the one that seemed final). Proposition 1 is not justified unless and until 2 is justified, which cannot happen unless and until 3 is justified, which cannot happen unless and until 4 is justified, which cannot happen . . . If this sequence never ends, it is only a pattern of *potential,* or *apparent,* justification. (Proposition 2 would justify 1, *were* the overall pattern to end. Proposition 2 *seems* to justify 1.) Such a sequence does not capture a pattern of real justification. So, 2 does not really justify 1.

Finally, then, we reach a skeptical conclusion. The skeptic argues that no such sequence ever ends. For one belief to be justified, some further belief or experience is needed. That further belief must be justified, too. But it is justified only if another belief or experience makes it justified. And the new belief or experience must be justified itself. Otherwise, it has no justification to transmit, as it were. Thus, another belief or experience must be added to the story. And so on. Hence, we derive this striking claim:

$S2_{gu}$ *But you are always merely guessing that p.*

You rarely think that you are guessing that p. But (according to $S2_{gu}$), you are wrong about that. You seem to not be guessing, because you advance 2 in support of 1. ("How could I be merely guessing that I am in London? Look at the care I am taking in mentioning my evidence.") But, given the unending nature of the sequence of propositions that ensues as you try to justify each previous proposition, 2 does not manage to justify 1. The skeptic says that 2 could justify 1 if that regress could be ended—but that it cannot be ended. (Note that, as with the skeptical challenges in Chapters 18 through 21, an externalist might not have allowed the regress to develop. He would deny that, in order to meet the no-guessing condition, you must continually find good reasons for your beliefs. What would he ask of you instead? Consult Chapter 14 for the answer to that question. Is externalism an attractive alternative to skepticism?)

In any event, here is our present skeptical conclusion:

$S3_{gu}$ *So, you never know that p. [From $S1_{gu}$ and $S2_{gu}$.]*

The regress is a sequence of attempts at justification—none of which succeed, precisely because there is never an end to the need for such attempts. The regress is, in effect, a very long guess—infinitely long, in fact, because each proposition in turn is, in effect, a guess (albeit a guess that does not feel like a guess). The regress argument begins with something that is not clearly puzzling. It is not obviously odd to say that 1 needs to be supported if it is to avoid being a mere guess. But the situation speedily becomes puzzling. Even if you supply more and more reasons, thereby feeling less and less as if you are guessing, you never overcome the original worry. For you are still guessing. Although your beliefs feel less and less like guesses, that is what they remain and remain. Maybe, as David Hume could have suggested (see section 20.3), that feeling is just a comforting but misleading *habit* you have gained. You would be contenting yourself with what is actually the false thought that you have sufficient support for your views. Your beliefs would feel justified. But they would be mere guesses in a life of mere guesswork.

The regress captures the idea that you could live your whole life trying to support the belief that you were in London (or New York, or Pittsburgh, or Sydney, say), yet never reach a stage at which the support you offered was sufficient. Only what is supported can support. So, no apparent support really ends the quest for support. Some piece of evidence, or some experience, is real support only if *more* evidence or experience is on the way. With your final breath, you can offer at best a claim for which support is still lacking. Had you lived one more minute, you could have offered apparent support for that claim. But then you would have needed to live one more minute, so as to provide support for that supposed support! And so on. Hence, do you need to live forever to justify even one belief? Would forever and a day be needed? Would even that be enough? If not, you can never do enough to justify even one of your beliefs. You cannot do enough to have knowledge. (You could reply, "But can't such efforts give me some—even if not perfect—justification?" The answer to that question depends on whether there can be less-than-perfect justification. And on that subject, see Chapter 17.)

22.3 Possible Responses to the Regress

Could you be justified in believing that you are in London (or New York, or any other city), without having to call on other beliefs or experiences? Suppose you think, "Of course I can. It is all too obvious that I am in London. I don't need any evidence for thinking that I am in London. I Just Know." The regress argument is fueled by the idea that justification always calls on new beliefs or experiences. To justify 1, 2 is needed; but 2 must then be justified, and 3 is needed for that; but 3 must then be justified, and 4 is needed for that; and so on. Is that underlying idea correct, though? Is all justification inferential?

The regress argument stands or falls with this thesis:

> UB   *For any proposition p, no matter how much justification you have for*
> *believing that p, it is not enough. Something else still needs to be justified*
> *if your belief is to be justified.*

UB implies that you have never provided quite enough justification for a given belief. Always, more is needed; always, there is *unfinished business*. Before a belief that p is justified, something else remains to be justified. (That "something" is often said to be epistemically *prior* to the belief that p.)

Standard responses to the regress argument question UB. (1) Maybe some beliefs are justified, but not by something else—hence not by something that then needs to be justified itself (Chapter 23). (2) Maybe some beliefs are justified by something else—but not by something that then needs to be justified itself (Chapter 24). (3) Maybe some beliefs are justified, but by something that is already justified (Chapter 25).

Other skeptical arguments also rely on UB (see Chapters 18 through 21). For example, according to the dreaming argument (section 19.3), your knowing that you are in London would depend on your knowing that you are not dreaming being there. If you say that you can see the Tower of London, the skeptic asks whether you know that you are not dreaming seeing it. For any supposed evidence e about the external world, he asks whether you know that you are not merely dreaming e. You are being asked to have one new piece of knowledge after another; only death need end such questioning. But, strictly speaking, even at death there will be unfinished justificatory business. The dreaming argument thus traps you in infinite regress. The same is true of our other skeptical arguments. You might like to verify this claim for yourself. (Does UB also help to generate the Gettier problem? In the dog/sheep case in section 5.1, do you fail to know that there is a sheep in the field, because you have not justified all of your relevant beliefs? And if—as UB implies—any situation will contain some pertinent beliefs that have not yet been justified, is the Gettier problem inescapable?)

In Chapters 23 through 25, we will explore the three classic nonskeptical responses to the epistemic regress argument. If one of these responses succeeds, therefore, that success threatens all our forms of skepticism. (It might also help to solve the Gettier problem.) The stakes are suddenly very high.

If everything depends on something else for its existence or nature, how did anything ever come to be in the first place? When was knowledge first created (if it ever was)? Is reality as a whole an infinite regress—one thing depending on another for its existence, on and on to infinity?

FURTHER READING

Passmore 1970, Chapter 2. (On regress in general.)
Moser 1985, pp. 23–26, 107–116. (On epistemic regress.)
Hetherington 1996. (On the possible link between Gettier cases and skeptical cases, mentioned at the end of section 22.3.)

23

Foundationalism

Do you know that you exist, if you do not already know what existence is? But do you know what existence is, if you do not already know that you exist? (Which existed first—the chicken or the egg?) Or do you know, in one all-embracing flash of insight, that you exist and what existence is? If you do not know what existence is, do you not know that you exist?

23.1 The Basic Idea of Foundationalism

The epistemic regress argument (section 22.2) is skeptical. Here is another way to capture its skeptical force:

1 *If all justification has to be inferential, then there is no justification.*
2 *All justification does have to be inferential.*
3 *So, there is no justification (and hence no knowledge). [From 1 and 2.]*

The support for 1 was the claim that if all justification is inferential, a regress ensues. The support for 2 was the claim that any putative justification you offer for a given belief needs some support of its own. (Note that the argument can be formulated in terms of knowledge as easily as in terms of justification.)

The most usual antiskeptical reaction to the regress argument is *foundationalism*. It says that not all justification is inferential. Equally, not all knowledge is inferential. Some is basic, noninferential—that is, foundational. In other words, some truths are justified noninferentially. Not all justifiers need to be justified by further justifiers.

Basic knowledge is like the foundation of a large building. Everything else in the building depends on it in order to stand tall. The foundation is as basic as it gets within that building. The foundation could stand without the superstructure; the superstructure could not stand without the foundation. Some knowledge is like that, according to foundationalism:

147

> BK   *(1) A given belief of yours is basic (noninferential, foundational) knowl-*
> *edge = df. (i) It is knowledge (in a way that might be described by some*
> *other, more specific, account of knowledge), but (ii) its being knowledge*
> *does not depend on its being justified by further knowledge. (2) At least*
> *some of your knowledge is basic.*

Which pieces, if any, of your knowledge are like this? What knowledge, if any, can halt the regress?

23.2 Cartesian Foundations

Descartes thought that the Cogito—"I think, therefore I am" (section 19.1)—could halt the skeptical infinite regress. He would claim that at the base of your attempts to know, either empirically or a priori, lies the Cogito. You know that you think; so you know that you exist (as a thinker). Even if other knowledge is in doubt, you know that you are using your mind. No knowledge is more basic than this. (But is even this knowledge possible? Can even "I think" be misinterpreted by you? It uses words; might you be misusing them? Do you know what thinking is? If you assume that you do, recall Chapter 21.)

That Cartesian picture implies that your knowledge of how things are depends on your knowledge of how you think they are. We turn to that picture more generally in section 23.3; right now, let's consider Descartes's version of it. For it is one thing to say (1); it is another to say (2):

1   *Even if you know nothing else, you know that you are thinking.*
2   *You know that you are thinking, and (on the basis of that knowledge) you can know a lot more besides.*

As section 19.2 explained, (1) will not displease most skeptics (although it might be contested by Chapter 21's rule skeptic). But they will certainly take issue with (2). And (2) is what is claimed by Cartesian foundationalists. They aim not merely to lay a foundation but to construct a building on top of it. They accord you basic knowledge, and they try to tell you how to derive the rest of your knowledge (your inferential knowledge) from that basic knowledge. (Perhaps the problem with the dog/sheep Gettier case in section 5.1 was that it can be difficult to use basic knowledge—such as knowledge of what *appears* to be in front of you—to derive nonbasic knowledge—such as knowledge of what *is* in the field.)

Cartesian foundationalism would ask whether, for instance, you can know that there *is* a red ball in front of you on the basis of the knowledge that you *think* there is a red ball in front of you. Can you know about an independent, real world on the basis of knowing what seems to exist around you? Descartes thought that he could know such things—but only after he had proven that God exists. (This proof was therefore the first step in his reply to his own external world skepticism, which we experienced in Chapter 19.) For an infinitely good and powerful God would not allow him to be perpetually deceived. Most of his beliefs about his surroundings would be true were God overseeing his efforts. And Descartes was confident that he could know of God's existence.

How did he argue for that significant claim? Well, said Descartes, he knows that he has an idea of God. He could not have made up that idea by himself; he could not have gained it by reflecting on his own merely finite qualities. His idea of God is of an infinite being. No finite being or world could give him that idea. Must there be an infinite being, therefore, so as to give Descartes the idea of an infinite being? Descartes thought so. He said that, because he knows that he has the idea of God, he knows that there is a God (giving him the idea).

And, with this reasoning, can the skeptical shackles be cast off? Can Descartes then reconstruct his body of knowledge as follows?

1   *I know that I have the idea of God.*
2   *So, I know that there is a God.*
3   *But God would not let me be deceived in many of my beliefs.*
4   *So, I know a lot.*

How plausible is such reasoning? Can knowledge of your own mind plus knowledge of God's existence give you knowledge of the world around you? What if you lack an idea of an infinitely good and powerful God? Can you still have knowledge? Or is ignorance the price to be paid for not thinking that there is a God?

Here is a possible (and much-discussed) worry about Descartes's project. He claims to know of God's existence. This claim is vital to his project. Once he thinks that he knows there is a God, he thinks that his reasoning will not lead him seriously astray: God will watch over him. But he reaches his claim that there is a God only after engaging in some reasoning (i.e., the reasoning that tells him that God exists). How can he know that this reasoning is to be trusted? If only the knowledge of God's existence ensures that he cannot be led badly astray in his subsequent reasoning, how much confidence should he have in his earlier reasoning (which he used before supposedly proving that God exists)? Might he, in effect, only be guessing that God exists? If he cannot know from the very beginning that God exists, how can he know anything, even after arguing for God's existence? Could the evil demon (section 18.3) be misleading him from the beginning? Might the demon be "covering his tracks," misleading Descartes into thinking that there is a God?

23.3 Sensory Foundations

Foundationalists often try to base all empirical knowledge, at any rate, on knowledge of appearances (any sensory appearances, not only visual ones). Knowledge of 1 would be said to depend on knowledge of 2, which would be said to depend on knowledge of 3:

1 *Here is a hand.*
2 *I am seeing a hand.*
3 *I am apparently seeing a hand.*

Proposition 1 is a claim about the objective external world; 2 is about your eyes linking you to that external world; and 3 reports on what is within your mind—seemingly, a sensory impression of an external world. With 3, there seems to you to be a hand present; you use that impression to justify 2, the belief that you are seeing a hand; and you use this belief to justify 1, the belief that there is a hand present. Thus, you end up basing your belief about the external world (your belief that 1) on a belief as to what seems to be the case (your belief that 3).

And, say these foundationalists, that is where it all stops. Knowledge of what world you *appear* to inhabit is the foundation for all of your beliefs about what world you *do* inhabit. Even a belief that you inhabit a real world at all would be based on apparent sensings of such a world. Your senses (or so it seems) would deliver knowledge of appearances—of how apparent things apparently look, smell, taste, feel, and/or sound. Then, with this knowledge, you can gain knowledge of a reality beyond your own mind (unless, of course, the external world skeptic from Chapter 19 is correct).

But is the relationship between what your senses apparently tell you and what is "out there" really so simple? Can foundationalists end the skeptical regress this easily? Can your senses give you basic knowledge? Here is a puzzle for foundationalism. (The puzzle has the form of a dilemma. That is, it offers a foundationalist two options, saying that he must choose one of them, and arguing that in either case he faces a problem: "You've got two choices—dead or dead!")

Here are the two options. Each concerns your supposed knowledge of 3 (the allegedly sensory foundation of your external world knowledge that 1). Either (1) 3 makes a substantive claim, purportedly applying the general concept of a hand in order to capture a truth about the world, or (2) it does not. Let's consider each of these alternatives in turn.

(1) Substantial Foundations

Assume, for argument's sake, that your sensory foundation (the belief that 3) is substantive—purportedly true. You take the general concept of a hand and try to apply that concept to something—most directly, perhaps, to a specific part of the overall visual array in your mind—accurately, it is to be hoped. This process (or one like it) is what gives you a belief that 3—and not a meaningless grunt, say. You have a visual experience to which you attach a meaning. You think of it as an experience that appears to be of a hand. Not a football, not a pig, not a book—but a hand.

Yet don't you need to justify that choice of concept? Don't you need to justify (at least to yourself) the application of the concept of a hand to part of your visual experience? You have decided that you seem to be seeing a hand—not that you are apparently seeing a small octopus or a large spider (in each case, one that has lost three legs). Doesn't this choice need to be justified? Don't you need to base your knowledge that 3 on some further knowledge, such as the knowledge that 4?

> 4 *Something should be thought of as a hand if it has, or appears to have, the*
>   *following features: . . .*

(Certainly the rule skeptic from Chapter 21 would think that 4 is essential. Do you think so, too?)

But if knowledge of 4 (or something like it) is needed in support of any knowledge of 3, knowledge of 3 is not basic. (By BK, being basic entails not needing to be justified by a further claim, belief, or proposition.) Yet 3 was supposed to be basic, according to the foundationalist. His example therefore fails him. His hunt for the basis of all empirical knowledge must resume. Your knowledge of the world around you will not ultimately rest on knowledge of what your senses seem to tell you. (But might there be other foundations for your external world knowledge? Is knowledge of 4 basic instead? On what, if anything, does knowledge of 4 depend? Might a priori knowledge—a kind of knowledge we met in Chapter 13—have a role to play here?)

(2) Insubstantial Foundations

Must the foundationalist therefore embrace the other alternative? Must he say that, in knowing that 3, you do not purport to apply the general concept of a hand? Let's assume, again for argument's sake, that he does say this.

Then, although you still have a visual experience that, on alternative (1), you would think is of a hand, there is now a sense in which your experience is not of a hand. As conceptualized by you, it is not of a hand. You are not thinking of it as being of a hand. That would be to "go out on a limb." You would risk misdescribing the content of your visual experience. And it was to avoid such mistakes that knowledge of 4 was apparently needed.

But then in what sense do you know that 3? How can you know that you are apparently seeing a hand? Won't you not even have a belief that you are apparently seeing a hand? To believe that you are apparently seeing a hand is to accept 3, rather than 3*, say:

3*   *I am apparently seeing an octopus that has lost three of its legs.*

Yet if (as hypothesized) you are not using the concept of a hand in order to cate-gorize or describe part of your visual experience, don't you fail to believe 3 rather than 3*? This is not to say that you believe 3*. A belief that 3* would still be a sub-stantive sensory belief. Hence, if you were to believe 3*, then (1)—the first horn of the current dilemma—would apply to you again. Thus, you must take no stand at all on what concept gives content or meaning to your visual experience. So you will not believe 3. You will not believe anything about what you are expe-riencing. You will experience without interpreting.

However, doesn't knowledge entail belief? (Section 3.1 urged that it does.) To know that p (for any p), don't you need to believe that p? If so, and if you do not really believe that 3, you also lack knowledge that 3. That is, a lack of belief that 3 entails a lack of knowledge that 3. Yet, by BK, if you do not know that 3, you do not have basic knowledge that 3. In other words, a lack of knowledge that 3 en-tails a lack of basic knowledge that 3. So, 3 will again fail the foundationalist. His hunt for the basis of all empirical knowledge continues. Once more, your knowl-edge of the world around you would not ultimately rest on knowledge of what your senses seem to tell you. On (2)—the second horn of our dilemma—you do not have knowledge of what your senses are telling you. They tell you nothing. At any rate, you are not "listening" to them. You are not interpreting their message.

This, then, is the dilemma for the foundationalist. First, he faces a choice in how he interprets your use of your senses. He says either that (1) your use of your senses gives you real sensory information, or that (2) it does not. Those options have the following consequences. (1) If your senses give you real information, that information must be justified (as being one piece of information, and not another)—in which case, the information is not basic. The skeptic's regress therefore continues. Your senses have not given you basic knowledge after all. (2) However, if your senses do not give you real sensory information, you have mere uninterpreted experiences—in which case, your experiences (and hence your senses) are not giving you knowledge, because they are not even giving you be-lief. And if they are not giving you knowledge at all, they are not giving you basic knowledge.

So, in either case (1) or case (2), the senses give you no basic knowledge. (What will do so? Or is there simply no basic knowledge?) But part of the episte-mological significance of the senses is that they seem like a basic way to gain knowledge of the world. If they do not give you basic knowledge of it, then, do they give you no knowledge of it at all? Does the skeptic triumph over the foun-dationalist?

How does a foundationalist avoid being dogmatic? Perhaps he says, "I believe that I am alive. And this is basic, or foundational, knowledge. (It doesn't get any more basic than that. This is the life.) But because the belief is basic knowledge, it rests on no further knowledge. So, there is nothing I can usefully say in support of it. How do I know that I am alive? I just do." Why isn't this assertion simply dogmatic? Yet if a belief is held dogmatically, doesn't it fail to be knowledge? And if it is not knowledge, it is not foundational knowledge.

FURTHER READING

Alston 1989, Chapter 1. (On the basic idea of foundationalism, in section 23.1; and on the issue of foundationalism and dogmatism, raised in the puzzle that ends this chapter.)

Descartes 1641, Meditation 3. (For his argument, in section 23.2, for God's existence.)

Van Cleve 1979. (On the argument of Descartes's, in section 23.2, for God's existence.)

Sellars 1963, pp. 128–134. (On the dilemma for foundationalism, in section 23.3.)

BonJour 1992, pp. 53–56. (On the possible importance of a priori knowledge to empirical knowledge, mentioned in section 23.3.)

24

Contextualism

For each area of possible knowledge, is there a final court of appeals as to what is known in that area? For example, is there an optimal way to determine what is known by the world's biologists? Should there be a Head Biologist with the job of resolving disputes as to whether a given biological claim can be admitted to the corpus of Biological Knowledge? Or should there be a Body of Mindful Biologists to resolve such disputes? Similarly, if we are looking for the last word on meanings, should we consult our dictionaries? Can they be doubted? And what if the dictionaries give different definitions? Who should resolve the disputes?

24.1 Real Doubts

Skeptics are dogged doubters. But might they be too dogged? Can doubt be taken too far? *Contextualists* think that it can. Let's consider their response to external world skepticism (hence to the regress skepticism described in section 22.3)—and see how they try to improve on foundationalism.

Suppose that you ask yourself whether you really do know that there is an external world. That is, do you know that 1 is true?

1 *There is a world (an external world).*

You argue for 1 by doing what you did in section 23.3. You target a more specific aspect of the world. "I know 1," you think, "if I know 2":

2 *Here is a hand.*

But how do you know that 2? (For now, ignore the skeptical dreaming worry from section 19.3.) Many epistemologists would suggest that if you know that 2, you know it on the basis of your knowledge of 3, which you base in turn on your knowledge that 4:

3   *I am seeing a hand.*

4   *I am apparently seeing a hand.*

But in this context of inquiry (where you ask whether you know 1 instead of presuming that you do), can knowledge of 4 ground knowledge of 3? Perhaps your belief in 4 can support your belief in 3 only if you already believe 1. If so, then (as I will explain) it is question-begging of you to "support" 1 with 4. You would be covertly "supporting" 1 with 1 itself!

By hypothesis, you suspended judgment as to whether 1 is true, neither believing nor disbelieving that there is a world beyond your mind. ("Is 1 true?" You shrug a shoulder or two.) But in that case doesn't 4 support only something like 5, rather than 3 or 2?

5   *Apparently, here is a hand.*

And 5 supports, at most, something like 6, instead of 1:

6   *Apparently, there is a world (an external world).*

Propositions 4 through 6 describe what is in your mind—the idea that there *apparently* is an external world containing a real hand. But can you use this idea to establish that there *is* an external world containing a real hand? By suspending belief in 1, you suspend belief in any such world. And once you no longer can call on 1, how does the fact that there appears to be an external world prove that there is one? Don't appearances need to be interpreted? And one, but only one, interpretation of them is that they reflect a reality beyond themselves. So, calling on any of the propositions 4 through 6 without presupposing 1 leaves you unable to prove 3, let alone 2. An apparent hand need not be a real hand. Maybe there are no real hands! If you suspend belief in 1, you suspend belief in what is a precondition of there even being any hands—the precondition being that there is an external world to *contain* the hands.

But you were trying to prove 2 in order to prove 1. The fact that there is a real hand was supposed to prove that there is an external, real world. So perhaps you cannot justify 1 in this way. Yet how else can you justify 1? Must you therefore discard 1, since the only possible way to justify it fails to do so? Must you accept external world skepticism?

A contextualist says that you need not discard 1. He says that what stops 4 from justifying 3 is the fact that, from the start of the argument, belief in 1 was suspended. Only because you did not assume that there is an external world were you unable to reason from 4 (a claim about an appearance) to 3 (a claim about a reality beyond appearances). And the reason you were not assuming that there is an external world was that you were trying to *argue* that there is one (and hence to justify the belief in one). If you are to argue for 1, you cannot assume 1. You had to suspend belief in 1 if you were to argue for it. (To "argue" for 1 from 1 plus other claims is not to argue for 1 at all. It is to presume 1.) Can we therefore draw the following cautionary moral about trying to justify 1?

> CM *If you treat 1 as needing to be justified, you will be unable to justify it. Once you concede that there is a need to justify the claim that there is an external world, you cannot justify that claim.*

So, do not try to justify 1, say the contextualists. Ignore the skeptic's demand. Assume that there is an external world. Doesn't everyone else do so? Except when you are around skeptics, you do not hear 1 being doubted. Is a skeptic's doubt therefore not a *real* doubt? When someone asks whether you know that there is a real world, does he only seem to raise a real doubt? Might he not really do so? (Ironically, can the skeptic face a skeptical problem about himself? Although he appears to raise a real doubt, he might not really be doing so at all. He tries to doubt that your apparent experiences of a real world are experiences of a real world. But does he succumb to this appearance/reality divide himself? Does his apparent doubt fail to be a real doubt?) Contextualists endorse RD:

> RD *Skeptical doubts are not real doubts.*

For contextualists, a skeptic's claim that "All of you are wrong to accord yourselves knowledge" is no more worrying than the joke, made by an American to an Australian (or vice versa), "You all drive on the wrong side of the road." If (almost) everyone drives on the one side, they *thereby* drive on the correct side for that country, that context. Contextualists think that much the same is true of people's allegiance to claims like 1. That is, because (almost) everyone thinks they know that 1, the skeptic is mistaken.

24.2 Contextual Doubts

What makes a doubt real? Is it enough that someone says something like, "I doubt what you say"? (Can someone say "I am listening to you" and not really be doing so? Is doubt like that?) Are there limits on what can be doubted? A contextualist says that there are. Real doubts occur within a context of inquiry. Real doubts are contextual, and this makes skeptical doubts unreal. For they do not occur within a context of inquiry.

How can that be so? Don't skeptical doubts occur within a skeptical context of inquiry? Isn't any doubt real within some context of inquiry? How can any doubt be legitimately ignored? Can we distinguish relevant doubts from irrelevant ones?

Maybe real doubts are those which people around you treat as pressing. But what if you are not keeping clever company? If you are surrounded by dullards, need you accept only what they accept? Can you choose to inquire more fully than they do? Is that a choice you should make? Even if you should, is there an upper limit to the number of extra questions you should try to answer? Notably, need you take skeptical questions seriously? Your friends might never do so, but does that remove your need to do so? What (if anything) makes a skeptical challenge optional? Is it the fact (as CM implies) that there is a sense in which skeptical doubts are unanswerable? Or is its unanswerability a reason to *respect* skeptical questioning?

The basic question is this. Who, or what, decides which doubts are real (and when and why will they decide it)? Or is there an independent Fact (existing where?) as to whether a given doubt needs to be taken seriously?

According to contextualists, there is no independent fact like that. Justification (they say) is context-relative. You have it, seek it, question its presence, or lack it only in a context of inquiry. Whether a specific doubt is real for you depends on your context of inquiry. If you are surrounded by skeptics, it can seem important to justify 1; if you are in the company of zoologists, it might not seem pressing to justify 1. So, look around you. Who is nearby? Should you move away from them? Should you do so if they ask you to justify the claim that there is an external world? Find people who will not make that request. Maybe you should seek only those who never challenge you on this issue. Would that be the right attitude?

But what determines whether you are in one context of inquiry rather than another? It is usually easy to determine what town you are in. Are contexts of inquiry so easily delineated? Maybe what matters is who your companions are and whether all of you are trying to answer the same questions. Is this such a clear criterion, though? Whether all of you are trying to answer the same questions depends on (1) which assumptions you and your companions share, plus (2) which theses all of you are not assuming to be true (and are, instead, investigating). You and the zoologists can take for granted that there is an external world, but you may debate how many ants there are (in that world). Still, is it always clear who *are* your companions in inquiry? Far away and unknown to you, another group is working on the same questions about ants. Are they part of your context of inquiry? Are their views on ants relevant to whether yours are justified? (If their findings conflict with yours, and you are unaware of that, does this defeat your justification for your findings? Chapter 10 bears on this question. Ignore it at your peril!)

What can that general picture of contexts of inquiry teach us about skeptics? Is there a skeptical context of inquiry? If enough skeptics meet, can they profitably debate whether they know of each other's existence? Or does there only seem to be a skeptical context of inquiry? Is there really a context of inquiry in which you can ask what the evidence is for thinking there is a real world? If so, is that real inquiry? Or is it mere mock inquiry? Does it deny the very point of inquiry? Imagine not having 1 as a shared assumption. Then what assumptions would you share? Basic assumptions create a context (a background) for inquiry.

Might some be so basic as to be mandatory? Once you cease assuming that there is a real world, how can you and others find common ground, so to speak, in which to plant your inquiries? What on earth, so to speak, is left once a belief as fundamental as 1 is no longer present? According to contextualists, nothing worth speaking of remains. Inquiry halts.

Thus, says the contextualist, you can reasonably ignore the skeptic's question. To take it seriously is to no longer assume that there is an external world. And perhaps such an assumption ends all inquiry. Does the skeptic leave us with nothing to say or think? (Perhaps all you can do is to rewrite everything you believe about how the world really is into claims about how it seems to be.)

24.3 Contextualism and Epistemic Regress

According to contextualists, then, skeptical doubts are not real. They are illusions of doubt, appearances of doubting that do not really capture the doubt they seem to capture. Surprisingly, though, contextualists still tend not to say that 1 is justified. You might have expected them to say that if there is no real doubt about 1, belief in 1 is justified. But usually they say no such thing. Instead, they reason as follows. You do not know that 1; you are not justified in believing that 1. Yet this is not a failing on your part and it should not please the skeptic.

Why is that? How can your lack of knowledge or justification fail to please the skeptic? Isn't it precisely what he claims?

Contextualism's point is that 1 is so fundamental to your thinking as to not *need* to be justified. It is, if anything, *a*justified (neither unjustified nor justified). Other (lesser?) beliefs, such as 2, are unjustified if not justified. They make claims that may or may not be true, that may or may not matter to you, and that may or may not have implications for many other beliefs. A belief like 1 is different—special, even. It "sets the scene" for other beliefs to be justified. Once 1 is in place, 4 can justify 3, hence 2. But (as we saw in section 24.1) until 1 is in place, 4 cannot justify 3, hence 2. Empirical knowledge and justification exist only once we assume there to be a world for such justification and knowledge to be about. Until we make such an assumption, we have no empirical justification or knowledge. Proposition 1 plays a vital role in the justification of other beliefs in spite of not being justified itself.

Thus, contextualists respond to skepticism with a *skeptical* solution (a form of solution that also appeared in section 20.3). They agree with skeptics that 1 is not justified or known. But they disagree with skeptics over the significance of that admission. First, they do not regard it as a *failing* to not be able to justify 1. Second, they deny that the absence of any justification for 1 renders all *other* external world beliefs unjustified and unknown. Unlike the skeptic, the contextualist says that you can know that there is a bird at your window even though you do not know that there is an external world! How can that be so? How can you know about things in the world without knowing that there is a world? Simple. Some claims need to be justified, some do not. Claim 2 does, claim 1 does not. (As to what would justify 2, a contextualist—with his respect for whatever beliefs people share—might approve of the social defeasibility account explained in Chapter 10.)

Consequently, contextualists make use of a thesis like CX:

CX   *A given belief of yours is contextually* special = *df. Although the belief is not justified, there are no real doubts about it. (That is, it is special within a given context c if and only if, although it is not justified within c, it incurs no real doubts within c.)*

CX and RD jointly entail that a belief in 1 is contextually special. Only a skeptic would try to doubt 1, but (by RD) his doubts are not real. (Can we draw a convincing line between real doubts and fake ones, though? If you say no, don't you thereby reject contextualism? But if you say yes, return to Chapter 16. *Where* is that line to be drawn? Can you think of an apparent doubt that is not clearly real and not clearly fake?)

This reasoning also reveals contextualism's response to the skeptical regress problem (Chapter 22). A contextually special belief is an unjustified justifier. Now, a belief in the existence of an external world—that is, a belief that 1—justifies other beliefs. (For instance, it helps to justify 2. Without 1, 4 is no evidence for 3 or 2.) But a belief in the existence of an external world justifies other beliefs without being justified itself (section 24.1). It can do this because (we are now told by contextualism) it is contextually special. So, we can even call it a *basic* belief. Contextualists end the regress with basic beliefs. Unlike foundationalists, though, they do not think of basic beliefs as basic knowledge (defined in section 23.1). Basic beliefs are not justified and not knowledge. They are just . . . special—grounding justification or knowledge without being justified or knowledge themselves. They are unjustified justifiers.

Something like 1, then, supposedly ends the regress—an otherwise endless search for justification. Do you agree with this contextualist suggestion? Can your search end with your most fundamental beliefs? For do those beliefs help to create the very contexts within which your questions about, and quests for, justification occur? Without them, would your thinking go nowhere?

But what is to prevent even your most basic beliefs from being mere dogmas? How do you know that they are not like that? If you do not, do even your most basic beliefs fail to provide a good answer to the skeptic? Have different beliefs been basic for different societies at different times—for example, during the Middle Ages, the belief that the earth was flat? Were such beliefs good bases for knowledge simply because they were taken for granted by so many people?

If an individual can be badly mistaken in her beliefs, why must the beliefs shared by a group of people be any more trustworthy? Perhaps you say, "But where there are several people, individual mistakes will be eliminated, canceled out." Why mightn't they be compounded instead? Suppose you reply, "There is a kind of safety in numbers." What kind of safety is that? Is it one that begets truth?

FURTHER READING

Moore 1959, Chapter 7. (For a famous attempt—using the example of hands, as in section 24.1—to know that there is an external world.)

Hetherington 1995. (On the idea, in section 24.1, that skeptics can face a skeptical problem themselves.)

Wittgenstein 1969. (For a famous example of contextualist thinking, in section 24.2.)

Moser 1985, Chapter 2. (On contextualism and regress, in section 24.3.)

25

Coherentism

You are prosecuting Ray: "Hey Ray, pray say where you were, on that day in May." (And so on.) As you question him, it becomes clear that he has an internally consistent and detailed alibi: "Let me tell you well; I ain't no criminell. It was hell, ringing that school bell. That's where I was; it's where I dwell." (And so on.) Does the consistency and detail of Ray's story justify its claims? If so, should you believe him? If not, why might you not do so? Would it be because, at various stages, his version of events clashes with yours? But why should you believe your own version over Ray's, especially if his is as internally consistent and detailed as yours? ("Say it ain't that way, Ray.")

25.1 The Basic Idea of Coherentism

Coherentism is the third nonskeptical reaction to the skeptic's regress argument (Chapter 22). The other two—foundationalism (Chapter 23) and contextualism (Chapter 24)—construct hierarchies. One posits basic knowledge (section 23.1); the other prizes basic beliefs (section 24.3). Coherentists are more egalitarian. For them, there are no basic beliefs and there is no basic knowledge; they do not stamp some few beliefs (or kinds of belief) as special.

Instead, says the coherentist, your beliefs are justified (if they are) by helping each other. None are epistemically prior; none are helped by, without also helping, others. A justified believer is a systematic believer. She has a system of beliefs that is internally coherent and harmonious:

> OH   A given belief of yours is justified in a coherentist way = df. It belongs to a
> coherent system of your beliefs.

A coherent system of beliefs is a set of beliefs, but not just any such set. It contains only beliefs that support each other and thereby justify each other. They stand in relations of mutual support and justification. But note that OH does not entail that your belief is justified in a coherentist way only if *all* of your beliefs cohere with each other. The system referred to in OH need not be the set of all of your beliefs, even at a given time. It might be the "serious" part, say—the beliefs that you bring to, and/or gain from, your inquiries into what is true. For example, your scientific beliefs need not cohere with—reinforce—your literary beliefs. (Should some systems cohere with each other, though? For example, need your scientific beliefs cohere with your religious beliefs?)

Here are two (small) sets of beliefs. In only one of them does there seem to be mutual support:

S_1 *{Numbers exist. 1 is a number. So is 2.}*
S_2 *{Numbers exist. Freddo is a frog. I'm alive.}*

In S_1, the beliefs seem pertinent to each other; in S_2, they do not. (Which of these two sets is more like the set of your beliefs? How do you know?)

25.2 Coherentism and Epistemic Regress

The coherence of a system of beliefs is participated in equally by all of the beliefs in the set. It is they that cohere; so it is they that are justified. This concept of coherence gives coherentists their distinctive reaction (as follows) to the regress argument.

Imagine having these two beliefs:

1   *Red balls exist.*
2   *Redness is like this: . . . To be a ball is to be like this: . . .*

Does 1 help to justify 2? Does 2 help to justify 1? Which proposition depends on the other in order to be justified? Or might each depend on the other?

Only coherentists can say that 1 and 2 might help to justify each other—with neither being already justified (justified before the other is justified). Foundationalists and contextualists puzzle, instead, over which proposition is the more basic of the two. Which one supports the other? they ask. Is 2 more basic? Seemingly it is, if in order to know that there are red balls you must already know what redness and ballhood are like. Or is 1 more basic? Seemingly it is, if in order to know what redness and ballhood are like, you must have already experienced some red things and some balls and have learned from them how to fill in the blanks in 2.

Or maybe there is no clear answer to those two questions. If there is not, is that because neither 1 nor 2 can be justified before the other? If neither proposition is more basic than the other, but we keep asking which is more basic, perhaps we are like someone who insists on an answer of either yes or no to the question "Have you stopped beating your wife?" asked of a man who never started beating his wife. Are 1 and 2 more of a package deal? Do you know 1 only because you already know 2? And do you know 2 only because you already know 1? Are they part of a single system of mutually supportive beliefs (your "physical world belief system")? The coherentist can say that they are. If foundationalists see your system of knowledge and justification as like a large building, one part of which is the foundation for the rest, coherentists think of this system as more like a strong spider's web. Each part supports each other part; the structure can be rebuilt in different places each day; and no one piece of material always anchors the rest of it.

25.3 Coherentism and Consistency

What is coherence, and what makes a set of beliefs coherent? (Can a set of beliefs properly be called a system of beliefs only if the set is coherent?) Presumably, not just any set of beliefs is coherent. So there must be restrictions on what makes a set coherent. One condition many coherentists impose is consistency. For instance, is S_3 incoherent because inconsistent?

S_3 *{Roosters crow. I hate anything that crows. I do not hate roosters.}*

Well, S_3 is incoherent if CC is true:

CC *A set of beliefs is coherent if and only if it is a logically consistent set of beliefs.*

But is CC true? It says that consistency is (1) sufficient, and (2) necessary, for coherence. Is it right about that?

(1) Sufficiency

Imagine Madam Zelda (from section 6.4), our ubiquitous fortune-teller, sitting down in her later years to write an autobiography. She ends the book with her predictions for the future course of the world. As usual, she has no apparent evidence for these predictions. But this does not stop her from believing them. What is more, they are logically consistent with each other. A world where they all came true would be a logically possible world. Is this consistency enough to justify her predictions?

   If not, it is possible to have a set of beliefs that are jointly consistent but not justified. Must you do more than be consistent in your thinking if you are to gain justified beliefs? (The set S_2 in section 25.1 is internally consistent. But do its beliefs really cohere? Are they at all justified by each other?)

(2) Necessity

Must you be consistent in your thinking if you are to gain justified beliefs? Can justification come from inconsistent thinking? Are there trivial inconsistencies and serious ones?

Recall Dr. Bio, our seal specialist (from section 6.4). He has been working hard, amassing a solid body of research material. His work has passed peer review, and several of his papers have been published in good journals. He decides to synthesize all of his work into a book on fur seals. The writing takes a year, but finally the deed is done. What results is a well-researched and well-argued discussion of fur seal breeding patterns. All that remains is for him to pen a preface. He begins with this disclaimer: "An all-too-justified belief in my own fallibility tells me to expect that somewhere in this book there is a false claim. So, that is indeed what I expect. But where is it? I have no idea. I accept everything I say in this book."

Whoa! Should he stop right there? Isn't he confronting himself with an instance of the preface paradox (described in section 1.2)? Is the result an inconsistent body of beliefs (the preface plus the rest of the book)? Yet isn't each of these beliefs justified? And mightn't this be because of the coherence that we may assume obtains between them in such a unified and rigorous book? Or does Dr. B's inconsistency render the entire book incoherent? Does it make his scientific claims about fur seals unjustified? If not, does this example show that it is possible to have an inconsistent set of beliefs in which each belief is still justified? (If you deny that possibility, go back to Chapter 17 and the lottery paradox.)

25.4 Coherentism and Fiction

Coherentism aims to account for justification purely in terms of what is internal to a system of belief. Ideally, you can survey all of your beliefs and, just by seeing how they relate to each other, decide whether you are a coherent believer. That is the spirit of coherentism. OH should be interpreted as saying that membership in a coherent system of beliefs is all that is involved in a belief's being justified. Nothing external to the system matters in this respect.

With this aspect of coherentism clearly understood, though, we now face what is, in effect, a skeptical puzzle about coherentism. Can coherentists distinguish between a body of justification and a piece of fiction? If they cannot, perhaps there is nothing that makes a coherent set of beliefs more likely to be true than an incoherent set. If that is so, does coherentism fail as a response to skepticism?

A detailed novel might construct a purely fictional story set in a purely fictional town. However, considered purely internally, couldn't the story be every bit as coherent as your belief system? For some examples, think of George Eliot's *Middlemarch*, J.R.R. Tolkien's *The Lord of the Rings*, or Jan Morris's *Last Letters from Hav.* Morris is an internationally known travel writer. But in her book she never tells us that there is no such place as Hav. It is easy to be fooled—as some people have been—into thinking that Hav exists! Yet, if these fictional worlds are just as internally coherent as your belief system is, how can coherentism accord you any more justification for thinking that you live in a real world than it accords a fictional character for thinking that *he* lives in a real world? Hence (in a skeptical vein), we might ask whether you can know that you are a real person in a real world. Can you know that you are not merely a fictional character in a fictional world?

You might respond, "But my beliefs are so coherent. That makes them justified. Doesn't that take me most of the way toward knowing where I am?" Well, does it? Mightn't a piece of fiction be no less internally coherent than a set of beliefs that are seemingly about the real world? Are some works of fiction, in fact, even more coherent than some realities? Might a coherentist be unable to say how your beliefs are any more justified than they would be if you were purely fictional? (Again, do you know that you are not purely fictional?)

Perhaps you continue, "What could be easier to avoid than this objection? I *do* have ways of knowing that my beliefs are not fictions. Let me count the ways!" And you would begin doing just that. Let's consider four possible suggestions as to what those ways might be.

1. One possible suggestion is that, unlike the fictional character's beliefs, most of your beliefs are *true*. Being fictional, most of the character's beliefs are false; being real, most of yours are true. In other words, most of your beliefs are true and this fact is part of the reason why your beliefs are justified.

But does this suggestion conflict (i.e., fail to cohere!) with OH? It makes justification depend on something external to your belief system. It distinguishes between systems on the basis of how many of their beliefs are true in the world outside. How can a coherentist adopt that approach? As OH implies, coherentism tries to account for justification wholly in terms of what obtains inside a system of belief; the justification is not supposed to depend on anything outside the system. (And in any event, is it so clear that having many true beliefs makes your beliefs justified? If you say that it is, make haste back to Chapter 6.)

2. Another possible suggestion is that you, unlike the fictional character, have acquired your beliefs *reliably*. Is this an advantage that you, as a real being, have over him?

Maybe it is, but can a coherentist make use of this fact? For doesn't it clash with OH? It links beliefs within your system to the world outside (specifically, to how reliably that world gave you those beliefs). So, it makes justification depend on something external to the system's internal coherence.

Of course, the suggestion avoids that problem if it requires just that your system contain *beliefs* about how reliably you have gained your beliefs. You might have beliefs about how reliably people form beliefs on the basis of their perceptions, for example. But can't a fictional character also have such beliefs?

(Anyway, is it so clear that your justification should be analyzed in terms of how reliably you gain beliefs? If you think that it is, return to Chapter 7.)

3. Perhaps the difference between your belief system and the fictional character's is that yours, unlike hers, is *causally* connected to the real world.

This suggestion, however, faces the same puzzle as the previous two. It makes your justification depend on something external to the relations of coherence within your belief system. It goes beyond those relations by asking whether the system was brought into existence by a real world. So, once more, OH (and the spirit of coherentism) has been left behind. (Moreover, as ever, how tempting is this causal suggestion on its own terms? If you are tempted by it, Chapter 8 is for you.)

4. Maybe your beliefs, unlike the fictional character's, are justified because of their *explanatory* power. Can you account for phenomena beyond the fictional character's explanatory reach?

Conceivably you can indeed account for such phenomena—but how does this fact help the coherentist? What would you be explaining? And can this question be answered in a way that coheres with OH?

First, are your beliefs explaining The World (that awe-inspiring reality containing you, your belief system, and much else besides)? For argument's sake, let's suppose so. On suggestion (4), this explanatory power is part of what justifies your beliefs. But if it is, then your beliefs are being justified partly by something external to the belief system containing them. They are being justified because (1) they cohere with each other, and (2) they explain aspects of The World outside. Yet (2) clashes with OH. The spirit of coherentism has been lost.

But, second, if we leave The World out of the story, what is left for your beliefs to explain? Won't they only explain each other? ("I believe this because I believe that.") And how can this kind of explanatory power distinguish you from a fictional character? Can't he, too, have beliefs between which there exist powerful explanatory relations?

Do these four suggestions (plus any others) therefore fail? Each of them seems to succumb to a dilemma. Either (1) the coherentist tries to make justification depend on coherence plus some kind of link to The World; or (2) he does not. Yet (1) if he does link justification to The World, does he fail OH, since he no longer lets justification be only a relationship *within* a belief system? And (2) if he does not make this link (that is, if he lets justification be just a relationship within a belief system), is he unable to show why your beliefs are more justified than those of some fictional character?

What is your reaction to this supposed dilemma? Do you still insist that there is a clear distinction between your belief system and the fictional character's? Where is it? Is the slippery slope puzzle from Chapter 16 relevant here? Is a belief system with one fanciful belief and ninety-nine nonfanciful beliefs nonfanciful? What of a system with two fanciful beliefs and ninety-eight nonfanciful ones? What of . . . ? When does a belief system contain justified beliefs? (And can it ever contain enough of them to avoid the Gettier problem in Chapter 5?)

Can Dr. Frankenstein create an adult person who already has an adult's knowl-edge? The person would have a set of beliefs. Can these be knowledge—just like that? Or do they fail to be knowledge, because they have not been formed in re-sponse to the world? Is a sustained personal history—such as is lacked by Dr. Frankenstein's creation—important to having knowledge of the world? If the creature spends a year saying exactly what Dr. Frankenstein says during that year, does it know as much as he does during that year?

FURTHER READING

BonJour 1985. Chapter 5. (On the basic idea, in section 25.1, of coherentism; and on coher-entism and regress, in section 25.2.)

Kornblith 1989. (On coherence and consistency, in section 25.3.)

Schlick 1959. (On coherence and fiction, in section 25.4.)

Klein and Warfield 1994. (On coherence and truth, in section 25.4.)

26

Pyrrhonian Skepticism

Human lungs function poorly in much of the world (underwater and high above sea level). Why should our brains interact with the world any better than our lungs do? Naturally, we think that our brains work well in many contexts. But are we impartial judges of our own prowess? Other animals sense some aspects of the world more accurately than we do. And different people possess differing levels of intelligence and awareness. Should we therefore treat our beliefs with caution? If so, how cautious need we be? (The giraffe said to the ant: "It seems to you like a mountain. To me, it's a small mound. Let's consult the hyena. He's medium-sized. So he'll tell us what to believe!")

26.1 The Basic Idea of Pyrrhonism

In response to some skeptical challenges (in Chapters 18 through 22), we have contemplated three potential ways to understand how beliefs can be justified or qualify as knowledge (Chapters 23 through 25). But even if none of those ways convince you, and hence even if you are not sure that you can have justification or knowledge, at least you still have your beliefs. "No one can take my beliefs away from me," you might say. Oh, can't they? Pyrrhonian skepticism (more succinctly, Pyrrhonism) thinks that it can do so.

Taking its name from Pyrrho, an ancient Greek philosopher, Pyrrhonism aims to divest you of all beliefs as to what is true in the world. If a Pyrrhonist has his way, you will retain no substantial beliefs. You will have only appearances—such-and-such seeming to be the case. Maybe you can have "subjective" beliefs, but these report nothing more than those appearances. There will be no "objective" beliefs purporting to describe how things really are. The belief-that-1 goes; a belief-that-2 could remain:

1   *That is a tree.*
2   *That appears (to me) to be a tree.*

26.2 The Pyrrhonist Argument

From different perspectives, things seem different. Hence, no single perspective captures how things really are. That is how it seems to Pyrrhonists. For example, you come to what seems to you like a tree. Proposition 2 is true; proposition 1 seems true. So, you believe 1. "No, stop right there!" calls the Pyrrhonist, whisking out his skeptical *modes* (various ways of inducing doubt). You duck and dodge, trying to retain a belief in 1. But he is relentless, an expert knife-thrower trapping you in a corner with his skeptical modes, aiming to systematically deprive you of belief. Here is how he reasons.

The object seems to you to be a tree only because you are a specific animal in a specific state and circumstance and because the object is in an equally specific state and circumstance. But your circumstance might have been different, and in such a way as to make 1 seem not to be true. If the light was different, the object might not look like a tree. Without leaves, it might not seem like a tree. With a different colored bark, it might look more like a statue than a tree. If you were unused to seeing trees, it might not seem like a tree. Had you been closer to it, or farther away from it, it might not have seemed like a tree. What if you had been distraught at the time? What if you had been dreaming? What if you had been drunk? What if you had been an ant? (Would an ant see the object as a tree?) What if your friend Jesse did not see the object as a tree? In these circumstances, 1 might not seem to be true. Is it therefore Amazing Luck that you are the right instance of the right kind of animal in the right state and circumstance to judge what the object is?

The Pyrrhonist's point is this. Can there be perspectives relative to which the object appears different from how it appears to you right now? Seemingly, there can. Shouldn't you respect such perspectives? Why should you think your current perspective is more accurate than the others? (Bear in mind that some of those other perspectives are your own, albeit in a different setting.) You think your current one is accurate. But, being a party to the dispute, you are not an unbiased judge. This is also true of anyone else involved in the dispute. There you are; there is Jesse. Is one of you more impartial than the other? Who is to say? Moreover, suppose you stand 10 feet from the tree; then you walk a little and stop 1,000 feet from it. The object looks different to you now. Is one "you" an "impartial" distance from it?

Would an impartial perspective be the perspective of someone (or something) with no existing view on whether 1 is true? (Must we proceed as if selecting a jury?) Even calling on a perspective like this will not satisfy Pyrrhonists, though. They say that as soon as the person (or the ant!) with the new perspective does decide whether 1 is true, he is no longer unbiased. He has become a party to the dispute. He either agrees with you (saying that 1 is true) or disagrees with you (denying that 1 is true). What makes the new perspective any better than yours and Jesse's? (It might be different. Must it be better?) Why should someone with a new perspective be called on to adjudicate? Suppose that the new perspective belongs to Ruth. Like you and Jesse, Ruth has a view on whether 1 is true. (She can adjudicate only by reaching such a view.) Once more, therefore, there is dis-agreement—this time, between Ruth and either you or Jesse. So, do we need yet another new perspective—perhaps someone with a fresh outlook—to objec-tively resolve matters?

Why bother? How could it help? If the owner of the new perspective—Deb, say—already has a view on whether 1 is true, she is a party to the dispute. This makes her ineligible to adjudicate. If she does not yet have any such view, this is only temporary. She will come to have a view (if only in the course of trying to adjudicate), at which point she is a party to the dispute. She is no longer impar-tial. Hence, Deb is ineligible to adjudicate. (Anyone who reaches no view at all on whether 1 is true never adjudicates impartially on 1, either!)

This pattern apparently continues without end. (Do we face a version of the regress argument from section 22.2?) At no time can you adjudicate on your own claim. You cannot be impartial. So a fresh perspective is needed (e.g., fresh evi-dence or someone else's views). But no new perspective is any more impartial than your own. (Nor is it any less so, of course.) There is no basic (foundational) perspective, because no one can impartially assume that her own perspective is authoritative. And there will be no contextual agreement or coherentist har-mony among the different perspectives. The only option left is a potential infin-ity of disagreements among people (and other animals?) with different perspec-tives—who continue their futile attempts to gain beliefs. But that is a regress. One person's, or animal's, perspective is accurate only if all other people, and all other animals, with their various perspectives, agree, or cohere, with it. However, no such universal agreement ever occurs.

Thus, no one with a single perspective at a given time can resolve whether 1 is true. Yet, once different perspectives are taken into account, neither 1 nor not-1 seems more probable than the other. The two possibilities seem to be what Pyrrhonists call *equipollent* (equally probable). So, you must suspend belief in both 1 and not-1.

Other types of beliefs are affected by the Pyrrhonist argument, too. For exam-ple, it applies to not only external world beliefs but also a priori beliefs (Chapter 13). Do you really believe 3?

3    $2 + 2 = 4$.

I presume that 3 seems to you to be true. Must it therefore be true? To some people, 3 does not seem true. Hence, is it arbitrary for you to believe 3? Are you ignoring evidence against 3? "But," you might reply, "only to poorly educated people does 3 not seem true. We can ignore their reactions." Who makes that de-cision? Who has been properly educated in this area? Does it happen to be those who agree with you about 3? Isn't that somewhat convenient? Would it worry you

that this claim sounds self-serving on your part? Might you just be ignoring in-
convenient evidence? How can you nondogmatically and fair-mindedly resolve
this dispute?

Similarly, do ethical beliefs and religious views succumb to Pyrrhonist reasoning? How would you apply the argument to 4 (or, for that matter, to not-4)?

4   *Bigamy is morally wrong.*

Is there no end to this kind of worry? For any proposition p, evidence for p is
p's seeming to be true; evidence for p makes p seem true. But, from some other
perspective, not-p will seem true. Different evidence can make not-p seem true.
Even when there is evidence for p, there might well be evidence against p. Can
we choose impartially between competing pieces of evidence? "Apparently not,"
say Pyrrhonists.

26.3 Pyrrhonism and Belief

Here is the heart of the Pyrrhonist argument. (1) Things seem thus-and-so to
you. (2) They would seem different to you, were your circumstances different.
Hence, (3) you can never form beliefs as to how things really are. You can only
ever believe that they seem thus-and-so—not that they *are* thus-and-so.

That reasoning seems logically invalid. Can't you believe that there is a tree
present, because there seems to you to be one present? It is your belief—no one
else's. Why care about other perspectives? ("I have my beliefs. You have yours. We
disagree; so what? We need not discard our beliefs!") How can it matter that, if
circumstances were different, no tree would seem to you to be present?
Circumstances are not different. Can't you form beliefs within a context, paying
no heed to how things would seem in a different context? Don't you do this every
day? If you were of a different religion, the world might seem different to you.
But you are not. Yet don't you still have beliefs? (Maybe none of your substantial
beliefs are impartial, though. Would that worry you?)

Can we make Pyrrhonist reasoning more tempting, then? I will mention two
conceptions of substantial belief that seem to make the inference from (1)-plus-
(2) to (3) logically valid.

(1) Multi-Perspectival Belief

A belief-that-1 has an objective content. Does its content (i.e., 1) therefore reflect
more than one possible perspective? After all, what it says is as purportedly true
for others as it is for you right now. A belief-that-2 is different in that respect. It
can seem to you that there is a tree present, even if it seems that way from no
other perspective. Because 2 reports only on an appearance from one perspec-

tive, it makes no claim about "public space"—a world of objective facts. But 1 does. It is ostensibly about a "shared" world—our world, not yours. Unlike 2, 1 purports to be about a world beyond how things seem to you right now. So, you believe 1 (as against 2) only by taking into account appearances other than the present one. If you do not do this, you are believing at most 2, not 1. A substantial belief (such as a belief-that-1) is *multi-perspectival,* aiming to reflect many perspectives at once. To have beliefs about a shared world is to "sum up" different perspectives on that world.

This account of belief does seem to make Pyrrhonist reasoning logically valid. If you were to have a suitably objective perspective on 1, and hence were to occupy more than one perspective on 1, wouldn't you experience competing appearances? For instance, you might experience 2 and 5:

5   *That appears (to me) to be a tall sculpture.*

We may suppose that proposition 5 reports what someone else experienced when confronted by the object to which you reacted with 2. But to experience 2 plus 5 (combining your current perspective with another) is to lack stable support for 1. Proposition 2 supports 1, but 5 does not. To believe 1 would be to believe on the basis of only some of the possible—and competing—relevant experiences. Wouldn't that course of action be rather arbitrary? (And even if reality does ever seem the same from all perspectives, is there a Humean worry about extrapolating from a stream of experiential data? Chapter 20 discusses that worry.) If such a course of action is arbitrary, is substantial belief therefore impossible? (You could say, "No. It seems to me that I have beliefs about how things really are." But does its *seeming* to you that you have such beliefs entail that you *do* have them? Chapter 21 touches on that question.)

(2) Undoubted Belief

Do you believe 1 only because it does not seem to you that 1 might be false? Yet if it seemed to you that 1 seemed false from other perspectives, wouldn't it seem to you that 1 might be false? And if you answer these questions with yes, shouldn't you be persuaded by Pyrrhonism? For Pyrrhonism aims to make it seem to you that there are perspectives from which 1 is seen as false. Again, then, can you really believe 1?

26.4 Pyrrhonism and Intellectual Tranquillity

You might worry about where Pyrrhonism leaves you. Don't. Don't worry; be (sort of) happy. Be content. Calm will come, suspect Pyrrhonists. ("Read All About It!") By losing beliefs as to how things really are, you achieve an intellectual quietude, a kind of tranquillity. Things still seem to you to be thus-and-so; accept those appearances at face value. But do not hunger for beliefs as to what lies behind the appearances. You will gain none. So, why seek them? Relax.

That is how it seemed to Pyrrhonists. Do you, too, feel some intellectual contentment? Does it seem to you that a life can be lived free of belief about objective reality? (Some say that Pyrrho himself tried to live like that. What would such a life involve? Would it be a life? On such matters, see section 20.3.)

Are Pyrrhonists thus the ultimate nondogmatists? For they did not even say that there are definitely no substantial beliefs. They said that it *seems* to them that there are none. But is even that conclusion plausible? If you were to follow Pyrrhonists in discarding beliefs as to how the world really is, would you relinquish all commitment to objective truth? You could not *believe* that there are objective facts. Yet don't they still seem to exist? If so, can you continue to act as if there are? Can you still *say* that there are? You could reply, "No. What we say reveals what we believe. If we cannot believe that there are facts, we cannot say that there are. Silence, please." Is that so? (If you think so, please revisit section 3.2.)

Regardless of whether you can literally live without beliefs, though, what do you think of the *spirit* of Pyrrhonism? Should you avoid assuming that your perspective on reality is always correct? Should you be prepared to discard beliefs, even favored ones? Should you always be prepared to inquire, and as impartially as possible? Should you take from Pyrrhonism a spirit of humility as an inquirer? After all, even if you think that Pyrrhonism goes too far, and that you can have some substantial beliefs, how well do you understand *which* beliefs to adopt? ("That's simple," you might say. "Some claims are better supported by evidence than others are. I'll believe those ones." Well, if I were you, I would now reconsider Chapters 14 and 15. In what ways are evidence and reasoning important? Is it so clear how best to use one's evidence?)

> *When someone disagrees with you about p, is your justification for p automatically weakened? When people disagree, must a compromise be sought? Is the truth always "somewhere in between"? Or is truth "nowhere"? If two young siblings disagree, should their parents believe neither of them?*
>
> *When something—such as a job application—goes against you, and you are a man, a woman, white, black, Asian, Hispanic, or a member of some other minority group, can you ever determine what the real reason is for the setback? Maybe it was racism. Maybe it was sexism. Then again, maybe your qualifications were not the best. Maybe your manners were not what was wanted. Maybe the interviewer had a headache when talking to you. Is there no end to this list of possibilities? Should you suspend all belief as to the real reason for the rejection?*

FURTHER READING

Cherniak 1986, pp. 125–127. (For the kind of puzzle that begins this chapter.)

Sextus Empiricus, *Outlines of Pyrrhonism*, I 1–163, in Bury 1933, pp. 1–93. (For the classic version of Pyrrhonism.)

Annas and Barnes 1985. (For a newer translation of Sextus, with commentary.)

27

Questioning Epistemology

Can a person know without knowing that he knows? One possible answer to this question is, "Yes. Bruce knows that it's raining outside, although he doesn't know that he knows it. How can he? He doesn't know what knowledge is." But can't it sound odd to apply that idea to oneself? *("I know that it's raining outside, although I don't know that I know it. How can I? I don't know what knowledge is.")*

27.1 The Problem of the Criterion

Let's end this book with three puzzles about epistemology itself. Our earlier puzzles have been about knowledge. The ones in this chapter concern attempts to theorize about knowledge.

The first is the *problem of the criterion*. (It was introduced in section 1.1; I'll call it PC for short.) It is the supposed problem of meeting the challenge that began this book—namely, the challenge of answering these questions in a reasoned way:

A   *What is knowledge?*
B   *Is there any knowledge?*

Now that you are at the end of the book, you might feel that you have good answers to A and B. (Do you? If so, which chapters have most helped you to reach those answers?) PC, however, denies that your answers could really be good ones. It reasons as follows.

1. To answer A is to offer a theory of knowledge (such as in any of Chapters 6 through 13, plus either Chapter 14 or Chapter 15). But how can you support, or justify, that theory? How can you answer A *well*? Would you need to test it on supposed examples of knowledge? For example, suppose you say (as is theorized in Chapters 6 and 7) that knowledge is a reliably acquired true belief. To support, or test, this theory about the nature of knowledge, must you apply it to specific

179

situations? Do you need to verify that in cases where you say that knowledge is present, as well as in cases where you think that knowledge is not present, your theory agrees with your assessments? Perhaps; yet doesn't this procedure require you to have already decided, in a careful way, where such examples are to be found? And isn't that what the other question, B, asks you to decide? Indeed, it is. So, in order to answer A well, you must have already answered B well.

2. To answer B is to decide where knowledge is (and where it is not) to be found. It is to decide who knows what when. But how can you support any such decision unless and until you have decided—in a careful way, of course—what knowledge is? Otherwise, how can you ever (nonaccidentally) categorize something as knowledge in the first place? But any decision as to what knowledge is constitutes an answer to A. So, in order to answer B well, you must have already answered A well.

3. But (1)-plus-(2) tells us that, in order to answer either A or B in a careful and thoughtful way, you must have already answered the other in that way. That is, to support an answer to either A or B, you must have already supported an answer to the other. How can you do that? By (1), in order to answer A well, you need to have answered B well. And by (2), in order to have answered B well, you need to have answered A well. Hence, by (1)-plus-(2), in order to have answered A well, you must have already answered A well! (To answer A well is in part to have answered B well, which is in part to have answered A well.) By analogous reasoning, we find that, in order to have answered B well, you must have already answered B well! (To answer B well is in part to have answered A well, which is in part to have answered B well.)

4. Doesn't (3) require something impossible? Nothing is ever answered before it is answered. Is it impossible, then, to provide a well-supported answer to either A or B? Is epistemology doomed? Is it destined to never satisfy its aim of carefully answering those fundamental questions? (Have your efforts as a reader of this book been in vain?)

Such is the problem of the criterion, a venerable epistemological puzzle. Do you see any way out of it? Which comes first—an identification of instances of knowledge (an answer to B), or a specification of the nature of knowledge (an answer to A)? According to PC, neither comes first. But if so (PC continues), there is a problem for your prospects of ever understanding knowledge. For don't you need to start your understanding by trying to answer either A or B? (Do you feel, at book's end, that you do not yet understand knowledge?)

PC is a higher-level skepticism. It argues that there is no *understanding* of knowledge—of what it is or where it is. To try to answer A is to seek a theory of knowledge. But to justify your answer, you need to test your theory on examples. That is, you need to answer B—and decide what *are* examples of knowledge. Yet your answer to B, too, is good only if supported. You might start confidently, saying, "I know that I am alive. I know that I am human." Still, won't you swiftly meet examples over which you hesitate, and about which you need to consult a theory of knowledge? Won't you need to put your answer to B on hold, pending a decision as to what knowledge is—that is, pending an answer to A? In this way, PC spins you back and forth between thinking about the nature, and thinking about the distribution, of knowledge:

> *A good answer to A requires a good answer to B requires a good answer to A requires a good answer to B requires a good answer to A requires . . .*

Will you forever fail to reach a good understanding of knowledge? (Is there a regress worry here, as in section 22.2?)

If you try to answer A, you are doing what we have done throughout this book. You are being epistemological, theorizing about the nature of knowledge. And, like a scientist proposing a theory of the origin of the universe, you would need to test your theory. The most obvious way to do so would be to apply the theory to supposed examples of knowledge. But this procedure involves you in answering B—and then PC applies to you.

At least, it applies to you unless you can answer B well without needing to answer A as well. So, is that possible? If you were to try to answer B without answering A, your approach could be called *bare particularism*. Particularism (as we saw in section 1.1) is the idea that B can be answered properly before A has been answered properly. Thus, it is one purported way to solve PC (which denies that either A or B can be adequately answered before the other). Bare particularism, though, tries to answer B while then *ignoring* A. And that is no way to solve PC. It "solves" PC only by ignoring PC. For instance, suppose you answer B with "For a start, I know that I am alive." A skeptic might then remind you of PC, responding like this:

> *Can you say what knowledge is? If not, you cannot justifiedly claim knowledge. You may as well be guessing that you know. So, you must start by finding a good answer to A. You need to understand, in a more theoretical way, what knowledge is. Until you accomplish that, whenever you claim knowledge (in response to B) you are really only guessing, perhaps being dogmatic.*

To which a bare particularist could reply as follows:

> *Look, I believe that I have some knowledge. What I lack is knowledge that I know. I lack it because I do not understand what knowledge is. That is why I cannot supply a good answer to A. But (and here is my bare particularism) I do not need to answer A. I can answer B adequately with a bare yes plus some good examples. I need to answer B more fully only if I need to know what knowledge is. But I have no such need; only epistemologists do. Right now, I am not being*

an epistemologist. I will therefore ignore A. I claim that I have knowledge, even though I admit that I do not fully understand what it is to have knowledge. I know; I just don't know that I know.

In an indirect way, though, such bare particularism still succumbs to PC. For, by avoiding answering A, you are not even trying to understand knowledge—and PC's aim was to leave you with no understanding of knowledge!

Here is the overall worry. (1) If, as a bare particularist, you try to answer B while ignoring A, do you thereby gain no understanding of knowledge? (2) Yet, if you do try to answer A, are you swept away by PC, denied any understanding of knowledge? (3) Hence, no matter how you approach questions about knowledge (either ignoring A or trying to answer it), are you bound to not understand knowledge? Does epistemology—since it *is* the attempt to understand knowledge—therefore stray beyond the limits of human understanding? Maybe you do have knowledge. Maybe there are facts you know. Yet perhaps neither you nor anyone else knows what it is for you to know. Maybe your being a knower cannot be understood. Might it be that knowledge can be possessed but not understood? You can own and use a car without understanding how it works; is knowledge like that?

27.2 Applying Pyrrhonism to Epistemology

Pyrrhonism (Chapter 26) is another epistemological idea that, if at all successful, seems to undermine epistemology. Pyrrhonists, remember, argue that there are no substantial beliefs as to how things really are. You can have what we might call subjective beliefs, reporting what appears to you to be true. But once you drop the qualifier "appears," and you try to form a belief as to what is really true, you seem to fail, say Pyrrhonists.

Now, epistemologists generally strive for beliefs regarding the epistemic world. For instance, if, in response to A, you say that there is a causal component in knowing that there is a sheep in the field (Chapter 8), or that such knowledge is present only if no false evidence is being used (Chapter 11), you are trying to suggest what knowledge is really like. You are not meaning to say only that it appears to you that knowledge is thus-and-so. You are saying that it *is* thus-and-so. (Isn't that the kind of answer that A seeks?) Just as knowledge is habitually taken to be true (Chapter 2), theorists of knowledge usually take their theories of it to be true—really true, not just apparently true.

But is an epistemologist ever entitled to such confidence in her theories—to accept them as really true rather than merely apparently true? Pyrrhonists would deny that she is entitled to this kind of confidence. Does their skeptical worry apply to any answers you might give to A and B (no less than to your claims about the physical world)? Pyrrhonism is fueled by disagreement between actual or possible perspectives. If there is disagreement about whether p is true, is it hard—even impossible—to maintain a belief that p? Pyrrhonists say that it is. How, then, would they react to the plethora of puzzles, questions, and possible theories in this book (and epistemology as a whole)? There is little agreement among theorists of knowledge about what knowledge is and about who has it in what circumstances. Do their disagreements prevent theorists from having beliefs about what knowledge is really like and about who has it? (Does analogous reasoning affect all researchers in all disciplines? Do their disagreements deprive them of beliefs—real beliefs? Are they producing only apparent beliefs—imitation beliefs? Even scientists disagree with each other. Are there therefore no scientific beliefs about the world? Can scientists report only how the world seems to them? Is scientific use of *hypotheses* particularly apt?)

If you came to this book already confident that people have knowledge, could you impartially assess the merits of the skeptical arguments in Chapters 18 through 22 and 26? Pyrrhonists will doubt it. Equally, if you already were, or have since become, skeptical in your thinking about knowledge, were you able to impartially adjudicate on the apparently nonskeptical ideas presented in Chapters 2 through 15 and 23 through 25? Pyrrhonists will doubt this, too.

27.3 Puzzling Theories

Regrettably, this book is about to end. Does this entail that the theorizing you have been doing while reading it should end, too? You have begun doing epistemology; when should you stop doing it? To try to answer A and B is to start thinking epistemologically. When can you nonarbitrarily, and profitably, cease such theoretical thinking?

As this book has made manifest, theories of knowledge raise puzzles—then more theories of knowledge, more puzzles, still more theories, still more puzzles, and so on. There are questions and there are attempts to answer them—and no such attempt is without its attendant puzzles. Are theoretical answers always provisional, wearing a garland of puzzles? If so, there will never be a time when the final puzzle has been eliminated. No wonder; mightn't any attempt to eliminate a puzzle (even what seems to be a final one) give rise to a new puzzle? Mightn't the supposed solution be puzzling itself? Aren't difficult and speculative subjects like that?

But if epistemology is like that, its questions can never be laid to rest. (Is this true of all other areas of human inquiry, too? Might questions and puzzles always ensure that theories are only theories, in science and elsewhere?) If you ever walk away from epistemology, confident of having solved its puzzles, will you be wrong? Will your answers only spark new puzzles? (Has that occurred as you have thought about the puzzles in this book?) If new puzzles will always arise, how can you ever, in good epistemological conscience, assume that you have found The Answer? Would there really be no puzzles left unanswered by your proposed answer? If there seem to be none, maybe this is because you have not looked hard enough for them!

Yet if you admit that puzzles remain, how can you, in good conscience, finish your theorizing? You would simply be giving up your quest for answers. Would you be ending your theorizing arbitrarily, clearly bereft of answers, consciously beset by puzzles? (How strong is your need to think about such matters? How strong is your need to understand?) Feel free to walk away, but do not assume that you leave with an understanding of knowledge. Perhaps you say, "If no such understanding is possible anyway, I'll cut my losses and leave well enough alone." You can do that, of course, but wouldn't it be nice to understand something about knowledge? And perhaps such understanding *is* possible. Only by doing epistemology, however, can you discover that it is. Fly back to Chapter 1, then, to continue what you have only just begun!

Has the experience of thinking so long and so hard about knowledge—trying to understand it—changed you at all? If it has, is this because you know more than you did before? Or do you know less but understand more? Do you know neither more nor less but understand more? Do you know more and understand less? Or do you know less and understand less? (Examples, please.)

FURTHER READING

Feldman 1981. (On knowing that one knows, an issue raised in the puzzle that begins this chapter.)

Chisholm 1989, Chapter 1. (On the problem of the criterion and its implications for doing epistemology, in section 27.1.)

Stroud 1989. (On the difficulty of completely understanding knowledge.)

Hetherington 1992. (On the difficulty of having knowledge or justified belief as an epistemological theorizer.)

References

Alston, W. P. 1989. *Epistemic Justification*. Ithaca, N.Y.: Cornell University Press.

Annas, J., and J. Barnes. 1985. *The Modes of Scepticism*. Cambridge: Cambridge University Press.

Annis, D. 1978. "A Contextualist Theory of Epistemic Justification." *American Philosophical Quarterly* 15: 213–219.

Armstrong, D. M. 1973. *Belief, Truth and Knowledge*. Cambridge: Cambridge University Press.

Audi, R. 1988. *Belief, Justification, and Knowledge*. Belmont, Calif.: Wadsworth.

Ayer, A. J. 1956. *The Problem of Knowledge*. London: Macmillan.

BonJour, L. 1985. *The Structure of Empirical Knowledge*. Cambridge: Harvard University Press.

———. 1986. "A Reconsideration of the Problem of Induction." *Philosophical Topics* 14: 93–124.

———. 1992. "A Rationalist Manifesto." In *Return of the A Priori*, edited by P. Hanson and B. Hunter, 53–88. Calgary: University of Calgary Press.

Bury, R. G., trans. 1933. Sextus Empiricus, *Outlines of Pyrrhonism*, Vol. 1. Cambridge: Harvard University Press.

Carrier, L. S. 1993. "The Roots of Knowledge." *Pacific Philosophical Quarterly* 74: 81–95.

Cherniak, C. 1986. *Minimal Rationality*. Cambridge: The MIT Press.

Chisholm, R. M. 1977. *Theory of Knowledge*. 2d ed. Englewood Cliffs, N.J.: Prentice-Hall.

———. 1982. *The Foundations of Knowing*. Minneapolis: University of Minnesota Press.

———. 1989. *Theory of Knowledge*. 3d ed. Englewood Cliffs, N.J.: Prentice-Hall.

Conee, E. 1988. "Why Solve the Gettier Problem?" In *Philosophical Analysis*, edited by D. F. Austin, 55–58. Dordrecht: Kluwer.

Descartes, R. 1641. *Meditations on First Philosophy*.

Dretske, F. 1971. "Conclusive Reasons." *Australasian Journal of Philosophy* 49: 1–22.

Elgin, C. Z. 1988. "The Epistemic Efficacy of Stupidity." *Synthese* 74: 297–311.

Feldman, R. 1974. "An Alleged Defect in Gettier Counterexamples." *Australasian Journal of Philosophy* 52: 68–69.

———. 1981. "Fallibilism and Knowing That One Knows." *The Philosophical Review* 90: 266–282.

———. 1985. "Reliability and Justification." *The Monist* 68: 159–174.

———. 1988. "Having Evidence." In *Philosophical Analysis*, edited by D. F. Austin, 83–104. Dordrecht: Kluwer.

Feldman, R., and E. Conee. 1985. "Evidentialism." *Philosophical Studies* 48: 15–34.

Fogelin, R. J. 1987. *Understanding Arguments*. 3d ed. New York: Harcourt Brace Jovanovich.

Foley, R. 1991. "Evidence and Reasons for Belief." *Analysis* 51: 98–102.

Gettier, E. L. 1963. "Is Justified True Belief Knowledge?" *Analysis* 23: 121–123.

Goldman, A. I. 1967. "A Causal Theory of Knowing." *The Journal of Philosophy* 64: 357–372.

———. 1976. "Discrimination and Perceptual Knowledge." *The Journal of Philosophy* 73: 771–791.

———. 1979. "What Is Justified Belief?" In *Justification and Knowledge,* edited by G. S. Pappas, 1–23. Dordrecht: Reidel.

———. 1980. "The Internalist Conception of Justification." In *Midwest Studies in Philosophy,* Vol. 5, edited by P. A. French, T. E. Uehling, Jr., and H. K. Wettstein, 27–51. Minneapolis: University of Minnesota Press.

Goodman, N. 1955. *Fact, Fiction, and Forecast.* 3d ed. Indianapolis: Bobbs-Merrill.

Hardwig, J. 1985. "Epistemic Dependence." *The Journal of Philosophy* 82: 335–349.

Harman, G. 1973. *Thought.* Princeton: Princeton University Press.

Hempel, C. 1965. *Aspects of Scientific Explanation.* New York: The Free Press.

Hetherington, S. C. 1992. *Epistemology's Paradox.* Savage, Md.: Rowman & Littlefield.

———. 1995. "Scepticism on Scepticism." *Philosophia* (forthcoming).

———. 1996. "Gettieristic Scepticism." *Australasian Journal of Philosophy* (forthcoming).

Hume, D. 1748. *An Enquiry Concerning Human Understanding.*

Kaplan, M. 1985. "It's Not What You Know That Counts." *The Journal of Philosophy* 82: 350–363.

Kim, K. 1993. "Internalism and Externalism in Epistemology." *American Philosophical Quarterly* 30: 303–316.

Klein, P., and T. A. Warfield. 1994. "What Price Coherence?" *Analysis* 54: 129–132.

Kornblith, H. 1989. "The Unattainability of Coherence." In *The Current State of the Coherence Theory,* edited by J. W. Bender, 207–214. Dordrecht: Kluwer.

Kripke, S. A. 1979. "A Puzzle About Belief." In *Meaning and Use,* edited by A. Margalit, 239–288. Dordrecht: Reidel.

———. 1980. *Naming and Necessity.* Cambridge: Harvard University Press.

———. 1982. *Wittgenstein on Rules and Private Language.* Cambridge: Harvard University Press.

Kyburg, H. E., Jr. 1961. *Probability and the Logic of Rational Belief.* Middletown, Conn.: Wesleyan University Press.

Lehrer, K. 1965. "Knowledge, Truth and Evidence." *Analysis* 25: 168–175.

———. 1971. "Why Not Scepticism?" *The Philosophical Forum* 2: 283–298.

Lehrer, K., and T. D. Paxson, Jr. 1969. "Knowledge: Undefeated Justified True Belief." *The Journal of Philosophy* 66: 225–237.

Levi, I. 1967. *Gambling with Truth.* London: Routledge & Kegan Paul.

Lewis, D. 1979. "Scorekeeping in a Language Game." *Journal of Philosophical Logic* 8: 339–359.

Lycan, W. G. 1977. "Evidence One Does Not Possess." *Australasian Journal of Philosophy* 55: 114–126.

Makinson, D. C. 1965. "The Paradox of the Preface." *Analysis* 25: 205–207.

McGinn, C. 1984. *Wittgenstein on Meaning.* Oxford: Blackwell.

Moore, G. E. 1959. *Philosophical Papers.* London: Allen & Unwin.

Moser, P. K. 1985. *Empirical Justification.* Dordrecht: Reidel.

———, ed. 1986. *Empirical Knowledge.* Totowa, N.J.: Rowman & Littlefield.

———, ed. 1987. *A Priori Knowledge.* Oxford: Oxford University Press.

———. 1989. *Knowledge and Evidence.* Cambridge: Cambridge University Press.

Nozick, R. 1981. "Fiction." In *The Mind's I,* edited by D. R. Hofstadter and D. C. Dennett, 461–464. Harmondsworth: Penguin.

Pappas, G. S. 1978. "Some Forms of Epistemological Skepticism." In *Essays on Knowledge and Justification,* edited by G. S. Pappas and M. Swain, 309–316. Ithaca, N.Y.: Cornell University Press.

Passmore, J. 1970. *Philosophical Reasoning.* 2d ed. London: Duckworth.

Plantinga, A. 1993. *Warrant: The Current Debate.* New York: Oxford University Press.

Plato. *Republic.*

———. *Theaetetus.*

Pollock, J. L. 1984. "Reliability and Justified Belief." *Canadian Journal of Philosophy* 14: 103–114.

Putnam, H. 1981. *Reason, Truth and History.* Cambridge: Cambridge University Press.

Radford, C. 1966. "Knowledge—By Examples." *Analysis* 27: 1–11.

Ring, M. 1977. "Knowledge: The Cessation of Belief." *American Philosophical Quarterly* 14: 51–59.

Sainsbury, M. 1988. *Paradoxes.* Cambridge: Cambridge University Press.

Sartwell, C. 1991. "Knowledge Is Merely True Belief." *American Philosophical Quarterly* 28: 157–165.

Schlick, M. 1959. "The Foundation of Knowledge." In *Logical Positivism,* edited by A. J. Ayer, 209–227. Glencoe, Ill.: The Free Press.

Sellars, W. F. 1963. *Science, Perception and Reality.* London: Routledge & Kegan Paul.

Shope, R. K. 1983. *The Analysis of Knowing.* Princeton: Princeton University Press.

Sorenson, R. A. 1987. "The Vagueness of Knowledge." *Canadian Journal of Philosophy* 17: 767–804.

Strawson, P. F. 1985. *Skepticism and Naturalism.* New York: Columbia University Press.

Stroud, B. 1984. *The Significance of Philosophical Scepticism.* Oxford: Oxford University Press.

———. 1989. "Understanding Human Knowledge in General." In *Knowledge and Skepticism,* edited by K. Lehrer and M. Clay, 31–50. Boulder: Westview Press.

Unger, P. 1968. "An Analysis of Factual Knowledge." *The Journal of Philosophy* 65: 157–170.

———. 1971. "A Defense of Skepticism." *The Philosophical Review* 80: 198–218.

Van Cleve, J. 1979. "Foundationalism, Epistemic Principles, and the Cartesian Circle." *The Philosophical Review* 88: 55–91.

Wittgenstein, L. 1953. *Philosophical Investigations.* Oxford: Blackwell.

———. 1969. *On Certainty.* Oxford: Blackwell.

Several of the articles listed above have been reprinted in anthologies. Three of the most helpful epistemology anthologies are as follows: (1) *Knowing,* edited by M. Roth and L. Galis (New York: Random House, 1970). (2) *Essays on Knowledge and Justification,* edited by G. S. Pappas and M. Swain (Ithaca, N.Y.: Cornell University Press, 1978). (3) *Empirical Knowledge,* edited by P. K. Moser (Totowa, N.J.: Rowman & Littlefield, 1986).

About the Book and Author

Despite the problems students often have with the theory of knowledge, it remains, necessarily, at the core of the philosophical enterprise. As experienced teachers know, teaching epistemology requires a text that is not only clear and accessible but also capable of successfully motivating the abstract problems that arise.

· In *Knowledge Puzzles*, Stephen Hetherington presents an informal survey of epistemology based on the use of puzzles to illuminate problems of knowledge. Each topic is introduced through a puzzle, and readers are invited to work their own ways toward a solution. Hetherington's light and undogmatic style encourages class discussion and independent thought rather than the memorization of "book" answers.

Covering all of the most important epistemological issues, informed by classical and contemporary literature, and rich in probing questions and suggestions for further readings, *Knowledge Puzzles* is a pedagogical breakthrough. Whether it is used as a main text or supplement, this lucid and engaging text will be welcomed both by teachers and by students.

Stephen Cade Hetherington is senior lecturer in philosophy at the University of New South Wales in Sydney.

Index